AF792697

ICONOGRAPHY
OF
SOUTHERN INDIA

G. JOUVEAU-DUBREUIL

ICONOGRAPHY OF SOUTHERN INDIA

TRANSLATED FROM THE FRENCH

BY

A.C.MARTIN

COSMO PUBLICATIONS

2001 INDIA

All rights reserved. No part of this publication may be reproduced, or stored in retrival system, or transmitted in any form or by any means without the prior permission of Cosmo Publications.

ICONOGRAPHY OF SOUTHERN INDIA

© COSMO PUBLICATIONS, NEW DELHI

First COSMO Print 2001

ISBN 81-7755-101-9

Published by

MRS. RANI KAPOOR
for COSMO PUBLICATIONS Div. of
GENESIS PUBLISHING PVT. LTD.
24-B, Ansari Road, Darya Ganj,
New Delhi-110 002, INDIA

Printed at

Mehra Offset Press

INDEX OF CONTENTS

Établissements André BRULLIARD. Saint-Dizier (Haute-Marne). — 1937

LIST OF FIGURES IN THE TEXT

APOLOGY

Not only among the educated Indian people, but among Englishmen there are many including myself who are « sufficiently ignorant of French to require the aid of a translation ».

When in 1915 I came across Professor Jouveau-Dubreuil's admirable work, I was nevertheless able to follow it sufficiently well to think it a pity that it should remain a sealed book to the majority of people in that part of India with the iconography of which it deals.

I submitted a translation of part of it to the author of the original who was kind enough to approve of my effort. He readily gave his permission to my continuing it on certain conditions, the most important one being that I should undertake to publish it. Having done so I was bound to go on.

My time was limited, so I called my son who had made better use of his educational opportunities than I had, to my aid. Without hesitation he condemned my work as being too literal. This saved me a lot of trouble at the time for it enabled me to sentence him to make the translation *de novo*, which penalty he could not evade without defiance of parental authority. In course of time it was done. We thus became partners in the obligation imposed by Professor Jouveau-Dubreuil to publish the book in English.

Our next difficulty was to obtain the blocks for the illustrations, without which the work would only be fit for bookworms. It was not till the glorious summer of 1925 during a short stay in Paris, that we discovered their fate.

They belonged to M. Guimet, the famous archaeologist, at whose instance Professor Jouveau-Dubreuil had so ably and arduously explored the subject. Mr. Guimet died and left his museum to the French Government. The Curator of the Archives was called up for service during the Great War, during which in company with so many heroes, he fulfilled the Great Sacrifice. R. I. P. His successor found that the blocks were lost.

We were still bound by our promise to the author and even if he should absolve us, we were unwilling to become « quitters ». So new blocks had to be made at great expense, which added much to the cost of this book.

The long delay was not without advantage, for in the meantime by residence among French people, my son added much to his proficiency in their language, while I took the opportunity of my short leave in England to learn a little English.

The result of all this may benefit our readers, but was deplorable to me personally, for to my horror, my son condemned his own translation and threw it at my head. With sweat sufficient to bring forth the infant Pulliar (see page 40) I laboured. This is the result.

For the text, my son who has adopted the diacritics and accents of the original with meticulous care, deserves the credit. For the translation of the voluminous footnotes, I take the blame. With those of Burnouf from Sanskrit poetry into French, I have assumed more freedom than I would with the author's text. The sense has not been altered and I hope my daring has not failed to preserve to some small extent at least, the spirit for which M. Burnouf had so remarkable a gift.

July, 1926. A. Ff. M.

ICONOGRAPHY

OF

SOUTHERN INDIA

INTRODUCTION

Southern India is rather a vague term. In this book it denotes the stretch of country along the Coromandel coast, from the mouth of the Northern Pennar river to cape Comorin. It is a region with certain distinctive characteristics. Its monuments belong exclusively to the Dravidian style, and its principal language is Tamil.

Elsewhere, there is a marked difference in the language, people and style of monuments. In those regions, Malayalam, Canarese or Telugu are spoken, and the monuments belong to the Chalukya or Northern Hindu style.

This work concerns the iconography of the country of Dravidian Architecture and the Tamil language, which comprises the ten districts of N. Arcot, Madras, Chingleput, S. Arcot, Salem, Coimbatore, Trichinopoly, Tanjore, Madura and Tinnevelly (1).

This iconography is almost entirely Hindu. The Musulmans and Christians have always been relatively few in this part

(1) Ramnad District is now made up of N. Tinnevelly and S. Madura. (Tr.) A few footnotes in this book have been added to those of the author of the original. Each of these for which the translators are solely responsible is marked (Tr.).

of Southern India. South of the Pennar river hardly a trace of Buddhism is found.

Some images of Jain śaints occasionally occur, sometimes standing naked, at others seated with legs crossed and with a halo surrounding their heads (1). But Jainism never seems to have flourished in this region.

From the time of the oldest historical documents, the Tamils have been what is called in India, Brahminical. Their religion is Hinduism, which we cannot define in a few words. In fourteen centuries this religion has become much modified, and has split up into numerous sects. Eminent teachers have preached ideas of a very exalted philosophy as appertaining to it, but these have only served to increase the differences of cults and dogmas.

We are concerned only with iconography, and therefore the matter becomes comparatively simple, for although the Hindus do not often agree about philosophic ideas, they have always been in complete accord on the manner in which their gods and religious scenes should be portrayed.

Iconography in Southern India is entirely religious, and as liturgical subjects cannot be treated according to the fancy of the artist, extremely strict rules always govern the method of representing the gods and the sculptors chisel is invariably guided with exact precision.

For example, in our days an artist who wishes to delineate *Pulliar* (*Gaṇêśa*) cannot depart from the exact form fixed by custom. Not only must he give the god an elephant's head, but he is compelled to direct the end of the trunk towards the left hand which holds a rice cake. One of the tusks must be broken, and that tusk must be the one on the right. The order of the emblems must not be inverted. The symbol called *aṅkuśa* must be in the second right hand and the *pâśa* in the second left hand.

A sculptor who wished to represent the god in any other way, would be accused of not knowing his profession, and of

(1) At Ariankuppam near Pondicherry, not far from the burning ground of the dead, there is a statue of this kind. It is about 1 ½ mètres high, and is protected by a hut which the Indians call *Brahmâ-Kovil*.

violating the most sacred laws of religion. The Brahmins would refuse to pay for such work, or to worship this heterodox divinity. An idol which was not made in accordance with the rules, would not be reverenced.

In the course of centuries the rules have been modified. If an ancient or modern relief of the same subject are compared, differences, often considerable, would be obvious ; but if instead of contrasting images of different eras, contemporaneous images are compared, it will be seen that they are identical, except in trifling matters.

It may therefore be taken as true that, with regard to the country of Dravidian Architecture and Tamil language : *when the same subject is represented on monuments of the same age it is depicted in the same manner.*

So in each period the way of portraying gods and religious scenes are ruled by strict laws. It is for this reason that iconography has become truly a Science.

This work on the religious iconography of Southern India is divided into two parts which differ in their object, method and results :

1st, the study of Modern iconography ;

2nd, the history of iconography.

Modern iconography can easily be studied in its entirety. All that is necessary is to obtain a good specimen of each of the modern images which represent gods or religious scenes which are the fixed patterns copied identically everywhere at the present time. By enquiry from artists, sculptors and painters the following facts may be ascertained about each image :

1. What it represents, and the legend to which it refers.

2. The name of the subject itself, and the technical names of the parts which compose it, such as people, dresses, emblems etc.

3. The rarity or frequency of the subject in modern iconography.

On the other hand, the study of ancient images is difficult and uncertain. To know exactly what those painters and sculptors wished to represent, it would be necessary that they should have written complete treatises on iconography, that their books should be extant in our own time, and present full proofs of authenticity.

We do not possess any work of the kind. We must fall back on other methods. In default of technical literature, a search has to be made in religious and literary writings for information on iconography. Archaeologists must seek for texts which they can apply to images.

Often no one can be found who is able to explain iconographical details. It frequently happens that several legends differing totally from each other can be applied to the same image. From the texts alone it is impossible to arrive at an exact knowledge of what the artist wished to delineate.

Finally, for this method to be of value it is important that texts used to interpret the images, should deal as nearly as possible with the same locality and be contemporaneous with the images themselves.

It is clear that it is not right to interpret a low-relief carved on the bank of the Cauvery by means of a text written on that of the Ganges, — again it would be illogical to interpret a 7th century image by a 10th century text.

For the iconography of Southern India it is evident that the greater part of the classic Sanskrit works of which translations are found in European libraries are of no avail, as they are in no way applicable to South India. It is Tamil literature that must be the subject of research. Unfortunately works written in the South of India are still very little known and their age uncertain. The greater part of them are modern and could only be used for modern iconography, for which no such help is required. The first thing would be to find the age of the Tamil works of which only copies are available. It would be necessary to make sure that these works had neither been altered nor interpolated. We shall not therefore try this plan (1), but make

(1) Quelques mois après la publication du présent ouvrage, en 1914, T. A. Gopinatha Rao faisait paraître le vol. I de son *Hindu Iconography* (The Law Printing House, Mount Road, Madras), dont le sujet était précisément l'étude de l'iconographie à l'aide des textes.

Le lecteur trouvera dans ce savant ouvrage d'innombrables renseignements tirés de textes inédits. Le vol. II parut en 1916.

use of a purely archaeological method, which is simply comparative iconography.

The age of the greater part of the sculptures which adorn Dravidian shrines can be ascertained with fair exactitude, because each low-relief is nearly always an integral part of the monument. The images which decorate the edifice were carved at the same time as the other ornamental parts of the design (pillars, capitols, brackets, attics, etc.) which declare the style of the building. We believe we have proved above that the style of a Dravidian monument is enough to give a clue to its approximate age.

We shall therefore arrange the images in classes according to the periods to which the monuments belong :

The *Pallava* period, 7th, 8th, and first half of the 9th centuries.

The *Chôḷa* period, second half of the 9th, the 10th, and 11th centuries.

The *Pâṇḍya* period, 12th, 13th, and first half of the 14th centuries.

The *Bijayanagar* (1) period, second half of the 14th, the 15th, and 16th centuries.

The *Madura* period, 17th century up to and including the present time.

Even a superficial examination of these images will show that the most ancient ones differ considerably from those of modern times, but the images of one period do not differ much from those of the epochs which immediately precede or succeed that period. That iconography has become modified in the course of centuries, and that the transformation has been slow and progressive, are therefore established.

The different phases of iconographical history form a continuous series down the centuries, so the last period of the series, modern iconography, may be completely known. Modern artists are the heirs of those of olden days, and the depositories of their traditions. Starting with modern iconography, we shall compare the images of each epoch with those that precede them.

(1) Also called Vijayanagar, *b* and *v* being interchangeable. The extensive ruins of this place are near the village of Humpi in the Bellary District. (Tr.)

It being evident that the traditions have become modified during the course of time, we shall be content to note the differences, without forming any hypotheses. To take an example: *Vishṇu* is usually recognized because he carries as insignia the *śaṅkha* and *chakra*, the conch-shell and the disk. The latter is a wheel, which in our times is surrounded by a scarf (*vastram*) and by four flames (*sudhar*) which issue from the rim of the wheel. In the *Bijayanagar* period (15th century) the wheel is without a scarf. In the preceding (*Pâṇḍya*) period (12th century) the flames issue also from the axle of the wheel. In the *Chôḷa* period (10th century) the wheel is still decorated, but it is seen end-ways. Finally, in the *Pallava* period (10th century) *Vishṇu*'s *chakra* is without flames. It may be said that there is not a single design which has not been subject to discernable transformation in the course of ages. It is important to follow from century to century the history of these modifications, in order to show clearly the identity of ancient images.

The study of comparative iconography is not limited to the textual rules which are used to represent religious subjects. It includes also statistics of these at the different periods of the art. In each epoch it is important to know which subjects were most often depicted, and on the other hand which were rare or even totally neglected.

It is not without use to know that the subject called *Sômaskanda* (*Śiva* with *Pârvatî* and *Subrahmaṇya*) is found over and over again in the Sivaite temples of the Pallavas. This design shows what was most essential in the religion of that period. Nor is it without interest to compare the different periods with each other, from the point of view of the statistics of religious subjects.

It is thus that we find that certain subjects often represented in our days seem quite unknown to ancient sculptors.

Is it not remarkable that the images of *Râma*, *Sîtâ*, *Lakshmaṇa* and *Hanumân* are nowhere to be found in temples prior to the 10th century? That *Kṛishṇa* and the bathing girls (*Jalakrîḍa*), *Kṛishṇa* playing the flute (*Vêṇugôpâla*) are never found in ancient temples and that the Vishnuvite symbol called *nâmam* never appears in sculpture until after the 15th century?

The importance of the study of iconography is useful not only for the history of the art, but for the history of literature and religion. Southern India is a country where monuments are very numerous, and of very great size. These monuments, which date from different times, are covered with sculptures which form an inexhaustible mine of historical documents.

But they have even greater interest when it is considered that they express the soul of the people. These are the manifestations of the human mind in a country which has long possessed an advanced and extremely particularized civilization.

CHAPTER I

SIVAITE ICONOGRAPHY

§ 1. — *Śiva.*

The Liṅgam.

Śiva (1) the great god of Southern India (where his Sanskrit names are *Mahâdêva, Mahêśa,* and *Mahêśvara*) is made manifest in the *Liṅgam.*

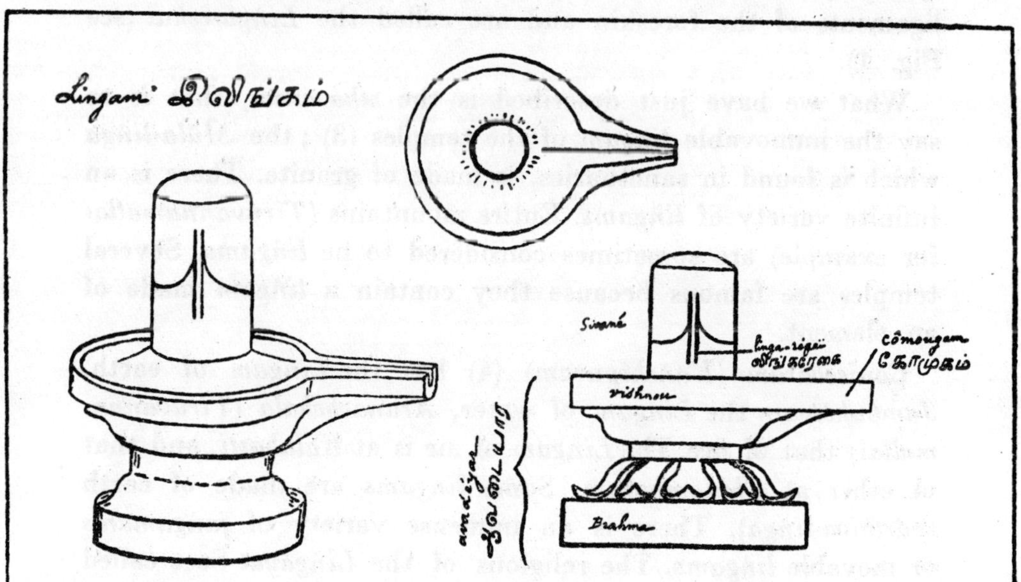

FIG. 1. — *Liṅgam.*

The shape of the *Liṅgam* is very variable. Figure 1 is the most ordinary. It is composed of two parts :

1. A pedestal called *avaḍeyar* (*pîṭha*) (2). This is sometimes

(1) In Tamil *Sivan,* from the Sanskrit *Śiva* (the propitious), also called *Sadâśiva* (the eternally happy), *Paramaśiva* (*Śiva* god of heaven), *Paramêśvara* (the sublime god), *Viśvanâtha* (the god of the world), *Îśvara* (the glorious), *Hara* (the almighty), etc.

(2) Some times also called *saluṅkha* or *vêdi.*

rectangular, but more often circular. Its usual shape is shown in Figure 1. The lower part is supposed to represent *Brahmâ*, and the upper part *Vishṇu*, these two acting as a support to the *Liṅgam* proper, which is *Śiva*.

The part played by the *avaḍeyar* is not only to support the *Liṅgam*, but to collect and draw off the fluids with which it is anointed (1). So, the upper part of the *avaḍeyar* is hollowed like a vase. A sort of gutter or spout called *komugam* (2) which ought always to point to the right of a person looking towards the shrine, acts as a drain for the liquids.

2. The *Liṅgam* proper. This is a cylinder placed upright on the pedestal the upper part of which is ended off by a spherical cap. It represents the Phallus : the vertical part of the cylinder is inscribed with upright grooves which indicate the ligaments of the foreskin and are called the *Liṅga-rekai* (see Fig. 1).

What we have just described is the *sthâvaram*, that is to say the immovable *liṅgam* of the temples (3) ; the *Mûla-liṅga* which is found in sanctuaries, is made of granite. There is an infinite variety of *liṅgams*. Entire mountains (*Tiruvannamallai* for example) are sometimes considered to be *liṅgams*. Several temples are famous because they contain a *liṅgam* made of an element.

Conjeevaram (*Kañchîpuram*) (4) has the *Liṅgam* of earth, *Jambukêśvara* the *Liṅgam* of water, *Arunachchala* (*Tiruvannamallai*) that of fire. The *Liṅgam* of air is at *Kalahasti*, and that of ether at *Chidambaram*. Some *liṅgams* are made of earth (*pârthiva-liṅga*). There is an immense variety of *jaṅgamams* or movable *liṅgams*. The religious of the *Liṅgâyat* Sect called *pandâram* and *andi* (mendicants) carry miniature *liṅgams*

(1) All statues in temples are thus supported by pedestals which act as receivers for the sacred oils. The *avaḍeyar* of the *Liṅgam* is nothing else, and does not have the signification of *yôni*.

(2) Called also *sômasûtra*.

(3) In large temples there are 108 *liṅgams*, each of which has a special name.

(4) Throughout this book the spelling of the name of this town is usually *Kañchîpuram* instead of *Conjeevaram*. The pronunciation of the *i* is the same as *ee*. (Tr.)

shaped something like an egg, which are kept in a silver box fastened to the arm, or neck, or in the hair.

Historical. — It is not a fact, as several authors make out, that the worship of the *Liṅgam* is a relatively recent acquisition of Hinduism. Iconography proves the contrary. From the beginning of the history of monuments in Southern India, the *Liṅgam* has been an integral part of Sivaite Hinduism (1).

In the *Pallava* monuments (7th century) the *Liṅgam* is found everywhere, and it is absolutely impossible to believe that it was only placed in the shrines at a later period.

Śiva, god of the *Liṅgam*, is seen here to be god the creator, and god of life. The beginnings of life are wrapped in mystery, and European Science is no better off in knowledge of this matter than the Hindus, who from the most ancient times have worshipped *Śiva* the supreme god, in the form of the *Liṅgam.* The worship of the phallus is the union of the mysteries of generation with those of divinity.

The shape of the *Liṅgam* being subject to many variations, it is not possible to give the history of it. We may however note that in *Pallava* temples the *Liṅgam* is not cylindrical, but prismatic (2). Such for example is the *Liṅgam* at *Kailâsanâtha* (the sanctuary of *Mahêndravaram*) (8th century) at *Kañchîpuram* (see Pl. I.), which is a prism with twleve facets. In the *Chôḷa* period, gigantic *liṅgams* were carved, such as those which are placed in the great *vimânas* of Tanjore and of Gangaikondapuram.

Ṛishabha.

In front of the *Liṅgam* a seated bull is nearly always to be seen. This is called *Ṛishabha*, but more usually *Nandi.*

(1) The legend of *Śiva* issuing from the *Liṅgam* is represented in the cave of the *Avatârs* at *Ellora.* The *Liṅgam* is sculptured in low-relief in No. 1 cave at *Bâdâmi* in a place where it forms part of the decoration, and so no one can maintain that it could have been added subsequently. The cave of the *Avatârs* and No. 1 cave at *Bâdâmi* certainly belong to the 6th century.

(2) It is strange enough that the phallus should be represented by a prism.

It is often confused with *Nandikêśvara*, the door keeper at *Kailâsa* with a bull's head on a human body, of whom mention will be made later. *Śiva*'s riding animal is also called *Nandi* (see Plate XVIII), otherwise called *Dharmadêva*, god of virtue.

Ṛishabha is always seated, never standing before the *Liṅgam*. It belongs to the kind of oxen which have humps on their backs, and is always a young bull with budding horns. Its presence in front of the *Liṅgam* is explained as the symbol of generic force. *Ṛishabha*'s head is turned towards the *Liṅgam*, and its feet except one of its fore feet, are gathered under the body. It always has a collar ornamented with bells, round its neck. (See Plate II.)

Historical. — In the Museum of the Louvre in Paris, in the collection brought back from Chaldea by the Sarzec mission (Excavations at Tello, A. O. 2354) there is a small low-relief showing a bull absolutely identical with *Nandi*. In Southern India it is incontestable that from the 6th century *Nandi* has been placed in front of the *Liṅgam*, and considered to be an emblem of *Śiva*. Time does not seem to have made much change in its shape.

We have said (1) that the 8 monoliths (7th century) at *Mavalipuram* (2) consist of 5 *rathas*, an elephant, a lion, and a bull. The last, placed towards the East between the *Bhîma-* and *Draupadî-rathas*, is a classic *Nandi*. In the cave near the light-house at Mavalipuram, at the end of the sanctuary there is a low-relief which represents *Sômaskanda* and *Nandi* seated at the feet of *Śiva* and *Pârvatî*. It is often found in the shore temple at the same place and in the *Kailâsanâtha* temple (both 8th century) at *Kañchîpuram*. The colossal *Nandi* at *Tanjore* is universally known (3).

(1) See Vol. I, *Archaeology of Southern India.* (Tr.)

(2) The correct name of this place is *Mahabalipuram.* We adhere to the corrupt form *Mavalipuram*, because it is so called by the dwellers in the neighbouring villages. The English name *The Seven Pagodas* is too cumbrous. (Tr.)

(3) In front of the temple of *Virûpâksha* (8th century) at *Pattadakal* near Bâdâmi, under an isolated pavilion there is a very large and beautiful *Nandi*, which recalls the one at Tanjore.

The Worship of the Liṅgam.

The office *Śiva-pûjâ* is performed three times daily — morning, noon and evening — in the sanctuary (*garbhagṛiham*) of the temple, by Brahmins called Saivas, who have been initiated (*dîkshâ*). *Śiva-pûjâ* comprizes three portions :

1. *Abhishêka* (sacred anointing), which consists of anointing the *Liṅgam* with milk, butter and sesamum oil (1).

2. *Dhûpa* (incense burning), which comprises burning perfumes (*sâmbirâṇi*).

3. *Naivêdya* (oblation), offering of food which must not contain the principle of animal life.

Besides this, prayers are recited, lamps lit and the *Liṅgam* decked with garlands of flowers, especially of the sort of jasmine called in Tamil *zambac* or *mugri* (Sanskrit : *mudgara*).

Śiva is very propitious to those who adorn the *Liṅgam* with flowers. The origin of the festival *Śiva-râtri* (*Śiva*'s night) is a proof of this. The *bhôja* (hunter) *Sivagossariar* killed such a number of birds in the forests that he was unable to carry so heavy a burden to the town of *Varanachy* before night fall. In order to escape from being devoured by ferocious beasts, he climbed with his bag into a *vepu* (*margosa*) tree. *Sivagossariar* slept badly, for it was new moon in the month of *Phalguna* (March), and the night was cold. In shaking the tree, flowers, leaves and drops of dew, fell on a *liṅgam* which was at its foot. This lucky chance caused supernatural favours to be accorded to him (2).

Tiruvanaikaval. — In the temple of *Jambukêśvara* the image of the adoration of the *Liṅgam* by an elephant is worshipped (Pl. III). At the foot of the tree, an elephant pours water with his trunk on a *liṅgam* which *Pârvatî* adorns with flowers.

Râma-Liṅgam.

When *Râma*, *Sîtâ*, *Lakhsmaṇa* and *Hanumân* were crossing

1) Officiating Brahmins never use coconut oil for this purpose.

(2) The Guimet Museum possesses a panel from a car, which shows this scene.

Râmêśvaram island after the defeat of *Râvaṇa*, they worshipped and adorned with garlands of flowers the well known *Liṅgam* called *Râmanâtha-svâmi* (God of Râma) which *Hanumân* had brought from the Ganges (Plate IV) (1).

Historical. — We have never seen *Râma-Liṅgam* depicted on any ancient temple. It is probably a local legend.

Śiva issuing from the Liṅgam.

The real presence of *Śiva* in the *Liṅgam* is proved by many legends, the two most famous being those of *Kaṇṇappa* and *Mârkaṇḍa.*

Kaṇṇappanâyanâr-purâṇam. — The hunter *Tinnen*, while chasing a wild boar one day, reached the banks of the river *Ponnamogaliar.* A small *Śiva* temple had been built near the spot. *Tinnen*, with another hunter *Kadden*, visited this shrine. Living always in the forests, he knew nothing of religious matters, but his friend *Kadden* explained to him that the god-head was incarnate in the *Liṅgam. Tinnen* felt within himself a burning devotion. Daily thereafter he offered the god water, flowers and even meat, since he knew not the rules of the cult. One day he saw drops of blood flowing from the eye of the god (2). Young *Tinnen* thinking that wicked persons had broken it, tore out one of his own eyes to replace the one which *Śiva* had lost. Next day *Tinnen* saw drops of blood flowing from the other eye, so he wanted to cut out his only remaining one, with a knife. Both his hands were required for this operation, for, after losing his eye sight he would not be able to find the eye-socket on the *Liṅgam* in order to put his eye into it. He therefore put his sandalled foot on the spot and was just going to insert the knife into his own eye (see Fig. 2) when *Śiva* coming out of the *Liṅgam*, stayed his arm.

So *Tinnen* was loaded with blessings and was given the name

(1) The shrine at *Râmêśvaram* is a very celebrated place of pilgrimage. Certain *pandârams* called *Kâchi-kaoris* go there in order to carry to it with particular devotion, a little water from the Ganges.

(2) *Śiva*'s face is sometimes drawn on the *liṅgam.*

of *Kaṇṇappa* (in Tamil *kannu* means eye), that is : He who gave his eye to the god.

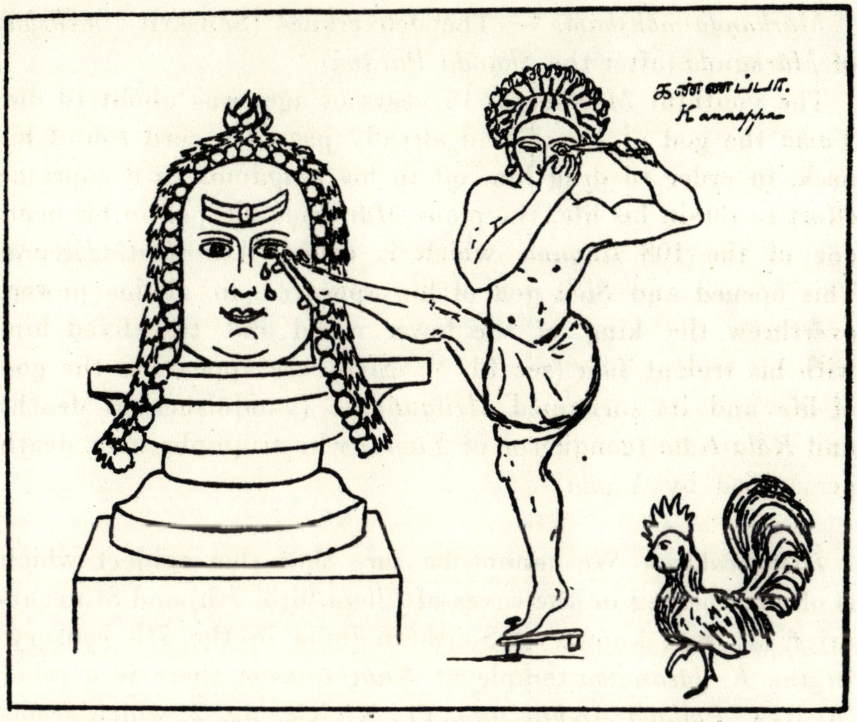

Fig. 2. — *Kaṇṇappa* (*Tinnen* offering his eye to the god).

The image of *Kaṇṇappa* cutting out his eye to offer it to the *Liṅgam* is very often reproduced in Southern India (1). It

(1) A sculpture in high relief (copied as a drawing by Regamey in the *Tour du monde*, XLIX, 1266th book, page 237) is found in the *Madura* temple. The story of *Kaṇṇappa* is very celebrated, but the greater number of Hindus do not know their religion and it is not surprising that no one was able to inform Mr. Guimet when he asked for an explanation of the scene.

« But here we have before us a sculpture of quite archaic character, of the type which reminds us of Etruscan or Pelasgian art. A sort of king with a satyr's head and pointed beard, stands like a dancer while he cuts out his eyes with a knife. In front of him on a little hillock a small recess is surmonted by a five headed serpent.

« Although there is agreement in what is told us about what this god is doing with his knife, our guides do not give us always the same name. Some say *Puruchambreyan*, others *Chikan*. Regamey who also sought enlightenment, tells us the name is *Vaden*. Probably, as usual, every one is right, meanwhile there is a character to identify. » (*Eight days in India*, by Emile Guimet : *Tour du monde*, XLIX, book 1266, p. 236.)

« What a number of details, allegories and scenes are to be seen... What then are the archaeologists of India doing ? To the task, gentlemen,

is particularly worshipped at *Kâḷahasti.* We have never found it in monuments prior to the 16th century.

Mârkaṇḍa-môksham. — The deliverance (Sanskrit : *môksha*) of *Mârkaṇḍa* (after the *Skanda Purâṇa*).

The youthful *Mârkaṇḍa*, 16 years of age, was about to die. *Yama* the god of Death had already passed a cord round his neck, in order to drag him off to his kingdom. In a supreme effort to retain his life, the pious *Mârkaṇḍa* clasped in his arms one of the 108 *liṅgams* which is called *Amurda-Gadêśvara.* This opened and *Śiva* god of life appeared in all his power, overthrew the king of the lower world and transfixed him with his trident *śûla* (see Pl. V). *Śiva* here appears as the god of life and its surnamed *Mṛityuñjaya* (vanquisher of death) and *Kâla-Kâla* (conqueror of *Yama*) who triumphs over death personified by *Yama.*

Historical. — We cannot be sure that this subject which is often repeated in the caves of *Ellora* (6th, 7th, and 8th centuries) (1), was known in Southern India in the 7th century. In the *Kailâsanâtha* temple at *Kañchîpuram* there is a relief (A. Rea, *Pallava Architecture*, Pl. XXXV, fig. 2) which seems to represent this scene. The sculpture has deteriorated so much, we cannot be certain on this point.

The Distinctive Characteristics of Śiva.

In South Indian iconography, *Śiva* is represented in human form sometimes with five faces ; hence the names *Pañcha-mukha* (one who has five faces) and *Pañchânana* (one who has five heads). He had three heads (the other two being *Brahmâ* and *Vishṇu*) after *Sarasvatî* and *Lakshmî* found him in the forest of *Taruka.* All the same, he generally has only one head. The dressing of

there is work to be done. » (*Eight days in India*, by Emile Guimet : *Tour du monde*, XLIX, book 1267, page 244.)

(1) At the back of the cave of the *Avatârs* the first low-relief shows this scene. It is usually admitted that the cave dates from the 6th century. This low-relief proves clearly that at that time, the real presence of *Śiva* in the *Liṅgam* was admitted. The same subject is also twice represented in the *Kailâsa* at *Ellora* (8th century).

his hair is a sort of tiara formed of plaited hair (in Tamil *sadai*, from the Sanskrit *jaṭâ*), so the god is also called *Jaṭâ-dhara*, *Kapardî* and *Piṅgara* (1).

In the middle of the knot of hair of the god, a head is found. It used to be a deaths-head. At the present day it is said to be the fifth head of *Brahmâ*, cut off by *Bhairava* (*Śiva*).

Śiva's head dress is ornamented with a crescent moon (whence his names *Chandra-śêkhara* and *Piraisûdi*) and the goddess *Gaṅgâ* who is delineated with clasped hands (2) and the body of a siren. So the god who carries *Gaṅgâ* in his head of hair, is called *Gaṅgaivênian* and *Gaṅgâdhara*.

Śiva's skin is white — doubtless because his body is covered with cow-dung ashes (*vibhûti, tirunîru*) in the manner of Sivaite holy men. His forehead is marked with the three white horizontal stripes worn by *Śivabhaktas* (worshippers of *Śiva*). They are made on the forehead by the three fingers (index, middle and ring) of the right hand after covering them with ashes. These three stripes are called *Vibhûtipundram*.

In the middle of the forehead a third eye is placed vertically, hence *Śiva*'s names : *Mukkanan*, *Virûpâksha*, *Tryambaka* (3). This eye of *Śiva* must not be confused with the small white or red circle (in Tamil *pottu*, in Sanskrit *tilaka*) which ornaments the foreheads of Hindus and takes the same place as the Buddhist *ûrṇa*.

Śiva's ears are always dissimilar. The right ear is long and hanging, and a small ring in the form of a snake is attached to its extremity (*nâgakuṇḍala*). The left ear on the other hand is ornamented with a big round buckle. This lack of symmetry is found in most ancient sculptures.

The snake is a very characteristic emblem of *Śiva*. *Vishṇu* is certainly shown lying and seated on *Adiśêsha*, *Kṛishṇa* dances on *Kâliya*, but *Śiva* alone is adorned with snakes, which serve him as bracelets (*vaṅgi*), scarves (*vastram*) or belts

(1) All Sivaite gods have the same head-dress of plaited hair. On the other hand *Vishṇu* and the Vishnuvite gods have a cylindrical tiara.

(2) In the fashion called in Tamil *kummudugirathu* and in Sanskrit *añjali*.

(3) In the oldest images of *Śiva*, at *Bâdâmi* and at *Ellora*, this is designed in a very neat fashion.

(*areynâmam*), so he is called *Poṅgaravanindu* (1). In the low-reliefs at *Bâdâmi* and *Mavalipuram* the snake is often the sole emblem of the god.

Śiva is frequently decked with the skulls and bones of the foes of the gods and of men. For this he bears the names *Kapâli*, or *Kapâla-mâlin* (adorned with skulls) and *Kaṅkâla* (adorned with bones).

The neck of *Śiva* is blue. We shall see that this is because at the time of the churning of the sea of milk, the god swallowed a poison which turned his throat blue, hence his names *Nîlakaṇṭha*

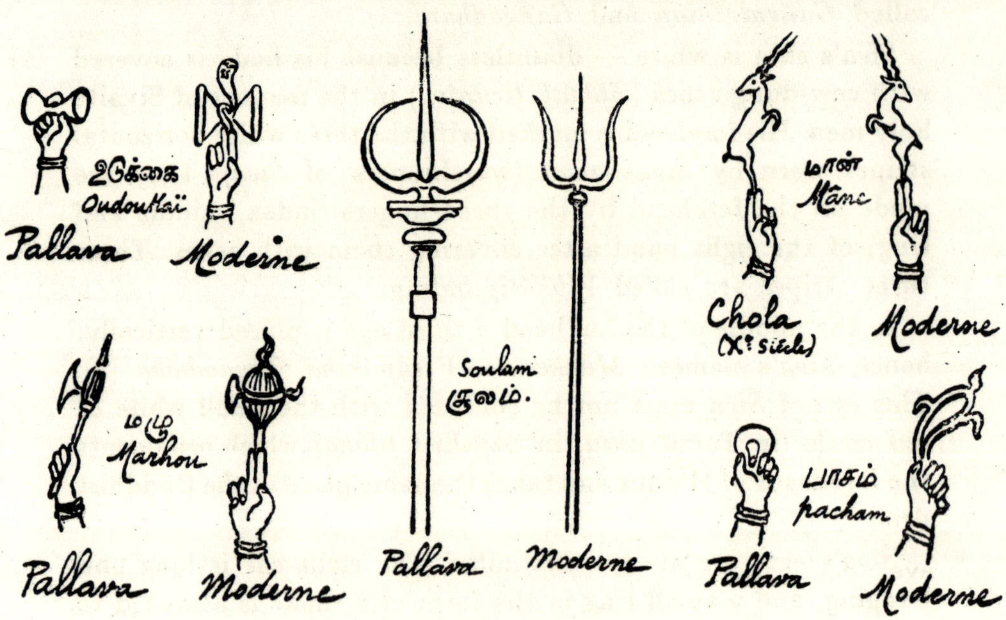

Fig. 3. — *Emblems of Śiva.*

and *Nañchuraikanda*. Usually *Śiva* has four arms, rarely more, and never only two.

Each of the arms carries a weapon or emblem which goes towards the characterization of the god. *Śiva*'s most particular weapon is perhaps the trident, *śûla* or *triśûla* whence the name *Śûlapâṇiyan* (he who holds the *śûla* in his hand).

The shape of the *śûla* (see Fig. 3) was quite different in the *Pallava* period. It has not really three points, because the centre

(1) *Gaṇêśa* and *Garuḍa* are also ornamented with snakes.

one is straight while the other two are joined together to form a circle.

The *śûla* recalls the Buddhist *triratna* : in fact in many cases it may be said that the *śûla* takes the place of the *triratna.* The latter often ornamented the upper part of the *horse shoe* of the Buddhist period. In the *Gaṇêśa* temple at *Mavalipuram*, the *śûla* occupies exactly the same position in the building (see Vol. I, *Architecture*, Fig. 33). Besides the *śûla*, the principal emblems of *Śiva* are four in number, which we will divide into two series :

1. The emblems of the right hand : the hatchet and the drum ;
2. The emblems of the left hand : the antelope and the cord.

This division is of some importance, as except for some out of the way instances in which the artist is at fault, these emblems are never invested although *Śiva* carries only two of them, as follows :

the hatchet (in the right hand), the antelope (in the left) ;
the hatchet (in the right hand), the cord (in the left) ;
the drum (in the right hand), the antelope (in the left) ;
the drum (in the right hand), the cord (in the left).

The hatchet (*mazhu*) and the antelope (*mân*) are emblems of *Śiva* in accordance with the following legend :

When *Śiva* lived in the forest of *Taruka* in the guise of a beggar, the wives of the *Ṛishis* fell in love with him, and almost lost their virtue. The angry *Ṛishis* dug a hole from which a tiger made by their magic arts sprang and attacked the god. He however seized the tiger, flayed it and dressed himself in its skin.

The *Ṛishis* sent an antelope against him, but *Śiva* caught it and held it in his left hand. They then threw at the god a hatchet made red hot in the fire, which the god kept as an emblem in his right hand.

In Sanskrit the hatchet is called *paraśu*, whence the god gets the name *Paraśupâṇi*. In our time the hatchet takes the form of a club (*gadâ*) and it looks like the emblem called *aṅkuśa* of which we will speak later.

The drum which *Śiva* holds in his right hand is the *uḍukkai* (Sanskrit : *ḍamaru*) used by religious mendicants. By its shape (which is that of a hyperboloid of an arc) it recalls an hour-glass, or the toy known in Europe as the diabolo.

Lastly the cord (*pâśa*) is a universal emblem of sovereignty. In olden temples it is a small kind of ring which the god holds by putting his index finger into it. In modern iconography it is a big buckle ornamented with three flames (*sudar*).

These are the principal insignia of *Śiva*, but the following may also be noted: 1. A small sort of *śûla* called *pâsupata*, which name is derived from the Sanskrit word *pâśupati* (the master of living creatures, and epithet of *Śiva*); 2. The vessel which holds fire (*ti*); 3. The cloud forming a flag whence the name *Jîmûtakêtu* (*Śiva*); 4. The beggars bowl (Tamil: *kabalam*, from the Sanskrit *kapâla*).

Finally, for which we have already given the reason, *Śiva* is clothed in the skin of a tiger.

Munmûrli or Trimûrti.

As we have said, *Śiva* is said to be the supreme god in Southern India. Plate VI represents a subject which shows well, that for Sivaites, *Brahmâ* and *Vishṇu* are divinities consubstantial with, but inferior to *Śiva*. *Śiva* is in the middle, and has but one leg, from his left side *Vishṇu* issues, and has only a left leg, while *Brahmâ* issues from his right side, with only a right leg. *Vishṇu* and *Brahmâ* seem to emanate from the same substance as *Śiva*.

Historical. — This subject was observed by Langles (*Monuments of Hindustan*) in the *Puthu-mandapam* at *Madura*. We have never seen it in more ancient monuments. In those of the 6th and 7th centuries the image of *Śiva* is often seen with *Brahmâ* on his right and *Vishṇu* on his left, but they look like acolytes or subordinates. It is to be noted that in the oldest Sivaite temples (of the *Avatârs* and *Kailâsa* at *Ellora*, and *Kailâsanâtha* at *Kañchîpuram*) the left side of the temple is given over to Vishnuvite iconography.

It is not impossible that the trinity had been thought of in the 6th and 7th centuries. The Hindus may have been inspired by Buddhistic, Egyptian and Christian trinities. All the same, it is only in modern iconography that the doctrine of the trinity is found expressed in the clear fashion that we have just seen (1).

In Hindu iconography *Śiva* is sometimes shown with three faces (*Trimukha*) as he was in the forest of *Taruka* near *Mayaveram*. More often the god has five faces (*Pañchamukha*).

Very probably it is a mistake to give the name *Trimûrti cave* to the three small cells to the North of the group at *Mavalipuram*. We have said before (2), that the Northern cave does not hold (as is thought) the image of *Brahmâ*. We think that the sculpture rather represents *Subrahmaṇya*. In fact we think that we can affirm that *Brahmâ* is always shown with three faces. The image in question has only one head, which is something like the one in the cave in *Trichinopoly*, which we think we are able to identify with *Subrahmaṇya*.

Brahmâ.

The following legend proves the superiority of *Śiva* : *Brahmâ* and *Vishṇu* each asserted that he was the greatest of the gods. To prove it, each tried to throw down a huge column. *Brahmâ* raised himself in the air and tried to reach the top of the column, while *Vishṇu* took the form of a boar, and dug up the ground to undermine the base. Their efforts were useless. Suddenly the column opened and *Śiva* appeared in all his glory. *Vishṇu* and *Brahmâ* recognised his divinity, and worshipped him.

The famous event which is the subject of this legend is commemorated every year on the *nakshatram* (star) day of the month of *Kartigai* (October-November) by the festival of *Paurnima*. It

(1) A single god with three heads representing *Śiva*, *Vishṇu* and *Brahmâ* is never found in ancient temples. In the cave at *Elephanta* there is a colossal image of a god with three heads, which is known as *Trimûrti*. Some authors (Langles for example) have doubted that this interpretation is well founded, but as the image is a little dilapidated, it is difficult to be sure.

The doubt would be cleared up, if instead of confining oneself to the cave of *Elephanta*, the iconography of the *Ellora* caves was studied. The same image will be found there in many places, notably in the sanctuary of that part of the *Kailâsa* called *Laṅkêśvara*. By examining the best preserved sculptures it would be clear that this subject represents *Śiva* with three faces.

It is possible that the god may here be considered as Creator, Preserver, and Destroyer. In any case it does not carry any of the insignia of *Vishṇu* or *Brahmâ*, but only those of *Śiva*. Probably this image was fashionable in the Bombay country in the 9th century.

(2) Vol. I, *Architecture*. (Tr.)

takes place at *Tiruvannamallai*, where *Śiva*'s image, appearing in a flaming column is a special object of worship (Fig. 4).

Every year at the time of this festival, a great fire is lit at the top of the mountain in honour of him who is called *Annâma-*

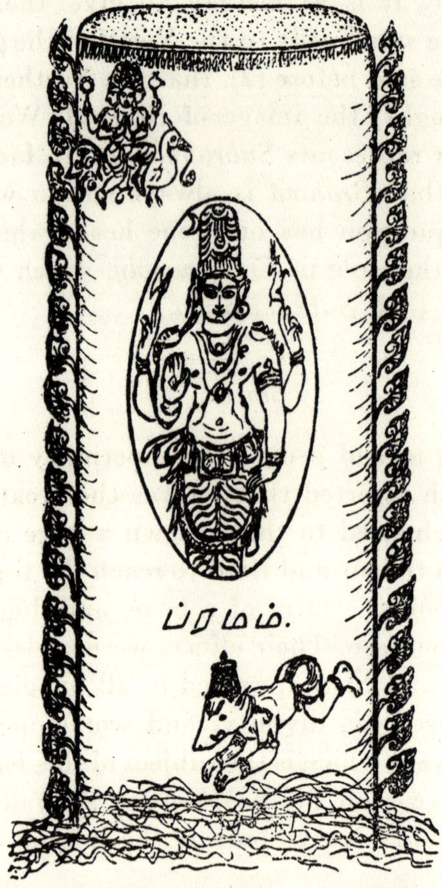

Fig. 4. — *Brahmâ* (*Śiva at Tiruvannamallai*).

***lainâtha* and *Aruṇâchalêśa*. The pilgrims pour *mantegu* (oil) into a large copper bowl. A huge roll of cloth is used as a wick for this enormous lamp.**

***Historical.* — This subject is depicted twice in the *Kailâsa-nâtha* temple at *Kañchîpuram* (8th century) (Pl. VII) (1). The same image occupies a niche on the North side of the great**

(1) In the cave of the *Avatârs* at *Ellora* (6th century) there is a large

vimâna at *Tanjore. Brahmâ* is there shown flying with wings. The column is one of fire, for in all the images the sculptor has never forgotten to adorn it with flames. The same subject is found on the *Sundara-Pâṇḍya-gôpuram* (16th century) of *Jambukêśvara* (Vol. I, Pl. XXXVIII, B).

Bhairava (the Redoubtable).

According to another legend *Brahmâ* and *Vishṇu* were disputing about their relative superiority. *Śiva* appeared in the

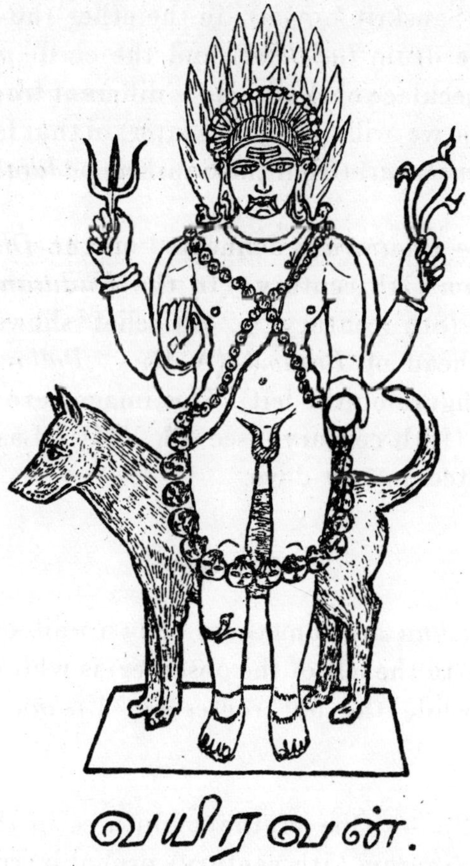

வயிரவன்.

FIG. 5. — *Bhairava, alias Vayiravan.*

low-relief representing *Śiva* appearing in the midst of the column. Some authors (such as LANGLES, *Monuments of Hindustan*) have confused this with *Narasiṁha* leaving the column. The scene is depicted in a practically identical way as in modern iconography. The same subject is carved in the *Kailâsa* at *Ellora* (8th century).

shape of *Bhairava ;* of the five heads of *Brahmâ* he cut off one and struck *Vishṇu* on the forehead with his trident. Drops of blood issued, and *Bhairava* made *Brahmâ*'s head which he had just struck off, drink them (1).

Bhairava is accompanied by his dog, which was an incarnation of *Kundôdaren* (he who carries *Śiva*'s umbrella). He lapped up the blood which fell on the ground (Fig. 5).

Bhairava is *digambara* (clothed in air), that is to say naked. He does not even wear the strip of cloth called *laṅguti*. In one hand he holds a vessel made of *Brahmâ*'s skull, and called *kabalam* (from the Sanskrit *kapâla*), in the other the *śûla*. The other hands hold the drum (*uḍukkai*) and the cord (*pâśa*). His scarf (*vastram*) is a necklace of skulls. He is different from *Bhikshâtanamûrti* (of whom we will take notice later) in that he does not wear sandals (*pâdarachchai*) (from the Sanskrit *pâdaraksha*).

Historical. — *Bhairava* is delineated on the *Dharmarâja-ratha* at *Mavalipuram* (7th century). In the *Kailâsanâtha* temple at *Kañchîpuram* (8th century) a low-relief shows *Śiva* cutting off the fifth head of *Brahmâ* (A. Rea, *Pallava Architecture*, Pl. XXXIV, figure on the left). This image is to be seen also at *Chidambaram* (13th century) (see Pl. VIII). Lastly, it is very often represented in our days.

Hari-Hara.

Śiva and *Vishṇu* are sometimes shown united in one person. The right side (to the left of the observer) is white and represents *Śiva* (*Hara*) while the left represents *Vishṇu* (*Hari*), and is painted blue.

Historical (2). — One of the sculptures in the *Dharmarâja-ratha* at *Mavalipuram* (7th century) probably represents *Hari-Hara*. A statue of *Hari-Hara* is in the most Southerly niche of

(1) It is added that he then placed *Brahmâ*'s head in his hair.

(2) This form of the divinity was known in the 6th century. An image of *Hari-Hara* is found at *Bâdâmi* in No. 1 cave (Pl. IX) and in No. 3 cave which bears an inscription dated 578.

the Western face of the base of the great *vimâna* at *Tanjore*. *Hari-Hara* is still worshipped in our times but is very rarely depicted.

Nadêsa (*master of the dance*), *Nadarâja* (*king of the dance*) (1).

Śiva is often shown dancing the *Tâṇḍava*. The reason is given in the following legend :

Śiva and *Kâlî* (his wife) quarrelled one day about their respective talent in dancing, each claiming to dance better than the other. They got *Vishṇu* to arbitrate. *Kâlî* imitated the gestures of her husband so perfectly that *Vishṇu* did not see any difference, and found it impossible to decide. But *Śiva* had recourse to a ruse. He lifted his leg much higher than the modesty of a female would allow. *Kâlî* did not dare to imitate him and so *Śiva* was declared victor.

In our times *Śiva* dancing the *Tâṇḍava* (2) is represented in many ways. Sometimes the god is seen in disorderly movement lifting his leg to the height of his head, but the image almost

(1) Called also *Nadêśvara*, god of the dance. *Nadêsa* comes from the Sanskrit *Naṭêśa* ; *Nadarâja* from the Sanskrit *Naṭarâja*.

(2) The following letter appeared in the *Madras Mail* of the 29th December 1925 : « *Sir*, — Siva, in his incarnation of *Natesa*, the special deity worshipped in the holy shrine of Chidambaram, which has, from time immemorial, been a visible symbol of a philosophic phase of the Hindu religion, is considered by the Saivites to have been born on the full-moon day of the month of *Margasira* and in the constellation of *Ardra* — the sixth lunar mansion, which falls on the 30th instant. On the night previous, the bathing of the image of the God *Natesa* takes place on a grand scale, with pots full of milk, honey, lemon-juice, ghee, oil, etc. When the bathing is over, the image being profusely decorated, is taken round in a grand procession. Subsequently, the *Anandatandavam* — the dance in ecstatic joy — follows the most impressive scene of the *Ardra* festival. Chidambaram is the place where, according to Hindu beliefs, persons, even of the lowest caste, have attained oneness with God, by sincere devotion and faith. *Nanda*, a *Paraiya* saint, attained eternal felicity by his intense devotions at Chidambaram. It is the only place in the whole of India, where no attempt has been made to import conventional ideas of Godhead, into the purely philosophic basis of the Hindu religion. The prominent idea, underlying the *Sthala Purana* of Chidambaram, is that the great God, having perceived his own self in Himself, is illuminated with wisdom, and dances with very joy on account thereof, and that the devotee who visits this temple, and witnesses this dance, is said to become himself absorbed in God.

S. Subramania Iyer.

Negapatam, Dec. 25. 1925. »

universal in Southern India is that which is worshipped at *Chidambaram* (Pl. X). The peculiarity of this image is the position of the left leg (*kâl*) and the left arm, which are thrown almost horizontally to the other side. The god in our days dances in the middle of an almost circular *tiruvachchi* which (like all *tiruvachchis*) is ornamented with designs like flames.

The god had dishevelled hair with an ornament of the crescent moon. The figure of *Gaṅgâ* appears in the knot of plaits (*jaṭâ*) which rise above his head. Of the four hands, the back one on the right holds down the drum (*uḍukkai*) adorned with snakes. The second right hand is lifted, the ends of the fingers pointing upwards in the position called *abhaya-hastam*. One of the left hands holds a vessel containing the sacred fire (*ti*) and the other left arm is carried to the front. The god is clothed in a tiger's skin.

His scarves (*urumalai*, *vastram*) are made of snakes and human heads (*muṇḍa-mâlâ*). The left foot is raised and the right one is placed on a giant (*asura*) called *Asamañja* or *Vyadhi* (the king of maladies) who lies prostrate, thrown down by the god, holding a snake in his hand. The antelope (*mân*) leaps about beside him.

Gandruvars (*Gandharvas*) fly in the air, musicians (*Kinnaras*) form a complete orchestra for the god's dance. Some beat drums (*dole*) beaten with the hand, or tambourines (*nagar*) beaten with sticks. The other musicians play the pipes (*lurti*), cymbals (*talam*) and all sorts of instruments, like the clarionet (*nagassaram*, *otu*) or the horn (*bouri*, *combu*, *tutarai*, *karna*, *pilaṅkojel*).

Bhadrakâlî, *Śiva*'s wife, is on the left of the god, while on the right *Vishṇu* declares the superiority of *Śiva* over *Kâlî* in the dance, and beats a drum.

Round *Śiva* are his worshippers, of whom we will speak later: *Patañjali*, the god with the body of a snake; *Vyâghrapâda*, the tiger-footed; *Nandikêśvara*, with the head of a bull; *Bhṛiṅgi* with three legs; the great Sivaite sages: *Appar*, *Mâṇikkavâchakar*, *Sambandar*, *Sundarar*; lastly the Brahmins of the very high and illustrious caste of *Dikshitars*, specially consecrated to the worship of *Chidambaramûrti* (*Nadêsa*).

There is not in all Southern India a sanctuary more reverenced than *Chidambaram*, where innumerable pilgrims bring their offerings. At *Madura* and *Srirañgam* the Brahmins prohibit access to the central enclosure, but it is not so at *Chidambaram*. The observer is allowed to penetrate as far as the famous *sabha*, the *kanaka*, the golden temple, and to see at a few yards from himself the effigy of *Sabhapathi* (*Nadarâja*), god of *Tillai*.

The festival of *Chidambaram* takes places in the month of *Mârgali* (December-January), whence its name *Mârgali-Tirumañjana* (procession of *Mârgali*).

Historical. — Statues of *Śiva* dancing in the same style as at *Chidambaram* are found in the niches of the *vimânas* at *Tanjore* and *Gañgaikondapuram*. In these two temples they occupy the most Westerly niche of the Southern aspect of the *vimâna*. This special pose was therefore known since the beginning of the 11th century on the banks of the Cauvery and the Coleroon. In these old images the gestures are much more elegant than in modern art.

We have nowhere found the image of *Śiva* dancing in the *Chidambaram* style in the temples of *Ellora*, *Bâdâmi*, *Mavalipuram* or *Kañchîpuram*. In all these monuments *Śiva*'s dance is in any and every style, except that of *Chidambaram*. At *Mavalipuram*, *Nadêsa* is seen on the first story of the *Dharmarâja-ratha*.

At *Kañchîpuram*, *Śiva* dancing, but not in the *Chidambaram* style, is found so often that we cannot mention all the places in which it may be seen (for example A. Rea, *Pallava Architecture* : in the *Kailâsanâtha* temple, Pl. XXVIII, XXXVIII, XL, fig. 2, LI, fig. 1, CXXIII, fig. 3, etc., and the *Tripurañkêśvara* temple, Pl. CIX, fig. 1) (1).

Gajâsura-saṁhara-mûrti (*Yânaiuritône*
(*Paramasivam flaying the Elephant*).

Śiva is often seen in modern art in the middle of an elephant's skin with his foot placed on the head of the pachyderm. A giant

(1) At *Bâdâmi*, *Nadêsa* is found on the right of the facade of cave No. 1 ; at *Ellora*, in all the Brahminical caves. Pl. XI shows *Śiva* dancing in the *Râmêśvaram* cave. *Nadêsa* is also represented in the Brahminical cave of *Aïwoli* near *Pattadakal*.

taking the form of an elephant (Sanskrit : *gaja*) pursued the devotees of *Śiva*, who ripped it open, transfixed the giant with his *śûla*, and made himself a garment of the elephant's skin.

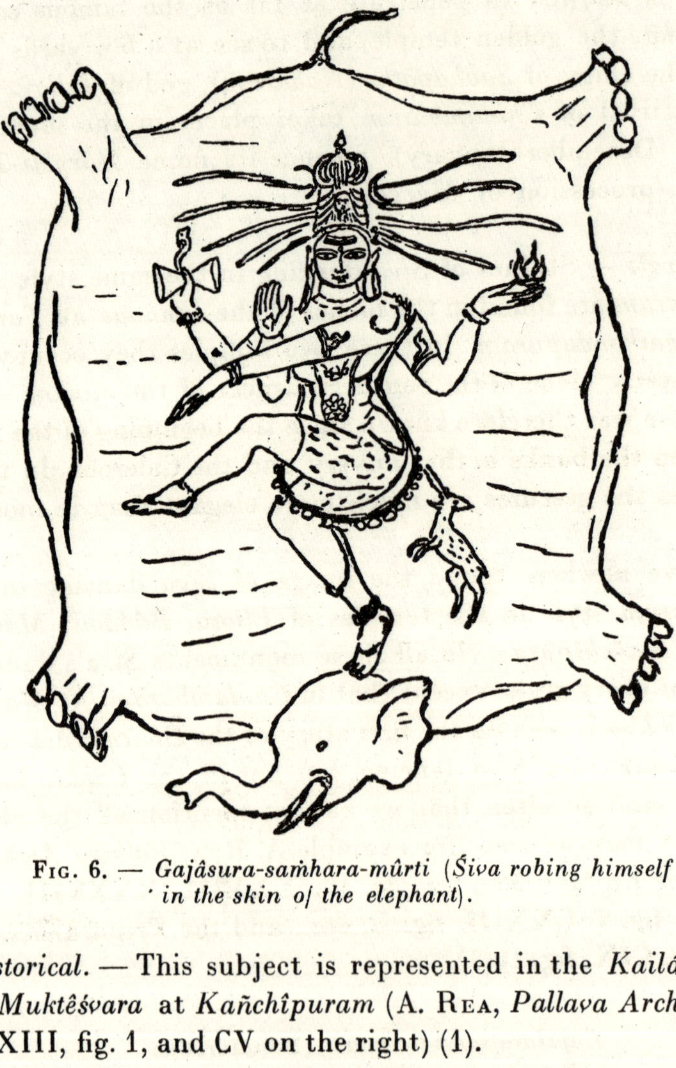

FIG. 6. — *Gajâsura-saṁhara-mûrti* (*Śiva robing himself in the skin of the elephant*).

Historical. — This subject is represented in the *Kailâsanâtha* and *Muktêśvara* at *Kañchîpuram* (A. REA, *Pallava Architecture*, Pl. CXIII, fig. 1, and CV on the right) (1).

Bhikshâṭanamûrti (*Pichandi*).

This is the name of *Śiva* begging, when under the form of

(1) At *Ellora* this is found everywhere. Pl. XII shows a large low-relief on the left of the entrance to the cave *Dhumar-Lêna* : *Śiva* transfixing the giant while he rips open the elephant.

Bhairava, having cut off *Brahmâ*'s head, he was smitten with madness and set out to beg throughout the world in the form of an *andi*. It was under this form that he went to the forest of *Taruka*, and that he seduced the wives of the *Ṛishis*, who sent against him the tiger, the antelope, and the incandescent axe.

Pichandi is always accompanied by the antelope (*mân*) which frolics near his right hand, in his left hand he holds a *śûla* which rests on his shoulder. In the other hands he holds the drum (*uḍukkai*) and the beggars bowl (*kabalam*). He is naked (*digambara*, clothed in air) and he has on his feet wooden sandals called *pâdaraksha*, such as devotees wear. They are fastened to the feet by a peg called *kamil* which passes between the toes.

Historical.— *Śiva* the beggar is represented in the *Dharmarâja-ratha* at *Mavalipuram* (7th century). On the *Kailâsanâtha* temple at *Kañchîpuram*, he is often seen surrounded by the wives of the *Ṛishis* of the forest of *Taruka* (see for example: A. Rea, *Pallava Architecture*, Pl. LXI, and XLVI, fig. 1). Plate XIII shows him on the Eastern *gôpuram* at *Chidambaram*.

Śiva in his chariot (Tripurasaṁhâra).

Śiva is sometimes depicted standing in a chariot driven by *Brahmâ*. The god carries the weapon *Pinâka* (1) and shoots arrows against the town of *Tripuram* where three giants had taken refuge.

History. — This subject is twice repeated in the *Kailâsa-nâtha* temple at *Kañchîpuram* (A. Rea, *Pallava Architecture*, Pl. XXXIII, fig. 6, and XXXIX, fig. 1). It is rare in our times (2). Several authors have confounded *Śiva* with *Râma* or *Arjuna*.

(1) *Pinâka* is the name of *Śiva*'s bow. The god is also called *Pinâkapâṇi* (he who carries *Pinâka*).

(2) This subject is found three times at *Ellora*, twice in the *Kailâsa*, and once in the cave of the *Avatârs* where it constitutes a large low-relief, the last on the right at the back of the cave (Pl. XIV).

Dakshiṇâmûrti.

Plate XV shows *Śiva* in the form of *Dakshiṇâmûrti*. He is called *Mahâ Yôgi* (the Great Ascetic) and is seated on a tiger's skin in the position called *Yôgâsana*, that is to say in the manner of *Yôgis*, under an *âlamaram* tree, which grows at the top of a hillock. A sort of belt (*aṅgostram* or *bahu-paddai*) holds up his knee. His plentiful hair falls over his shoulders. As a *guru* he teaches his doctrine to his disciples who are collected round him (1).

Historical. — In our opinion this image is very interesting because of its incontestable resemblance to the first sermon of Buddha before his first five disciples. In the ancient images of the *Kailâsanâtha* temple (8th century) at *Kañchîpuram* (Pl. XVI) and of the *Koraṅganâtha* at *Srinivasanalur* (10th century) (Vol. I, *Architecture*, Pl. XXX. A.) hinds are always seen at the feet of the god. The presence of these hinds can only be explained in one way. The first sermon of Buddha took place in the deer park. These animals represented by Buddhists have survived

(1) In the *Bhâgavata Purâṇa* (Burnouf's translation), book IV, chap. VI, is the following passage :

« 31. The gods saw a fig tree...

« 32. It was a hundred *yôjanas* high and its branches had a spread of seventy five. It threw around it an immovable shade. It harboured no nest, and never was penetrated by heat.

« 33. Under this tree, born of the great contemplation of the *Yôga*, who is the refuge of those who desire salvation, the *Suras* saw *Śiva* seated, looking like the god of death, who had put away his wrath.

« 34. He showed himself in peaceful guise, served by *Nandana*, and by other great *Siddhas*, calm like himself, his friend (*Kuvêra*) the chief of *Guhyakas* and *Yakshas*, seated by his side.

« 35. The supreme Lord walking in the way of knowledge, in the austerities of *Yôga*, accomplished in his affection for the universe which he loved, the salvation of the worlds.

« 36. He carried the *Liṅga* sought by the penitents, a club, ashes, a thick tuft of hair, an antelope skin, and the disk of the moon ; his body was the colour of red chalk.

« 37. He was seated on the seat of ascetics, made of the *Darbha* plant ; to *Nârada* who questioned him he explained the *Vêda* eternal, while harkened the sage.

« 38. He had placed on his right thigh, his lotus-like left foot ; on his left knee his left arm, on the upper part of his right arm, his rosary. (The gesture called) the seal of reasoning, his right hand did make. »

in the old images representing *Dakshiṇâmûrti*. But there was no reason to show hinds at the feet of *Śiva*, and so in our days they have entirely disappeared (1).

Gaṅgâdaram.

In *Pallava* temples low-reliefs of *Śiva* drawing the Ganges out of his hair are often found. The god holds a tress of hair in his hand. The goddess *Gaṅgâ*, whose body is like a siren's, appears with clasped hands. This subject is that of the unique low-relief (Pl. XVII) found in one of the two *Trichinopoly* caves (that which has inscriptions) (7th century).

It is seen very often in the *Kailâsanâtha* temple at *Kañchîpuram* (8th century). (See A. Rea, *Pallava Architecture: Kailâsanâtha*, Pl. LIX, LVII, XLIV, fig. 2, and CXXIII, fig. 2; *Muktêśvara* temple, Pl. CIV and XCVII, fig. 2) (2). But the interest of this image lies in the fact that although it is very wide spread in ancient sculpture, it is quite unknown to modern artists.

Śiva and Pârvatî riding on the bull.

On the other hand, *Śiva* and *Pârvatî* riding on a bull are never seen in ancient South Indian temples (3), although in our days it is one of the images most often repeated. This white bull, the riding animal or *vâhana* of *Śiva*, according to the legend is *Dharmadêva*, god of virtue. But it is usually called *Nandi*. Plate XVIII represents this subject. On each side of the divine group, Brahmins offer fruits and perfumes, and carry banners of a special sort called *alavatomes*.

Sômaskanda.

In our days (Pl. XIX) *Śiva* with *Pârvatî* (*Umâ*) and a small child *Subrahmaṇya* (*Skanda*) are still represented.

(1) In the *Kailâsa* at *Ellora* there is a large low-relief (the one opposite to that of *Śiva* clothing himself in the elephant's hide) of *Dakshiṇâmûrti*, the likeness of which to Buddha's image is striking.

(2) It is also found in the *Kailâsa* at *Ellora*, and once on the *vimâna* at *Tanjore* (10th century).

(3) Très fréquent au contraire à Ellora et dans le Nord.

Historical. — *Sômaskanda* is never seen any where in the caves of *Ellora* and *Bâdâmi*, but on the other hand this image is the great master design of *Pallava* iconography. It is so often repeated in the *Kailâsanâtha* temple at *Kañchîpuram*, that it is useless to count them. It is enough to say that the reproductions of this design are innumerable there.

It seems that it represents the essential part of *Pallava* Sivaism about 700 A. D., for the image is usally found in front of the *liṅgam*, on the wall which forms the back of the sanctuary (see Pl. I). *Śiva*, and *Pârvatî* who carries *Subrahmaṇya* on her knees, are seated on a bench. The attitudes of the divine family are full of calmness and nobility. *Śiva*'s left arm is in the same position as that of Buddha begging. The other arms carry no emblems except snakes. *Vishṇu* and *Brahmâ* stand, one on the right, the other on the left, a little behind *Śiva* (Pl. XX).

Râvaṇa below Kailâsa.

Śiva's heaven is a white mountain (whence the name *Rajatâdri*, mountain of silver), where *Kailaiyâli* (the god of *Kailâsa*) lives with his wife, his children, his worshippers and the company of *Gaṇas* (*Kailâsa* is called *Gaṇaparvata*, the mountain of *Gaṇas*). At the entrance of the *Pudumantapam* at *Madura* is a very fine statue showing the giant *Râvaṇa* under *Kailâsa*. The following is the explanation which modern sculptors in this country give of this subject :

The pious *Râvaṇa* with the object of getting near *Śiva*, wanted to make *Kailâsa* come to him, to this end he prayed long, but uselessly. As the mountain would not come to him, he resolved to go to it, and take it home with him. When he began to lift *Kailâsa*, *Pârvatî* noticed that the mountain was shaking, and drew her husband's attention to it. *Śiva*, placing his foot on *Kailâsa*, put it straight again. *Râvaṇa* was underneath and remained a prisoner. Fearing that he had angered the god he stayed quiet and began to pray. Then *Śiva* released him and gave him a sword (*ayudam*) and heaped blessings on him (1).

(1) Outside Southern India the legend is quite different. We borrow the following passage from Mr. Cœdès : « One day while traversing *Garavana*

Historical. — The subject is not to be seen in the *rathas* or caves at *Mavalipuram* and *Trichinopoly*, but it exists in low-relief in the small temple (not as old as the *rathas*) on the top of the rocks near the light-house at *Mavalipuram*, above the cave of *Durgâ*. It is found at *Kañchîpuram* in the *Kailâsanâtha* temple (A. Rea, *Pallava Architecture*, Pl. CXXIII, fig. 5), and in that of *Tripurâṅkêśvara* (Pl. CIX, fig. 2) (1). The giant who is under *Kailâsa* is always depicted with ten heads and twenty arms. In ancient low-reliefs he is seen from the back.

§ 2. — *Pârvatî.*

Pârvatî-kalyâṇa.

The marriage of *Śiva* and *Pârvatî* is often represented in our days. Pl. XXII shows the marriage of *Pârvati* under the form of *Mînâkshî* (the goddess with eyes of a fish) (2) guardian protectress of *Madura*.

The marriage of *Śiva* and *Pârvatî* is commemorated by the *Tirukalyâṇa* (divine marriage) festival.

Historical. — This subject is found in the *Kailâsanâtha* temple at *Kañchîpuram* (8th century). (A. Rea, *Pallava Architecture*, Pl. XLII, fig. 2) (3).

in his marvellous chariot, *Râvaṇa* suddenly saw the *Pushpaka* stop, for it had arrived at the foot of the mountain on which *Śiva* was playing. The *Râkshasa* got angry and taking the mountain in his arms, shook the rock. At this quaking the *Gaṇas* trembled and *Pârvatî* clung to *Mahêśvara*. Then *Mahâdêva*, the first of the gods, crushed the mountain with his toe as if in sport, at the same time he broke the arms of *Râvaṇa*. »

(1) At *Ellora* this is one of the most often repeated subjects. It is found in all the Brahminical caves : *Ashes of Râvaṇa*, *Kailâsa*, *Râmêśvaram* and *Dhumar-Lêna*. A low-relief in this last cave (Pl. XXI), situated on the right of the entrance, is one of the largest and most beautiful at *Ellora*.

(2) There is a pretty story told and known to but few, to explain the meaning of the name *Mînâkshî* : « As the mother fish swims in the river with her little ones who follow behind crying in their distress, she is not able to do anything for them. She turns her head and looks at them and they are comforted. So *Mînâkshî*'s glance is sufficient to comfort her followers. » (Tr.)

(3) It is often represented at *Ellora* : one finds it carved in large high-relief in all the Brahminical caves. The god and goddess hold hands, and *Vishṇu* pours lustral water for consecration, in the presence of all the other divinities.

Ardhanâri or Parâṅgadâ.

Śiva and *Pârvatî* are sometimes united in the form of a single androgynous deity. The right hand side of the divinity (which is to the left of the observer) represents *Śiva* and the left side *Pârvatî*. It is *Śiva*, *Ardha* (half) *Nâri* (woman). It is easy to recognize this deity. On the male side, the axe, the drum (*uḍukkai*) and snakes are seen. On the female side the breast is prominent,

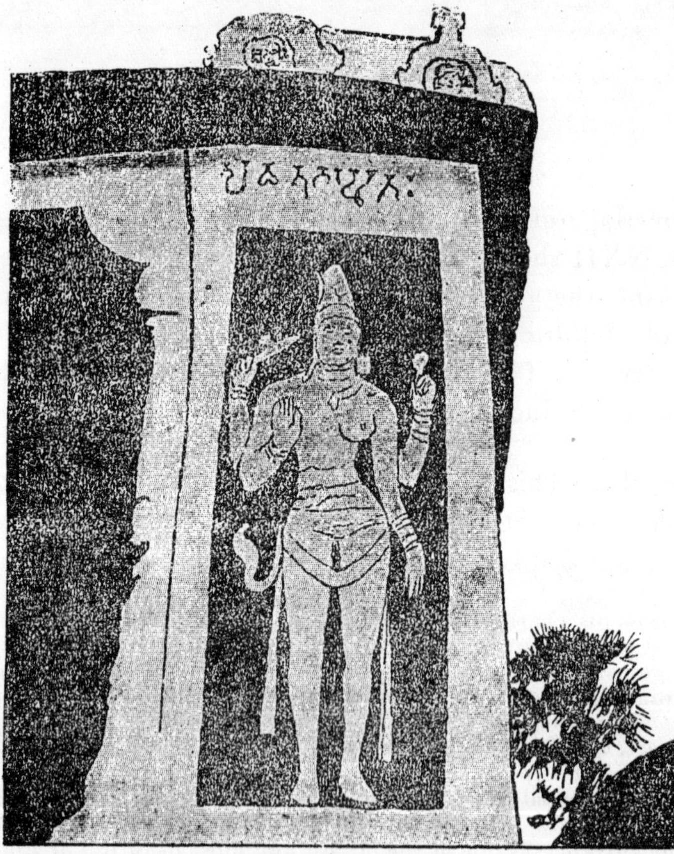

FIG. 7. — *Ardhanâri at Mavalipuram (7th century).*

the waist pinched in, the hip enlarged and covered with a cotton cloth (*podavê*). A flower is carried in the hand, bracelets and anklets deck the arm and leg.

Historical. — *Ardhanâri* is found at *Ṃavalipuram* on the *Dharmarâja-ratha* on the ground floor at the right of the Eastern facade (Fig. 7 and Pl. XXIII), and at *Tanjore* (last niche on the right of the West facade). Somewhat rare in our times (1).

Pârvatî (2).

This is the wife of *Śiva*, the latter bearing the name of *Pârvatî-*

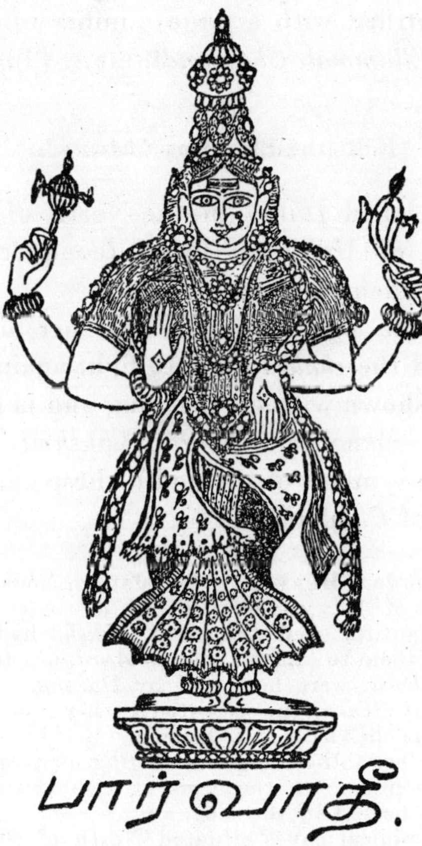

FIG. 8. — *Pârvatî.*

(1) This image is perhaps the oldest known, if one agrees with the story of the Hindu ambassador to Bardisanes (about 220 years A. D.) who describes a cave in the North of India containing an image of a god, half man half woman (STOBOEUS, *Physics*, published by Gaisford, p. 54, and PRIAULX, *L'Inde et Rome*, p. 153). It constitutes a large low-relief in cave No. 1 at *Bâdâmi* (Pl. XXIV).

(2) « The mountaineer », called also *Umei* (Sanskrit: *Umâ*), *Têvî* (Sanskrit: *Dêvî* goddess), *Ammei* (mother), *Śakti* (energy), *Gauri* (the daughter), *Kâmâkshî* (one whose looks are amorous), *Mînâkshî* (the fish-eyed).

kojunan (the husband of *Pârvatî*), and the daughter of *Takshen* (*Daksha*) (1).

She is represented sometimes with two arms, holding in her right hand the flower called *Seṅgarhunîrppû*, sometimes with four arms, carrying the Sivaite insignia *pâśa* and *mazhu* (Fig. 8).

Several festivals are sacred to *Pârvatî ;* those of *Quêdaravurdan*, *Paṅguniuttiram*, and *Adi Puran* are celebrated in *Śiva* temples at the *nakshatram* called *Puran*, in the month of *Adi* (July).

Pârvatî is identified with a large number of deities, particularly with *Kâlî*, *Ellammal*, *Châmundî*, etc... (2).

Kâlî (the Black) or *Châmundî*.

This goddess called *Durgâ* in the North of India, is known in her character of *Mahisha-mardinî* (conqueror of the giant *Mahisha*). She is identical with *Pârvatî*.

According to the legend, *Vishṇu* lent her his weapons, the *śaṅkha* shell, and the *chakra* disk, to fight against *Mahishâsura*. She is therefore shown with his insignia, and is the only goddess who carries the *śaṅkha* and *chakra*. (*Lakshmî*, wife of *Vishṇu*, never carries the symbols of the god.) These emblems are therefore distinctive of *Châmundî* (3).

(1) *Bhâgavata Purâṇa*, Burnouf's translation, book IV, chap. I :

« 47 *Daksha*, son of *Aja*, wedded *Prasûti*, daughter of *Manu* (*Svâyambhuva*) : sixteen beautiful eyed daughters, *Daksha* had by her.

« 48 Thirteen of them to *Dharma*, one to *Agni*, one to the *Pitṛis* jointly, and the last to *Bhava*, were bestowed by *Daksha*.

« 64 *Satî*, wife of *Bhava*, tho' devoted to her spouse divine, to bring forth a son his equal in virtue, was unable.

« 68 For *Daksha* her father, angry with *Bhava* (*Śiva*), unmerited insult in wrath put upon him. *Satî*, the bride of a short time, abandoned her body, and merged herself in the *Yôga*. »

(2) In the Brahminical caves situated North of the *Pennar*, there is often found a series of « mothers » placed between *Śiva* and *Pulliar* or *Bhṛiṅgi*. These goddesses carry a small child in their arms, and hold the emblems of the principal Brahminical deities. The mothers are *Mahîśvarî*, *Brahmâṇî*, *Indrâṇî*, *Kumârî*, *Varâhî*, etc. The vehicles (*vâhanas*) of the respective gods are found at their feet. The statues exist in the Brahminical caves at *Aïwoli* (near to *Pattadakal*), at *Ellora* in the caves *Ashes of Râvaṇa* and *Râmêśvaram* at the entrance and at the left of cave No. 22.

In the Buddhist caves at *Ellora*, a series of goddesses each corresponding to a Buddha is found. The Brahminical craftsmen have probably imitated the Buddhists in this matter.

Nothing of the sort is found in Southern India.

(3) The following passages are found in Mr. Burgess' work *The Cave*

Châmundî rode a lion in her fight with *Mahisha*, who had a buffalo's head. So *Châmundî* is represented sitting on a lion (*siṁha*) transfixing with her *śûla* the buffalo-headed giant. Flames appear behind her head and two pointed teeth issue from the corners of her mouth. She has a dozen arms, which brandish an axe (*paraśu*), a club (*gadâ*), a sword (*khaḍga*), a bow, a shield, a little bell (*ghaṇṭâ*) and lastly the shell *śaṅkha* and the disk *chakra* (Pl. XXV). She is also seen standing on the buffalo head of *Mahisha*.

Historical. — The image of *Kâlî* is one of those most often found in *Pallava* temples. In the *rathas* of the Seven Pagodas, the most Northerly of the group, which was been wrongly called *Draupadî*'s, is sacred to *Châmundî* who is represented all over it : in the sanctuary, on the facades, notably on the Eastern one where *Kâlî* is standing on the buffalo's head. This image is identical with that carved on the facade of the *Trimûrti* cave (Pl. XXVI).

A low-relief showing *Kâlî* is also found in the Vishnuvite *Varâha* cave. Lastly, in the cave near the light-house, wrongly called *Yamapuri* (because *Mahishâsura* was confused with *Yama*) there is the justly famed low-relief which represents *Kâlî*'s fight (Pl. XXVII) (1).

The goddess has not the same air of ferocity which is given to her in modern iconography. On the contrary, her face is calm, and her figure gracious. There are many representations of *Kâlî* in the *Kailâsanâtha* temple at *Kañchîpuram* (A. Rea, *Pallava Architecture*, Pl. LVI and XXXIX). In all ancient images *Châmundî* bears the Vishnuvite emblems *śaṅkha* and *chakra.*

temples of India, p. 117 :

« At the back (of the *Draupadî-ratha*) is a statue of *Lakshmî* the consort of *Vishṇu*, standing on a lotus, four armed and bearing the *chakra* with other emblems in her hand. »

Page 151, about an image sculptured in the *Varâha* cave :

« It may rather be considered as a representation of *Durgâ*, though the *śaṅkha* and discus rather belong to *Lakshmî*. »

The author of these lines seems to be ignorant of the fact that it is *Durgâ* (*Châmundî*), and not *Lakshmî* who carries the emblems *śaṅkha* and *chakra*.

(1) At *Ellora* the combat of *Kâlî* is also seen in the *Kailâsa* court on the left of the entrance.

The figure A, pl. XXXVIII of Vol. I, shows an image of *Kâlî* of the *Pâṇḍya* period.

Now-a-days she is considered to be a *grâma-dêvatâ* (village divinity) and is specially worshipped by the *sureurs* sellers of *kallu* (palm juice), who ornament the front of their shops with *Kâlî*'s image.

§ 3. — *Pulliar.*

(*Gaṇêśa.*)

The most renowned sons of *Śiva* and *Pârvatî* are *Gaṇêśa* (*Pulliar*), the elder, and *Subrahmaṇiar*, the younger, who are often depicted at their father's side : *Pulliar* on the right and *Subrahmaṇiar* on the left of the god. The third son of *Śiva* is *Vîrabhadra*. The name *Pulliar* is a corruption of the Tamil word *pilleyar* (the son). It designates the god more usually known in India by the names *Gaṇêśa* (from *gaṇa*, company, and *iśa*, chief) and *Gaṇapati*, with reference to his attribute of leader of the company of *Gaṇas* (little spirits of *Kailâsa*).

God of prudence and wisdom, he has great power to triumph over difficulties. Thus he is fervently worshipped under the names *Vighnêśvara* and *Vinâyaka*, that is to say, « conqueror over difficulties ». The distinctive character of *Pulliar* is that he has the head of an elephant on a human body. So he is surnamed *Anaimukavar* (from the Tamil word *anai*, meaning elephant), *Gajamukha*, *Gajânana* (from the Sanskrit word *gaja*, elephant), and *Tumbikkayan*, one who has a trunk (from the Tamil word *tumbikkai*, trunk). This peculiarity is explained in several ways.

Pârvatî while bathing longed for a son ; a sweat covered her body, and when she was wiping it off, she found a child in the hollow of her hand. *Śiva* in astonishment asked her : « Who is this child ? — *Pillai âr ?* » The *Dêvas* came to pay hommage at his birth. *Śani*, the genius of the planet Saturn, whose look reduced to ashes whatever he gazed at, stayed behind with head cast down. *Pârvatî* taking his reserved manner to be an insult, abused him roundly. Driven to desperation at last, he looked at *Pulliar*, whose head was reduced to ashes. To console *Pârvatî*,

Śiva ordered *Śani* to cut off the head of the first living being found lying down towards the North.

The animal was an elephant; so its head was fitted on to the body of the child.

According to another story, *Śiva* and *Pârvatî* saw the elephants disporting themselves in a forest. They felt constrained to follow

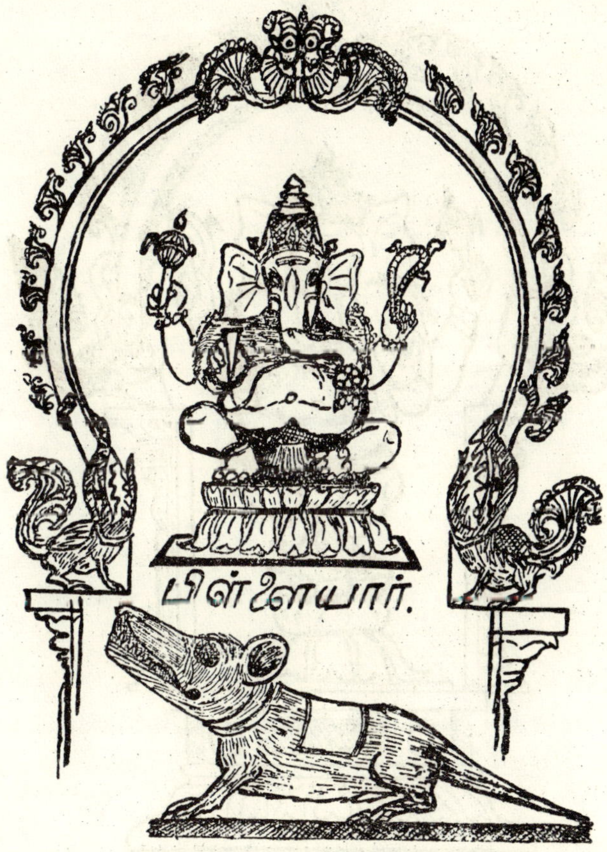

Fig. 9. — *Pulliar.*

their example, and the son conceived under these circumstances was born with the head of an elephant.

The anniversary of his birth is celebrated by the *Pillaiyâr-Chatturtti* festival (the fourth day after the new moon of each month, but specially in the month of *Avani* (August-September).

Pulliar's exploit was fighting the giant *Gujaimugâsura* (*Gajamukhâsura*), the elephant-headed demon. The latter had obtained the privilege of not being killed either by a beast, a man, a god or a demon. *Pulliar* not being one of these, as he was half god, half elephant, was the only one who could deal with him victoriously. The giant broke the god's right tusk, but *Pulliar*, using it as a javelin transfixed *Gajamukha*, who transformed

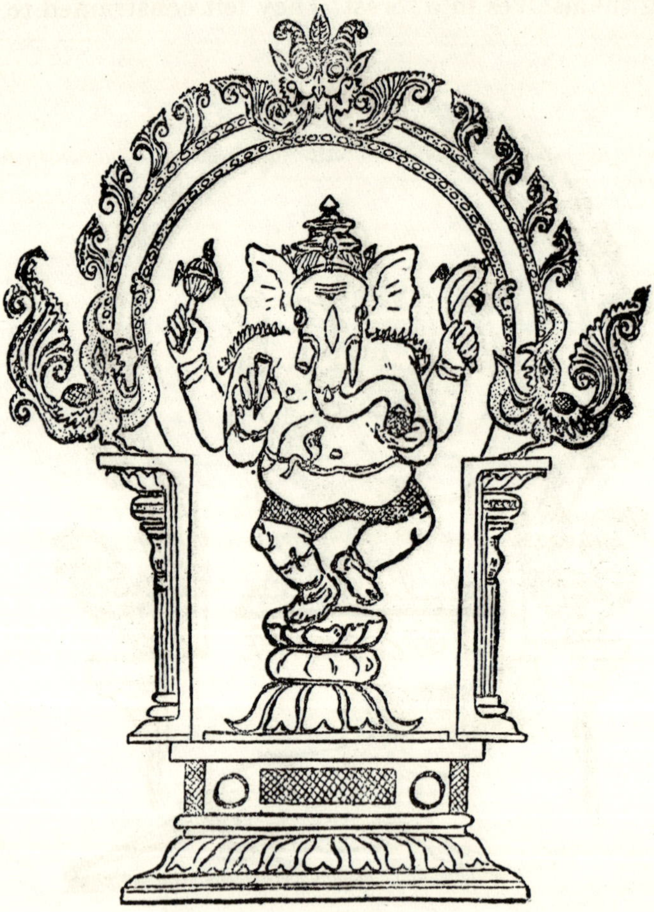

Fig. 10. —. *Pulliar dancing.*

himself into a rat (*yêli*) and became the vehicle (*vâhana*) of the god.

The god is usually represented seated (Fig. 9), but sometimes standing or dancing (Fig. 10) and then he has the name *Kuttâdam-Pulliyâr*. When he is riding the rat he is called *Âkhuratha* or *Âkhuvâhana*. His body is obese ; it is white, doubtless because of cowdung ashes. His belt is a snake. Bells are fastened to his trunk and ears. He has four arms ; one right hand bears the symbol *aṅgusam* (*aṅkuśa*) which is not exclusive to the god with the elephant head. It is a Sivaite emblem, and is sometimes carried by *Śiva*, and nearly always by *Pârvatî*. One of his left hands carries the cord *pacham* (*pâśa*). So *Pulliar* is called *Aṅgusapachamêndi* (he who carries the *aṅgusam* and *pacham*).

The second right hand holds his tusk (Tamil : *tandam*, Sanskrit: *danta*) broken off by *Gajamukha*. Lastly, the second left hand holds a cake made of rice flour (*ṁôdaka*), for the god is very partial to rice (*ariziounde*) whence his name *Môdakapiriyan*. The end of the trunk of *Pulliar* is always placed on this rice cake.

Historical. — Images of *Pulliar* are not very numerous in *Pallava* temples. There is not one at *Mavalipuram*. At *Trichinopoly* and *Vallam* there are low-reliefs which represent this god carved on monolithic temples dating from the 7th century. At *Trichinopoly* there is a large image of *Pulliar* in the cave without inscriptions, where he is seen standing, surrounded by *Gaṇas*. His emblems are hardly visible, for the stone is worn, and one of the arms is broken off. It is beside *Subrahmaṇiar*, near *Śiva*'s shrine.

At *Vallam* (Pl. XXVIII) he is seated. His trunk is directed to the right, and not to the left as in our times ; he does not bear the modern emblems *pacham* and *aṅgusam*, but holds something vague, which may be his tusk.

In these two images he is not accompanied by his rat (1). In temples of the Tamil country anterior to the 12th century, the vehicles (*vâhana*) of the gods are never seen, neither *Subrahmaṇiar*'s peacock, nor *Brahmâ*'s swan (*haṁsa*), nor the parrot of *Kâma*. Vedic gods are never seen mounted on their respective animals. *Śiva* never rides his bull. *Kâlî* is the only one who rides, mounted on her lion (*siṁha*).

On the other hand the *vâhanas* are always seen at *Ellora*. It is therefore a Northern Indian custom which was introduced in the South, about the 12th century.

(1) At *Ellora* he is often represented. He has as emblems an axe, a flower, and a vessel full of cakes. His rat is not seen there either. In fact these ancient images are very different from modern ones, and in our days no one would consent to worship them.

§ 4. — *Subrahmaṇiar.*

(*Subrahmaṇya or Skanda.*)

Śiva's second son is *Subrahmaṇiar* (1) who is also called *Supraya-kumâra* (the young child), *Murugan* (the younger son), *Kandasami* (*Skanda-svâmi*), etc...

He was begotten by *Śiva* for the purpose of destroying the giant *Surapatma*, who had obtained from *Śiva* the power to rule the universe. With the aid of his brothers *Siṅgamugâsuran* and *Târagâsuran* and of his sister *Assomuguy*, he maltreated the *Ṛishis*. These complained to *Śiva*, who opened the eye which is in the middle of his forehead, thence came a spark called *Porri* which fell on to the lake *Saravanapoyigai*. This spark changed into six children who were nursed by six of the *Ṛishis*' wives (who were subsequently changed into stars, the Pleiades).

Śiva sent *Pârvatî* to see the children and as she wished to embrace them all at the same time, they were immediately combined into a single body with six heads. *Śiva* commanded the giant thus made to fight against *Surapatma* who entrenched himself in the fortress of *Vîramâyêndrapuri*. *Subrahmaṇiar* first conquered *Târagâsuran* (*Târaka*). When he attacked the giant *Sura*, the latter changed himself into a tree, but *Subrahmaṇiar* drove his lance called *Vêl* into the heart of the tree which split into two pieces, one of which was changed into a peacock, and the other into a cock. Ever since *Subrahmaṇiar* has the peacock to ride upon, and the cock ornaments his standards. The birth and feats of *Subrahmaṇiar* earned him the following epithets : *Śaravana* (born in the lake of that name), *Kârttikêya* (nursed by the six *Kṛittikâs*, the Pleiades), *Gaṅgeyan* (born in the arms of *Gaṅgâ* or *Pârvatî*), *Arumukha* or *Shanmukha* (who has six faces), *Dvâdaśakara* (who has 12 arms), *Dvâdaśâksha* (who has 12 eyes), *Târakajit* (the conqueror of *Târaka*), *Vêlayuda* (he who is armed with the *vêl* : the lancer), *Surasaṁhâra-mûrti* (the

(1) Two different derivations are given for this name : 1. *Śubhra-maṇya*, (diamond like) ; 2. *Su-brahmaṇya*, protector of the Brahmin caste.

conqueror of *Sura*), *Mailêrivêlan* (the lancer who is mounted on the peacock).

Subrahmaṇiar is shown as a beardless young man (Fig. 11), his forehead is marked with *vibûdipundram.* The lance (*vêl*) rests on his right shoulder. He has four arms. The two front hands (*kayi*) are respectively in the positions called *abhaya-hastam* (the right one and) *varada-hastam.* The two back arms both carry insignia representing thunder-bolts (*vajra*) whence the name *Vachirayudam.*

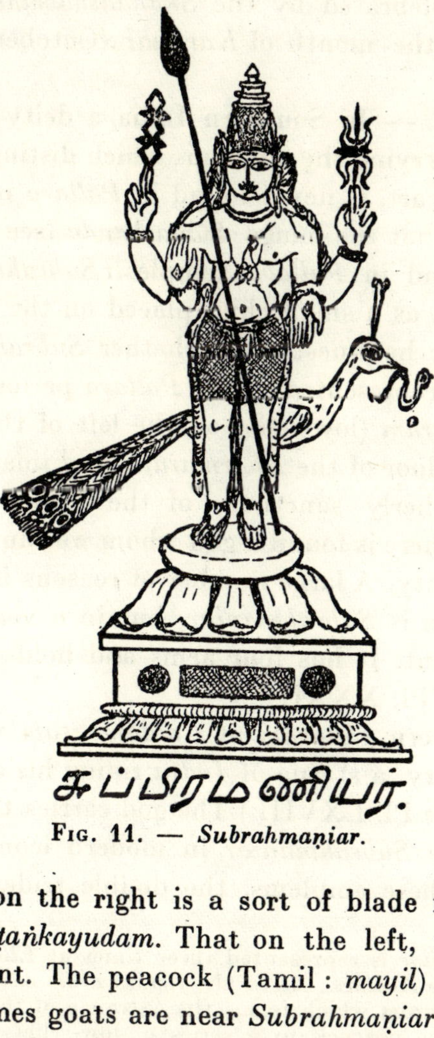

Fig. 11. — *Subrahmaṇiar.*

The emblem on the right is a sort of blade made by three lozenges called *ṭaṅkayudam.* That on the left, named *triśûla*, is a double trident. The peacock (Tamil : *mayil*) stands behind the god. Sometimes goats are near *Subrahmaṇiar* (1) which were given to him when he went to visit *Dêvalôgam.*

(1) For example in the *Ramêśvaram* at *Ellora.*

Subrahmaṇiar is often riding on a peacock (Pl. XXIX). The bird's tail spread fan-wise forms a multi-coloured aureole round the god. *Subrahmaṇiar*'s two wives are represented one on each side of the god. *Vaḷḷi-ammai* is on the right, she is brown and sometimes rides a lion. The other *Dêvayânai* is of a bright colour, and her riding animal is an elephant.

When *Subrahmaṇiar* is shown with six faces (Pl. XXX) he is called *Arumugam* (*Arumukha*).

The anniversary of the victory of *Subrahmaṇiar* over the giant *Sura* is celebrated by the *Skandashashṭhî* festival, which takes place in the month of *Kartigai* (October-November).

Historical (1). — In Southern India a deity accompanied by a peacock or carrying the emblems which distinguish *Subrahmaṇiar* in modern art, is never found in *Pallava* or *Chôḷa* temples. We have seen that the image *Sômaskanda* (see Pl. XX) is very frequently found in *Pallava* temples. *Subrahmaṇiar* (*Skanda*) figures in them as a small child placed on the knees of *Pârvatî* (*Umâ*). It may be questioned whether *Subrahmaṇiar* in adult form was ever represented in the *Pallava* period.

At *Mavalipuram* (low-relief on the left of the Eastern facade of the ground floor of the *Dharmarâja*, and image at the back of the most Northerly sanctuary of the *Trimûrti* cave) and at *Trichinopoly*, there is found a god whom we cannot identify with any modern deity. A large number of reasons induce the beliefh that this image is *Subrahmaṇiar*, but in a very different style from the present. It has four arms and holds insignia difficult to distinguish (Pl. XXXI).

On the Eastern *gôpuram* at *Chidambaram* which dates from the 12th century, a statue of *Indra* riding his elephant is found in a niche. (See Pl. LXVIII.) The god carries the same emblems as characterize *Subrahmaṇiar* in modern iconography. This is logical since these emblems, the double trident and the three

(1) *Subrahmaṇiar* is represented three times at *Ellora* : 1. at the back of the cave of the *Avatârs* ; 2. in the *Ramêśvaram* cave ; 3. on the facade of the small *gôpuram* which forms the entrance of the *Kailâsa*, when he is seen riding the peacock in a series of low-reliefs consecrated to the Vedic gods. It seems that at *Ellora* he was considered a secondary deity, and he never carries any of the emblems of which we have spoken.

sparkling squares, are emblematic of thunder-bolts (*vajra*) and *Indra* was considered in olden days to be the god of the sky, who hurled thunder-bolts.

It would appear therefore the *Indra*'s emblems were affected after the 13th century by *Subrahmaṇiar*. Besides, the two wives of *Subrahmaṇiar* ride respectively on an elephant and a lion. The elephant is the mount of *Indra* and the lion that of *Indrâṇî*, his wife. Lastly, the image of *Arumugam* (*Subrahmaṇiar* with six faces) seems very modern, as it is not found in ancient temples.

Palani-Andavar.

Subrahmaṇiar is worshipped at *Palani* (to the West of *Madura*) in the guise of an *andi* (beggar), whence his names *Palani-andi Palani-vêlan* (the lancer of *Palani*). *Palani-Andavar* (1). (Pl. XXXII) is represented almost naked, his only clothing being a strip of cloth called *laṅguti* made of a napkin (*kaupinam*) upheld by a cord (*annâkavur*). His breast is decked with chaplets (*rudrâksha*) and with the Brahminical thread (*punul*).

His feet are shod with *pâdarachchai* (from the Sanskrit *pâdaraksha*). The lance rests against his right shoulder, and his right hand holds a club (*daṇḍa*).

Historical. — We have never seen an image of *Palani-Andavar* in an ancient temple.

§ 5. — *Vîrabhadra.*

According to a Tamil legend *Śiva*'s father-in-law *Daksha* entered an assemblage one day, where his son-in-law who was present, did not rise to salute him. *Daksha* was furious, and gave himself up to evil deeds to cause harm to *Śiva*. He made use of a certain process in black magic called *yâgam*, which consists of burning wood and pronouncing certain *mantiras* before the flames, designed to cast spells.

(1) *Andavar* means « the lord ». (Tr.)

Śiva was immediately seized with violent pains, and sent his eldest son *Pulliar* against *Daksha*, who successfully bribed *Pulliar* by an offering of cakes. *Śiva* then sent his second son *Subrahmaṇiar*, who knew this god's character and won his friendship by giving him dancing girls. Meanwhile the effect of the *yâgam* caused *Śiva* such suffering that a profuse sweat covered his body.

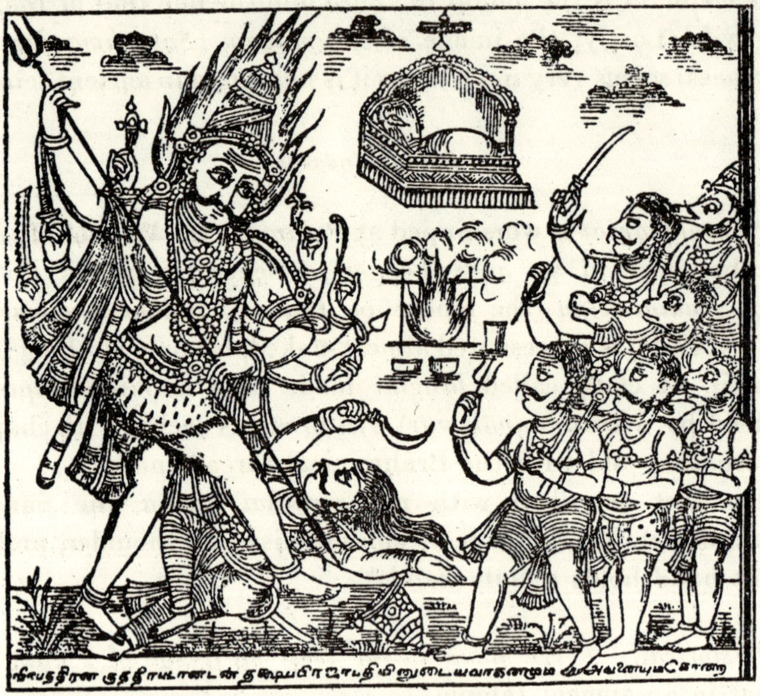

FIG. 12. — *Vîrabhadra demolishing the sacrifice of Daksha.*

From the drops of sweat which ran down from *Śiva*'s brow, came the giant *Vîrabhadra*, who making *Daksha* stop his sacrifice (Fig. 12), cut off his head and threw it into the fire. *Pârvatî* prayed her husband to give back his life to her father. *Śiva* acquiesced, but as *Daksha's* head had been burnt up, it was replaced by that of a ram (1).

(1) The version of the *Bhâgavata Purâṇa* is appreciably different. *Bhâgavata Purâṇa*, book IV (translation of BURNOUF) :

« Chap. III. 2. ... When *Daksha* was raised by *Brahmâ* the Most High, to be the chief of all chiefs of creation, he was filled with pride overweening.

« 3. After performing the ceremony of *Vâjapêya*, and overcoming those who knew the better *Brahmâ*, he began the sacrifice called *Vṛihaspatisava*.

Vîrabhadra's appearance is terrifying (Fig. 13). He is decked with collars of skulls (*muṇḍa-mâlâ*). Flames spring from his hair,

« 5. *Satî* the divine, daughter of *Daksha*, who had learnt in heaven from the conversation of the dwellers in the air, of the great sacrificial ceremony her father was performing,

« 7. ... spoke thus being full of desire, to the chief of the *Bhûtas*, her husband :

« 8. « Thy father-in-law the *Prajâpati*, a great sacrifice now is performing. Let us then go together, o *Vâma* (*Śiva*), if such is thy wish. »

« 15. Thus pressed by his wife *Giritra*, the friend of those who follow him, remembered the painful words like sharp arrows, with which the *Prajâpati* had wounded him in the presence of the Creators of the Universe, and smilingly replied :

« 20. ... « His daughter though thou be, thou must not have regard for thy father *Daksha*, who hates me, nor for those devoted to him. He it was, at the time of the sacrifice made by the Creators of the Universe at which I attended, who harmed me with words outrageous, which I did not deserve. »

« Chap. IV. 3. ... Her heart with vexation and anger was torn, sighing as if her heart would break, *Satî* proceeded to the household of her father, by her woman's passion her mind led astray, abandoning him beloved by virtous men, who out of his own love, had given her half of his body.

« 6. The precinct of the sacrifice she entered, that place loved by those of the Brahmins the *Ṛishis*, by all the immortals, where the victim is killed after consecration, by the recital of *Vêdas*, where the instruments of the ceremony, of clay and of wood, of brass and of gold, of the herb called the *Dharba*, and also of skins, are carefully kept.

« 7. No one present when she entered, dared to receive with respect the goddess disdained by her father, fearing to offend the celebrant of the sacrifice.

« 9. Seeing the sacrifice in which *Rudra* took no share, and the lack of respect shown by her father *Daksha* to *Vibhu* (*Śiva*) the divine, the scorned sovereign goddess, in the midst of the assembly, gave way to her wrath, as if she willed to destroy the worlds in her anger.

« 24. Heaping insults on *Daksha*, in the midst of the sacrifice, she sat on the ground without sound, and turned to the North ; to her lips she put water ; wrapped in yellow silk robes and shutting her eyes, she entered the way of the *Yôga*.

« Chap. v. 1. On learning from *Nârada* of the death of *Bhavânî*, which the contempt of the *Prajâpati* had caused, and defeat of his company of servants, *Bhava* felt a boundless rage.

« 2. Furious and biting his lips, he who bears the burden of the worlds, the redoubtable god, suddenly rose, drily laughing the while, he tore off the tuft of his hair, the terrible illumination of which was like claps of thunder and fire, and hurled it to the ground.

« 3. From this knot sprang a giant whose body touched the sky, accoutred with a thousand arms, darkly tinted, like three suns shone his head, whose teeth were huge, whose hair was like a flaming fire, carrying a necklace of skulls and weapons of various kinds, ready to strike.

« 4. With folded hands he cried : « What must I do ? » The chief of *Bhûtas* made happy, replied : « Redoutable warrior ! *Daksha* and his sacrifice destroy, you are the chief of my braves, a part of myself. »

« 5. On receiving the order from the angry god, the giant marched

formidable fangs protrude from his lips above which are heavy moustaches. He carries *Śiva*'s emblems, but he is distinguishable from him and from the other gods, because his principal arms carry weapons, namely a sword and a shield (*kêdayam* or *parisai*). By his side *Daksha* with a ram's head, stands with folded hands.

round the sovereign lord, god of gods, in token of respect, and then felt himself unequalled in courage, and able to sustain the attacks of those most mighty.

« 6. Followed by the servants of *Rudra*, who made violent noises, he gave vent to a terrible yell, and wielding a spear able to demolish the Destroyer of worlds, he rushed forward ; the anklets which adorned his feet clashing as he went.

« 22. Trampling the breast of *Daksha* under foot, the three-eyed giant cut at his head with trenchant blade, but failed to sever it completely.

« 23. On seeing the body, the skin of which could be pierced neither by arrows nor swords, *Hara*, the master of creatures, vastly astonished, meditated long.

« 24. But the god who is the master of all creatures, noted the way in which the victim of the sacrifice was slain, by the same means he took the head of *Daksha* off from his body. The sacrificer now became the victim.

« 25. Seeing this action, the *Bhûtas*, *Prêtas*, and *Piśâchas* praised the god saying : « Good ! Good ! » but the others exclaimed otherwise.

« 26. In his wrath he threw the head into the Southern fire, after thus destroying the sacrifice of the gods, he went away to the home of the *Guhyakas*.

« Chap. VI. 1. ... Then all the companies of the *Dêvas* put to flight by the armies of *Rudra*, worshipped *Svayambhû* and told him all that has happened.

« 4. When the sovereign creator heard the tale of the gods, he spoke thus :

« 6. « If you wish to revive the sacrifice, be sure to placate the god who has been deprived of his wife. »

« 8. After giving this counsel to the *Suras*, *Aja*, accompanied by the gods, the *Prêtas* and the chiefs of creation, left his dwelling to go to that of the enemy of *Pura*, on the most beautiful of mountains, on *Kailâsa* loved by the lord supreme.

« 42. *Brahmâ* said :

« 50. ... « O intelligent god, revive the sacrifice of *Prajâpati* which thou hast destroyed before it was finished, that sacrifice, I mean, in which the wicked priests the celebrators refused thee thy share, and bring it to its conclusion thyself.

« 51. Let him who caused its celebration, live again ! »

« Chap. VII. 1. Satisfied by the words which the uncreated god used to supplicate him, *Bhava* smiling said :

« 3. « Let the chief of the creatures whose head was burnt up, now take the head of a ram. »

« 7. ... The warriors of *Indra*'s army and the *Ṛishis* went once again to the sacrifice of the *Dêvas*, and with them went the god and the *Vêdas*.

« 8. Everything was done according at the order fo the ever happy *Bhava*, to the body of *Daksha* he adapted the head of the ram destined for the sacrifice. »

Historical. — *Vîrabhadra* is represented in the temple of *Kailâsanâtha* at *Kañchîpuram* (A. Rea, *Pallava Architecture*,

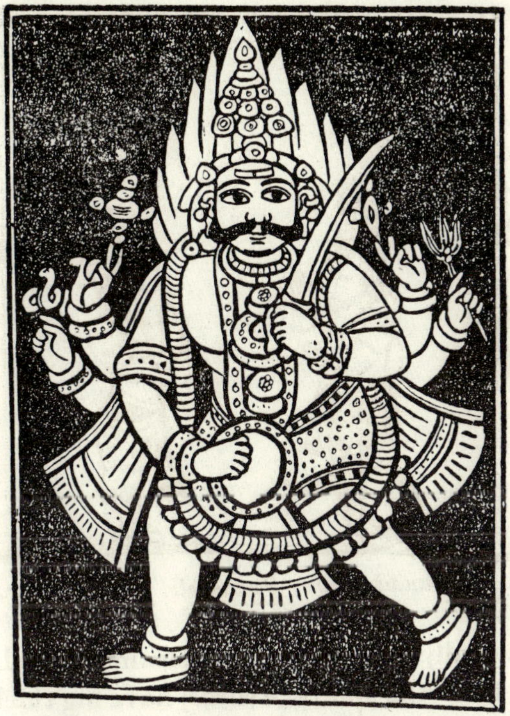

வீரபத்திரன்.

Fig. 13. — *Vîrabhadra.*

Pl. XXXVI, fig. 1 : panel 16th from East and on South side of court).

§ 6. — *The Sivaite Saints.*

Patañjali or Padañjeli.

In modern art *Śiva* is often surrounded by a following of acolyte deities. *Patañjali* is a little god, the lower part of whose body ends as the tail of a snake. He was a *Yôgi*, and not wishing to crush insects with his feet, he obtained from *Nadarâja* the *varam* to be changed into a reptile (1).

Padañjeli's hair is plaited and piled on his head, his hands are clasped before *Śiva*, and he wears a pointed beard (Fig. 14).

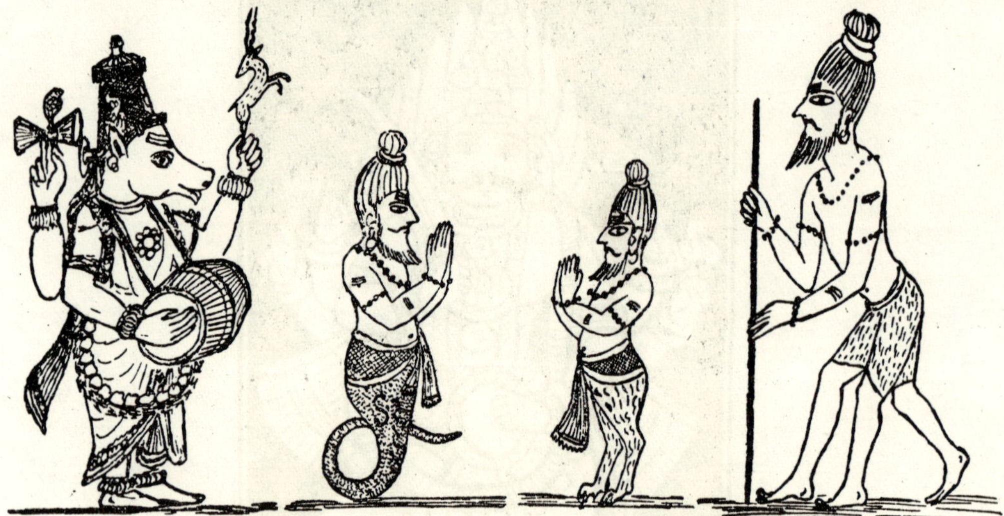

FIG. 14. — *Nandikêśvara, Padañjeli, Viagrapadar, Bhṛiṅgi.*

Hindu gods usually have their faces clean shaved like Brahmins. On the other hand the giants (*Asuras*) have big thick moustaches, and the *Ṛishis* all have beards.

Historical. — We have never found in ancient low-reliefs any personage which can be clearly identified with *Padañjeli*.

Viagrapadar or Vyâghrapâda.

This is a small god with the feet (*pâda*) of a tiger (*vyâghra*) (Fig. 14). The upper part of his body is identical with that of *Padañjeli*. His business was to go and gather flowers for *Nadarâja* in order to protect him from the pricks of thorns, the stings of insects or the bites of snakes etc. *Nadarâja* gave him tiger's feet.

(1) *Padañjeli* may be the same as *Patañjali*, the author of *Mahâ-Bhâshya*, the commentator of *Pâṇini*'s grammar, who according to the legend, fell from heaven into the hollow of *Pâṇini*'s hand in the form of a small snake, whence his name (*pat*, to fall ; *añjali*, hollow of the hand) ?

Historical. — It may be *Viagrapadar* who is seen on the right of the 16th low-relief at the Eastern end of the Southern face of the *Kailâsanâtha* temple court at *Kañchîpuram.* (See A. Rea, *Pallava Architecture*, Pl. XXXVI, fig. 1.)

Bhṛiṅgi or Maharuchi.

As to the upper part of his body this *Ṛishi* is like *Padañjeli* and *Viagrapadar*, but he is much taller ; his hair is plaited and piled up in a knot. His forehead is marked with the three white stripes of *Śiva*, he has a pointed beard, and is decked with necklaces of *rudrâksha* beads (Fig. 14) ; frequently his hands are clasped in the position called *kummudugirathu* (Sansrkit : *añjali*), but often he carries a stick. *Bhṛiṅgi*'s distinctive characteristic is his thinness. He has three legs, the reason for which is as follows :

Bhṛiṅgi wished to worship *Śiva*, but not *Pârvatî.* She was furious and took away all his flesh (1). *Śiva* seeing that he had nothing but bones, and so no longer could stand, gave him a third leg to support him.

Historical. — We have never seen a personage with three legs on any ancient sculpture (2).

Kârikal-Ammei.

One sometimes sees in the company round *Śiva*, a woman in a very emaciated condition. This is not *Bhṛiṅgi*'s wife. as might be supposed. She is called *Kârikal-Ammei*, the goddess worshipped at *Kârikal*, and bears the name *Punnidavadiar* (*Punîtavatî*), the wife of a Brahmin merchant called *Paramadattan.*

One day she gave to a beggar a mango which was intended for

(1) It is supposed that the human body is composed of two substances : flesh which is the feminine part, and bones which form the masculine part.

(2) At *Ellora* (notably in the cave *Ramêśvaram*) and at *Bâdâmi* (cave No. 1, low-relief representing *Ardhanâri :* see Pl. XXIV), a personage who is completely deprived of his flesh is to be found, sometimes with his family. This skeleton, for the skin only remains on the bones, is none other than *Bhṛiṅgi.*

her husband. When he asked for the fruit, she gave him several, which she obtained miraculously. Her husband, in face of this prodigy, saw in her a goddess and ceased to treat her as his wife. In despair she prayed heaven to take away her flesh. The mango feast at *Kârikal* commemorates this legend in the month of June.

Nandikêśvara.

We have already said that *Ṛishabha* and *Dharmadêva*, the bull which sits in front of the *liṅgam*, and the bull which *Śiva* rides, must not be confused with *Nandikêśvara.* He has a bull's head on a human body with four arms. The back arms carry the drum (*uḍukkai*) and the antelope (*mân*) emblems of *Śiva.* The front arms are usually occupied in beating a long sort of drum called *matalam* (Fig. 14).

Historical. — The second panel on the Western face of the *vimâna* of the temple of *Kailâsanâtha* at *Kañchîpuram* represents *Śiva* dancing. On the left of the god, *Nandikêśvara* is seen dancing too (1). (See A. Rea, *Pallava Architecture*, Pl. LVIII.)

Appar.

Plate XXXIII represents the four great Sivaite sages who are often shown beside *Śiva.* They are *Appar*, *Sundarar*, *Sambandar* and *Mâṇikkavâchakar.* All four composed religious hymns. The first three were apostles of Sivaism and opponents of Buddhism and are the authors of the book called *Dêvâram*, a collection of prayers which are chanted after the office of *Pûjâ* in *Śiva* temples. The fourth, *Mâṇikkavâchakar*, is the author of a collection of religious hymns called *Tiruvâchakam*, and of the erotic poem *Tirukôvei.*

Appar, also called *Tiru-Navukarassu*, born in the South of India in the end of the 6th century, was first Buddhist, then a Jain, and finally Sivaite. He is depicted with shaven head, leaving

(1) In the cave No. 1 at *Bâdâmi*, low-relief of *Hari-Hara* (Pl. IX), a little godling with a bull's head stands by *Śiva*'s side.

only the knot of hair behind called *kuḍumi-muḍi* ; his head and arms are decked with chaplets (*rudrâksha*) ; his hands are joined in the position called in Tamil *kummudugirathu* (Sanskrit : *añjali*). On his right shoulder rests a trowel called *ojavaram*, with which he used to dig up herbs in the pagoda in which he lived.

Sundarar.

Sundaramûrti-Svâmi, born about 800 A. D. (1) at *Tirunavalur* in the Karnatic, was brought up in a royal family, but took to an ascetic life on attaining his majority. One day by means of his religious hymns he stopped a flood of the Kaveri river. He died at the age of 18 years at *Tiruvañjaikkaḷam.*

He is represented with a tiara on his head, as a sign of his noble birth. In his right hand he holds a flower of nenuphar (*tamarapushpa*), and his left hand rests on a stick of special form carried by ascetics, which is called *yôgatandu.*

Sambandar.

Tiru-Jñâna-Sambandar-Svâmi lived about 600 A. D. From the age of 5 years he took to a mendicant life. He is therefore represented as a young child. Peacock's feathers adorn his head. In his hands he carries cymbals made of metal disks tied together by a cord. This musical instrument is called *talam.*

Mâṇikkavâchakar.

Mâṇikkavâchakar was born about 800 A. D. at *Vadavur*, on the banks of the Vaigai near Madura, and was minister to *Arimarddhana-Pâṇḍya*, king of Madura. He was ordered by the king to buy horses, but used the money for the glory of *Śiva.* The king's stables however were miraculously filled with horses, which subsequently turned into jackals.

Mâṇikkavâchakar combatted the Buddhists who came from Ceylon, and Jainism. He wrote a book in favour of Sivaism called *Tiruvâchakam.* This work contains moral precepts.

(1) The dates of these saint's births are not accurately known.

Mâṇikkavâchakar died at *Chidambaram* at the age of 32 years. He is represented carrying a chaplet and a book of *olai* leaves (1). His festival called *Avani-Mulu* takes place during the *nakshatram* of *Mulu* (August).

Arupathumuvar.

Among the other personages in *Śiva*'s following, *Kundodaren* (*Kundodara*) who carries *Śiva*'s sunshade must be mentioned. Also the *Arupathumuvar*, the 63 Sivaite saints of whom *Tandesvara* is the principal.

(1) Hindu books are written on palm leaves called *olai*.

CHAPTER II

VISHNUVITE ICONOGRAPHY

§ 1. — *Vishṇu.*

Vishṇu (the penetrating), also called *Perumâl* (the lord), *Gôvinda* (he who brings heaven within reach), *Hari*, etc., is usually represented in human form. His head is encircled with the tiara (whence *Vishṇu*'s epithet : *Kirîṭin*) which is also worn by deities attached to *Vishṇu.* The shape of this tiara has undergone considerable change in the course of centuries (Fig. 15).

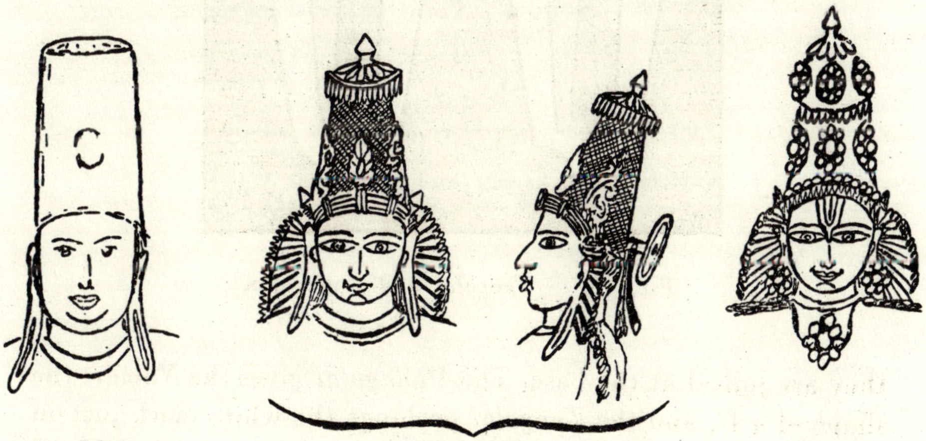

Fig. 15. — *Tiara of Vishṇu.*

In the *Pallava* period it was a simple cylinder. In the middle ages it was something like a truncated cone. Now-a-days it is like a kind of sugar-loaf ornamented with jewels, and is called *kridam* (1).

The god's ears are long and pendulous. The colour of his skin

(1) This shape is not unlike that of the tiara which *Indra* wears in the Greco-Buddhist sculptures (*Visite d'Indra,* photo. 1058, 1.M. list).

is always blue except in the incarnation of *Râma*, whose skin is always green, and of *Kṛishṇa* whose colour is black or blue, and sometimes white and rosy.

In our days, *Vishṇu*'s forehead is always marked with the sign called *Tirunâmam*, or simply *Nâmam*, from the name of a kind of chalk (which comes from *Tirupati*), with which the Vaishnavas trace the sign on their foreheads. It consists of three vertical stripes ; the middle one is red, and is called *Tiruchurnam* (holy chalk), because it is made of a mixture of lime and saffron. The other two stripes on each side of the first are much broader and are joined below. They are white and are called *Gôpichandana*.

There are two kinds of *Nâmam* according to the way in which

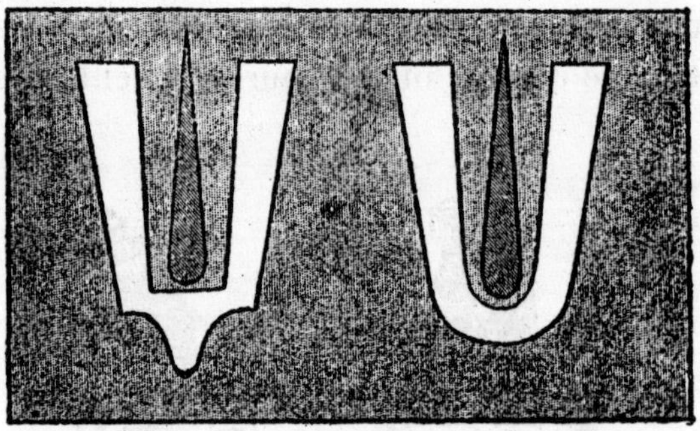

FIG. 16. — *Teṅgalai and Vadagalai.*

they are joined at the base. The *Vadagalai* gives the *Nâmam* the shape of a *U*, and the *Teṅgalai* prolongs the white mark just on to the nose and takes the form of a *Y*, worn by the disciples of *Manavala* (Fig. 16).

The *Nâmam* is fairly important in iconographical history as a chronological character. In *Pallava* temples *Vishṇu*'s forehead is always absolutely unmarked (1).

It is always so until the 15th century. It appears that the *Nâmam* appeared in the *Bijayanagar* period. It is the rule today. The sign is therefore comparatively recent. In any case we think

(1) It is the same in all the ancient temples at *Ellora*, *Bâdâmi*, etc.

we can assert that when the *Nâmam* is seen on an image, it is later than the 15th century (unless the mark was added afterwards on to the image).

Vishṇu's face is always beardless. His eyes are like lotus flowers, whence the epithets *Puṇḍarîkâksha* and *Jalajalôchana* (the god with lotus eyes). *Vishṇu* always has four arms, whence his name *Chatur-bhuja.* He is often fashioned making the gestures *abhaya-hastam* and *varada-hastam*, of which we shall speak later.

Sometimes he holds in his hand a lotus flower *padumaṇi* (from the Sanskrit *padma*), *tamarasi* or *kamala.* He has five weapons (*pañchâyudha*) : the bow, the sword, the club, the conch and the disk :

1. The bow (in Sanskrit *śârṅga*, whence *Vishṇu*'s name *Śârṅgapâṇi*) called *Kôdaṇḍa* (*Râma* too his called *Kôdaṇḍarâma*).
2. The sword (Sanskrit : *khaḍga*) called *Vidyâdhara.*
3. The club (*gadâ*) called *Kaumôdaki.*
4. The conch called *Pâñchajanya*, known by the Tamil name *Saṅgu* (from the Sanskrit *śaṅkha*), the shell of the sea-mollusc *Murex Tritonis*, which can be used as a trumpet.
5. The disk (*Sudarśana* or *Vajra-nâbha*), known by the Tamil name *Chakram* (from the Sanskrit *chakra*), which is a weapon. (*Vishṇu* is also called *Nêmiyon*, he who carries the disk.)

The last two weapons, the conch and the disk are characteristic of the god ; besides they have valuable chronological importance, and deserve special study.

It is easy to ascertain the age of a sculpture by examining these emblems, which form one of the means of fixing the dates not only of the statues of *Vishṇu*, but also those of *Kâlî*, since we have seen, in both ancient and modern sculpture, *Kâlî* always carries the *Saṅgu* and the *Chakram.*

Figure 17 shows the evolutionary law of the *Chakram.* In all the low-reliefs at *Mavalipuram* (7th century) and in the *Kailâsanâtha* temple at *Kañchîpuram*, the disk *Chakram* is a disk absolutely devoid of flames, which the god holds between his thumb and index finger (1).

(1) In the *Kailâsanâtha* temple at *Kañchîpuram*, *Vishṇu* is often seen holding a *Chakram* ornamented with flames, but they are never carved on the stone. They have been added in cement when the temple was repaired at a more recent period.

Some centuries later, this wheel was ornamented with flames called *sudar*, some placed on the edges of the disk, and others proceeding from both ends of the axle. Besides, it is no longer held between the thumb and first finger, but is balanced on the ends of the first and middle fingers. Again, the wheel is usually seen end on.

On the side which represents *Vishṇu* in the statue of *Hari-Hara* in the most Southern niche of the Western facade of the *Tanjore* temple, a *Chakram* of this kind is to be seen.

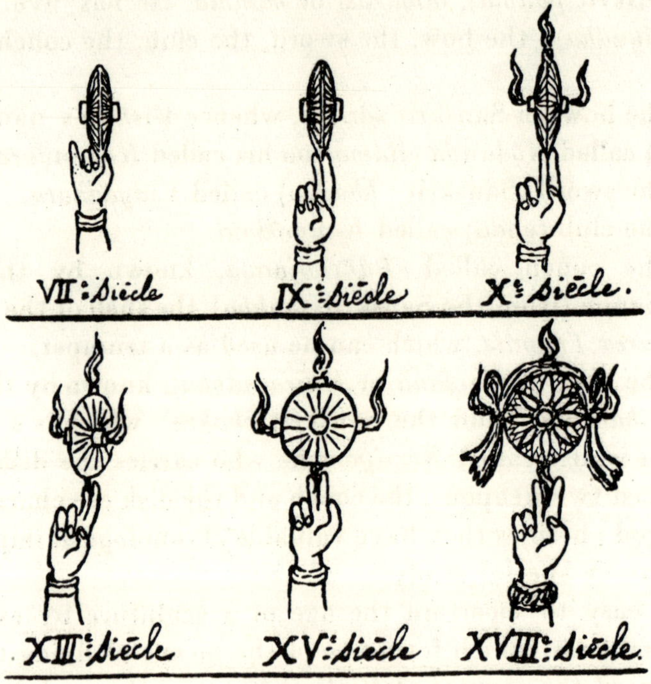

FIG. 17. — *Evolution of the Chakram, the disk of Vishṇu.*

Plate XXXIV represents a statue of *Vishṇu* in a niche of the Eastern *gôpuram* at *Chidambaram* (13th century). The *Chakram* is of the sort we have just described. The Madras Museum has several statues of *Vishṇu* showing flames issuing from the axle of the *Chakram*, which is seen broad-side on.

In the *Bijayanagar* period the flames issuing from the axle disappear. Lastly, in the *Madura* period, a scarf (*vastram*) is added round the wheel the two ends of which hang down below the flames which issue from each side of it (Fig. 17, 18th century).

In our days the *Chakram* is a circle with four (1) flames (*sudar*)

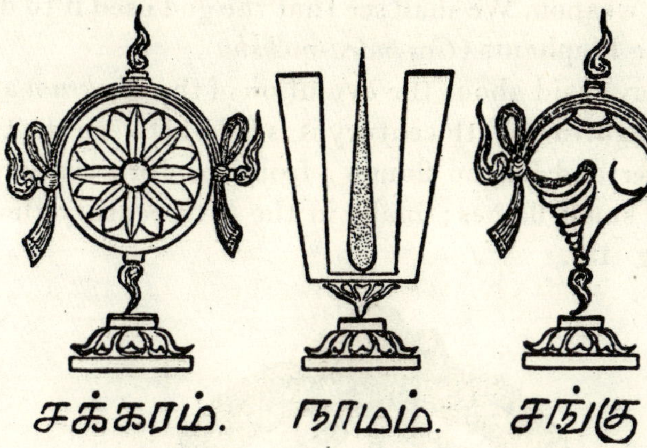

Fig. 18. — *Vishnuvite emblems: Chakram, Nâmam and Saṅgu.*

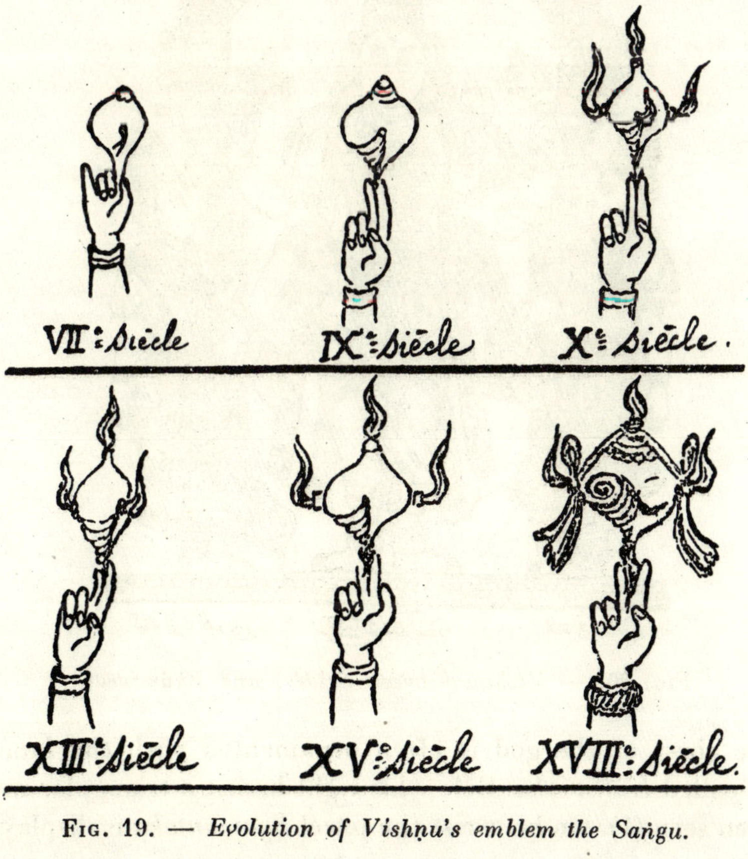

Fig. 19. — *Evolution of Vishṇu's emblem the Saṅgu.*

(1) Only three flames appear on the *Chakram* up to the 15th century. But the *Saṅgu* has four in the 10th century, reverting later to three only until the 15th. (Tr.)

issuing from its edges, and round the circle is the scarf (Fig. 18). It is a cutting weapon. We shall see that the god used it to deliver the king of the Elephants (*Gajêndra-môksha*).

What we have said about the evolution of the *Chakram* applies also to the *Saṅgu*. In the 7th century it is held between the thumb and first finger and has no flames; from the 10th century it is adorned with small flames; finally in the 17th century the scarf as added (Fig. 19).

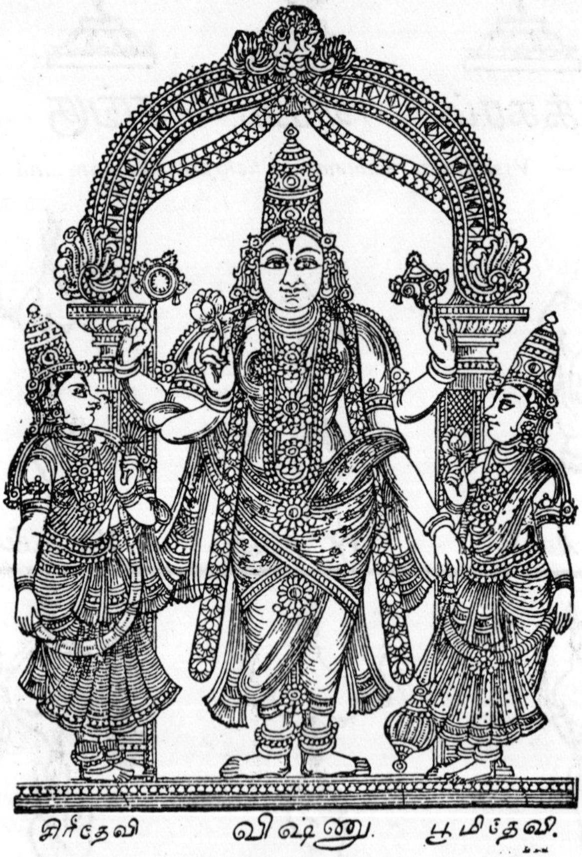

FIG. 20. — *Vishṇu between Śrîdêvî and Bhûmidêvî.*

The chest of the god is often ornamented with the famous jewel called *Kaustubha*. Below his right breast a triangular mark is often seen (1). On his wrist the jewel *Syamantaka* is displayed.

(1) According to writings *Vishṇu* ought to wear on his chest a knot of curled hair called *Śrîvatsa*.

Vishṇu and the *Vishṇubhaktas* (worshippers of *Vishṇu*) are adorned with chaplets of beads of *tulasi*, called *tulasimanittâvadam* (1).

The lord is often represented as in Fig. 20. He stands between two goddesses, *Śrîdêvî* (*Lakshmî*) and *Bhûmidêvî*. They are distinguished one from the other by the fact that *Śridêvî*, goddess of the sky, is always on the right of the god, she holds lotus flowers (*tamarapu*) in her left hand. *Bhûmidêvî*, goddess of the earth, stands on the left, and carries on her right hand a jasmine blossom (*malligai*).

In modern images the upper part of the body of both these goddesses is covered with a sort of corslet called *ravukai*, over which is a cloth (*poduvai*). Their ears are also profusely decked with ear-rings. This is not the case in the 14th and 15th century images, when both goddesses have bare breasts. *Śrîdêvî* alone has a horizontal ribbon called *kachu* or *kañjagam* over her breasts. *Bhûmidêvî* (the goddess on the left of the god) has her breasts quite naked. Besides, *Śrîdêvî* has round ear-rings, while *Bhûmidêvî* has pendulant ears without any ornaments, in those periods.

In this image *Vishṇu* seems to be bigamous, a very ancient particular. In the *Kailâsanâtha* temple at *Kañchîpuram*, a low-relief represents *Vishṇu* seated between his two wives (A. Rea, *Pallava Architecture*, Pl. XLI, fig. 1). It is customary to place for the lord's use, a pair of sandals (*sada*) called *Sadagopam*, in front of *Vishṇu*.

Around the god are frequently represented the bird *Garuḍa*, the monkey god *Hanumân*, *Tumburuvar* (*Tumburu*) with the head of a horse, *Nârada* playing a musical instrument like a *vîṇâ*, the *Pannirendu-âjvâr* (2), his twelve apostles : 1. *Poigai-âjvâr*, 2. *Pûtattâjvâr*, 3. *Pêyâjvâr*, 4. *Tirumarhisai-âjvâr*, 5. *Nammâjvâr*, pourtrayed sitting under a tree in the guise of a *guru*, with a book in his hand ; 6. *Kulasêkharajâjvâr*, 7. *Periya-âjvâr*, 8. *Thondaradippodi-âjvâr*, 9. *Tirupân-âjvâr*, holding in his hand a *vîṇâ* (a sort of guitar) ; 10. *Tirumangai-âjvâr*, who

(1) We have seen that Sivaite chaplets are made of *rudrâksha* seeds.
(2) The Tamil letter transliterated *j* by the author, in the word *âjvâr*, is often *zh* or *rl* or simply *l* in other books. (Tr.)

holds a sword and shield ; 11. *Andâlammani*, a woman who vowed herself to the god at *Śrîraṅgam ;* 12. *Madhurakavi-jâḷvar* who has a *talam* (a kind of cymbal) in her hand.

Besides these are the Vishnuvite sages : *Srimanthamuni*, *Sriâḷavandar*, *Mudaliandar*, *Suratâjvâr*, *Puleilogâsavariar*, *Tirukachchinambi*, *Srimanavâla-mamuni* and lastly *Sribachiakkhâra* (the Commentator) who is none other than the illustrious *Râmânuja*. This last is also *Odeyavar* (Pl. XXXV). He is represented seated with legs crossed and hands folded, on his right arm rests a fleg which bears the Vishnuvite insignia (*Saṅgu*, *Nâmam*, *Chakram*). The *Nâmam* is the *Teṅgalai* one. *Odeyavar* is the greatest Vishnuvite apostle. The ceremony called *Tirumanjanam* is celebrated in his honour.

Śrî-Raṅganâtha.

The highly renowned temple of *Śrîraṅgam* on the island of that name near the confluence of the Cauvery and Coleroon river opposite Trichinopoly, is dedicated to an image of *Vishṇu* much venerated in the South of India. The god (Pl. XXXVI) sleeps lying on a serpent with five heads, which serves as a canopy. This serpent is called *Śêsha* (durable), *Adiśêsha* or *Ananta* (the eternal) ; so the god who sleeps on *Ananta* has the name *Ananta-Śayaṇa*. The two wives of *Vishṇu*, *Śrîdêvî* and *Bhûmidêvî*, sit at his feet.

The right hand of the god is always placed between his head and its pillow. He has often only two arms ; when he has four, the extra two carry the *Saṅgu* and *Chakram*. Often too (but this is not the rule) the stalk of a lotus issues from *Vishṇu*'s navel, and on its flower *Brahmâ* is seated.

At *Chidambaram* a statue of *Raṅganâtha* is found a few yards from the sanctuary of *Nadarâja*.

Historical. — It is impossible to pass over in silence the fact that in Buddhist caves, the iconography of which is inspired by the doctrines of *Mahâyâna*, notably at *Ajaṇṭa* the *Nirvâṇa* of Buddha is represented in a manner which recalls the sleeps of *Vishṇu*. The head of the sleeper is always to the right of the observer, and the feet to the left.

At *Mavalipuram* (7th century) an image of *Vishṇu* lying on a serpent (Pl. XXXVII) (1) is found opposite to the large low-relief depicting the combat of *Kâlî* and *Mahishâsura.* An image of *Raṅganâtha* is also found in the *Vaikuṇṭha-Perumal* temple (A. Rea, *Pallava Architecture,* Pl. LXXXII, fig. 2) (2).

Nârâyaṇa.

Raṅganâtha must not be confused, as is sometimes (3) done, with *Nârâyaṇa.* The latter is a young child who sucks the toe of his left foot. He lies in the middle of a banian tree leaf, Tamil *vaṭa* (*Ficus indica, bengalensis*) ; in this form *Vishṇu* is called *Vaṭapatraśayi* (he who sleeps on a *vaṭa* leaf) (Pl. XXXVIII). It is under the form of *Nârâyaṇa* that *Vishṇu* created the world (4). We have never seen the image of *Nârâyaṇa* on ancient monuments.

Vaikuṇṭha-Nâtha (*Vishṇu,* god of *Vaikuṇṭha*).

Vaikuṇṭha is the paradise of *Vishṇu,* who bears the title of *Vaikuṇṭha-Perumal.* He is seated on the serpent *Ananta* or *Adi-śêsha,* and the hood of the cobra (*nâga*) spreads out to form a canopy over *Vishṇu*'s head, who in this form is worshipped as lord of the supreme beatitude (*Paramapadanâthan*).

Historical. — This image is found in the *Vaikuṇṭha-Perumal* temple at *Kañchîpuram* (A. Rea, Pl. LXXI, fig. 4) (5).

(1) At *Ellora* in the cave of the *Avatârs, Vishṇu* is seen lying on a snake which however has a human head and bust.

(2) In the *Kailâsa* of *Ellora* (end of 8th century) there is a low-relief of *Raṅganâtha. Brahmâ* is seated on the lotus flower which issues not from the navel but from the half-open stomach of *Vishṇu.* It is only later that the god's feet are held by two women.

(3) « On the left or South wall is a large bas-relief of *Nârâyaṇa* or *Vishṇu* reclining upon the snake *Śêsha* » (Burgess, *Cave temples of India,* p. 146).

(4) This name is however used in a more general sense. The epithet is used for the invocation of *Vishṇu* in the famous prayer called *Ashṭâkshara* (the 8 Sanskrit letters) : *Om ! Nâmô Nârâyaṇâya !* Om ! adoration to *Nârâyaṇa !* (in Sanskrit spelt in 8 letters.) (Tr.)

(5) There is a very large low-relief which deals with this subject in No. 3 cave at *Bâdâmi* (6th century, Plate XXXIX). Dr Gustave Le Bon points out (*Les Monuments de l'Inde*) that Buddha is seated in the same identical position on a serpent as represented among the carvings of the *Amarâvâti* tope (2nd century).

Varadarâja (*Vishṇu* riding on *Garuḍa*).

The vehicle (*vâhana*) of *Vishṇu* is a minor deity, half man, half eagle (of the *Falco pondicherianus* species) called *Garudan* (Sanskrit : *Garuḍa*) or *Suparṇa*, the son of *Kaśyapa* and *Vinatâ*. Its

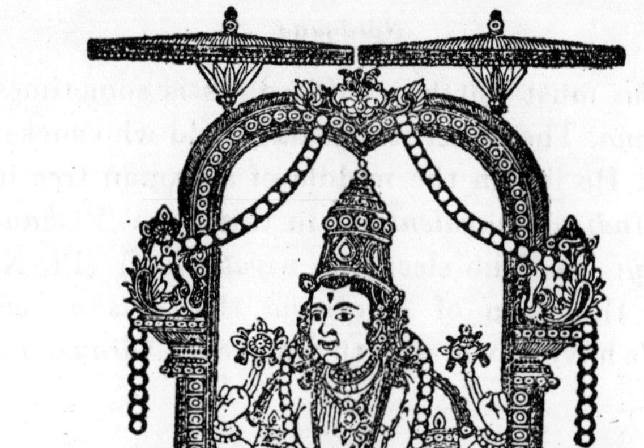

வரதாசப்.பெருமாள்.

FIG. 21. — *Varadarâja at Conjeevaram.*

nose is curved in like a beak and it has large wings. Today there is worshipped notably at Conjeevaram (*Kañchîpuram*) under the name of *Varadarâjasvâmi* (he who grants favours) (Fig. 21).

The image is ancient, as it is found at *Kañchîpuram* in the

Pallava temple of *Vaikunṭha-Perumal* (8th century) (A. Rea, *Pallava Architecture*, Pl. LXXXII, fig. 1, and LXXXII, fig. 2). It also is to be seen at *Chidambaram* on the Eastern *gôpuram* (13th century) (Pl. XXXIV). It is noteworthy that in this sculpture *Vishṇu*'s *Chakram* is seen along its edge, and that the flames issue from the axle of the wheel.

Garuḍa is also represented holding in his hand the *amurda-kalasam* which he got as his share after the churning of the sea of milk.

Gajêndra-môksham.

Modern artists often represent the deliverance (*môksham*) of the king of the Elephants (*Gajêndra*) (Fig. 22).

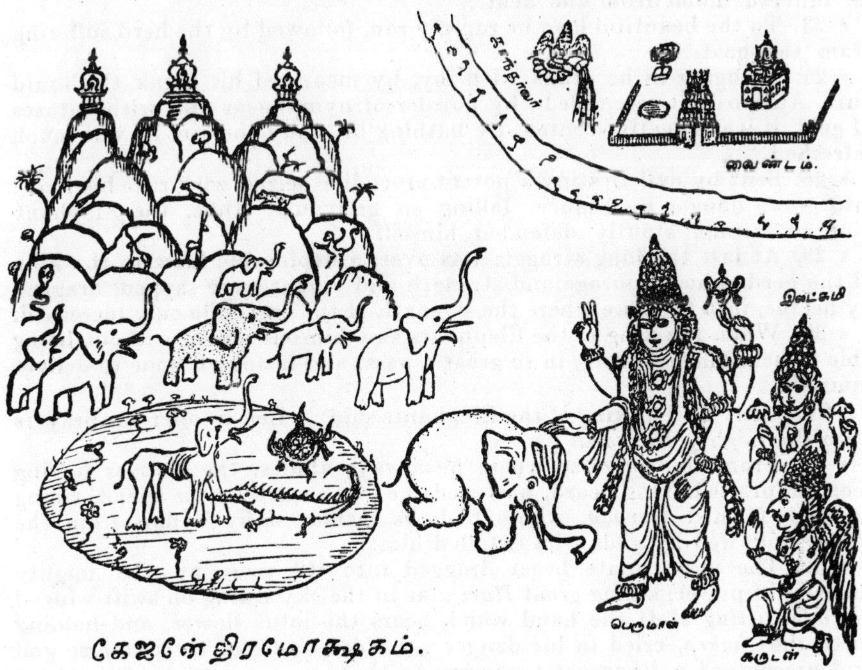

Fig. 22. — *Gajêndra-môksham (Deliverance of the king of the Elephants).*

There lived in a pool a very wicked crocodile. The king of the Elephants, the friend of *Vishṇu*, passing by the pool was held prisoner by the crocodile which seized his foot in its teeth. But the lord came down from *Vaikunṭha* on the shoulders of the bird

Garuḍa, and smiting the crocodile with his disk *Chakram* he delivered the king of the Elephants (1).

Historical. — It is possible that this is the subject represented

(1) *Bhâgavata Purâṇa*, BURNOUF's translation, book VIII, chap. II:

« 1. ...There is a famous mountain, which goes by the name *Trikûṭa*...

« 2. ... its triple summit of silver, of brass and the third of gold lit up the sea to the limits of the far distant horizon.

« 5. In its vales abode the *Siddhas*, *Châraṇas* and *Gandharvas*, *Vidyâdharas*, *Mahôragas*, the *Kinnaras* and *Apsaras*, who took their pleasure therein.

« 7. Numerous herds of untamed beasts, its valleys filled ; birds of voice harmonious peopled the gardens of gods, formed of every sort of tree.

« 14. Golden lotuses balanced on an extensive mere.

« 19. The Elephant lord one day, who lived in those mountainy vales, walked there with this numerous wives.

« 22. In the company of other Elephants, their females and their babes, he suffered much from the heat...

« 23. To the beautiful lake he rapidly ran, followed by the herd suffering from the heat...

« 24. Plunging in he drank with joy, by means of his trunk, the liquid pure. Ambrosia it resembled ; by powder of nymphaeas and with lotuses of gold, it was sweetly scented. By bathing his body therein, he was much refreshed.

« 26. Sent by evil Destiny a potent crocodile seized with rage his foot ; into grave danger by chance, falling so grievously thus, the Elephant king so strong, stoutly defended himself.

« 29. At last the long struggle was over, a deplorable blow to the king of the herd, whose courage and strength and vigour were sapped, dragged by his foe, into the lake where the strength of the crocodile only increased.

« 30. When the king of the Elephants saw himself fallen, without being able to help himself there, in so great a pass, and losing all hope to deliver himself...

« Chap. III. 2. The king of the Elephants said : « Let us offer our prayers unto the mighty *Bhagavat* god. »

« 31. From the universe where he always abides, the distress having seen, his praise having heard, hastened the god to deliver his friend, riding on eagle-formed *Garuḍa*, whose body is fashioned by hymns from the *Vêdas*, followed by gods who extolled him.

« 32. The unfortunate beast dragged into the mere by the mighty monster of power, seeing great *Hari* afar in the sky riding on swift winged *Garuḍa*, lifting aloft the hand which bears the lotus flower, and holding forth the *Chakra*, cried in his danger : « *Nârâyaṇa !* of the universe god and preceptor ! o *Bhagavat !* worship to thee ! »

« 33. *Hari* the uncreated, seeing his plight descended at once, and pitying pulled him out of the lake, along with the horrible monster. The crocodile's throat having cut with the *Chakra*, the Elephant king he restored to the gods (*a*). »

(*a*) The sharp edged quoit, still used by the Sikh regiments of the Indian army, is probably the modern representative of the *chakra*. The whole object of the Burnouf foot note is to prove that the *chakra* is a cutting weapon. (Tr.)

in a low-relief in the *Vaikuṇṭha-Perumal* (A. Rea, *Pallava Architecture*, Pl. LXXXIV, fig. 1) (1).

The Avatârs.

The descents (*avatâra* means descent) or incarnations of *Vishṇu* on the earth are so named. Ten principal ones are enumerated : *Matsya*, *Kûrma*, *Varâha*, *Narasiṁha*, *Vâmana*, *Paraśurâma*, *Râmachandra*, *Balarâma*, *Kṛishṇa* and *Kalki*.

It was probably only in the 12th century that a certain number of legendary exploits were grouped together, catalogued and assigned to *Vishṇu*. This methodical classification of legends was very favourable to the development of Vishnuvism. There are about five of these incarnations which would have remained almost unknown to artists, if they did not form part of the classical series, such are the *avatârs* : *Matsya*, *Kûrma*, *Paraśurâma*, *Balarâma* and *Kalki*.

The other five may be divided into two groups ; *Varâha*, *Narasiṁha* and *Vâmana* occupy the first place in the iconography of ancient temples. Modern temples are covered with sculptures referring to the legend of *Kṛishṇa* and *Râmachandra*.

Whatever the reason may be, it is incontestable that the series of the *avatârs* is never represented on temples older than the 12th century (2).

According to the legend, the incarnations *Matsya*, *Kûrma* and *Varâha*, took place in the age *Kṛitayuga* ; *Narasiṁha*, *Vâmana*, *Paraśurâma* and *Râmachandra*, in the age *Trêtâyuga* ; *Balarâma* and *Kṛishṇa*, in the age *Dvâparayuga* ; finally *Kalki* will come to pass in the age *Kaliyuga* (3).

(1) It is found on the North side of the *Deogarh* temple in *Lalitpur* (United Provinces) (Burgess, *Ancient Monuments of India*, Vol. II, Fig. 252). In this sculpture it is a serpent (*nâga*) and not a crocodile which holds the elephant prisoner. Lastly it is to be noticed that there is a distinct resemblance to the worship of Buddha by the elephant *Nalagiri*.

(2) At *Ellora* in the cave of the *Avatârs* and in the *Kailâsa*, a series of low-reliefs exclusively devoted to *Vishṇu* is found. But only four of the incarnations are to be seen : *Varâha*, *Narasiṁha*, *Vâmana* and *Kṛishṇa*.

(3) The present age. (Tr.)

1. *Matsyâvatâra.*

Tamil legend : The warriors *Nadhukaïtabha* inhabiting the region called *Pâdâlalôgam*, situated under the waters, stole the four *Vêdas* from *Brahmâ* who was unable to go to the bottom of the water to look for them. So *Vishṇu*, incarnated himself as a fish, conquered the *Madugadaivar*, and brought back the *Vêdas* (1).

(1) *Bhâgavata Purâṇa*, Burnouf's translation, book VIII, chap. xxiv :
« 8. While the Creator desired repose, and gave way to the sleep which time led to him, the powerful *Hayagrîva* stole away the *Vêdas* which had issued from the mouth of the god, and which lay by his side.
« 9. The beneficent *Hari*, who is the lord, hearing what the chief of the *Dânavas*, *Hayagrîva* had achieved, arrayed himself as a fish called *Śapharî*.
« 10. At that time a certain *Ṛishi* among the kings called *Satyavrata*, a great man and devoted to *Nârâyaṇa*, was undergoing a penance which consisted on living on nothing but water.
« 11. This same was he who, when born in the present *Mahâkalpa*, in the character of the son of *Vivasvat*, and under the name *Śrâddhadêva*, was raised by *Hari* to the rank of *Manu*.
« 12. One day when plunged in the river *Krîtamâlâ*, he made his libations, it happened that a little fish called *Śapharî*, was found in the water held in his hands.
« 13. *Satyavrata*, who was king of *Dravida*, released into the river as he poured the water from his hands, the fish which had thrown itself into them.
« 14. The fish said with mournful voice to the king who was moved to much pity : « How o King ! is it that you who take pity on the unfortunate, thus abandon me, poor, and timid, in the waters of the river to the large fish which prey on my kind ? »
« 15. Not knowing that it was a god who, in order to show him favour, had assumed the form of a fish, the king thought only of saving the little animal.
« 16. No sooner had he heard its plaintive prayer than, touched with compassion, he took it in his bowl and carried it off to his hermitage.
« 17. The animal there grew so fast in a single night, that it found no room in the bowl, and spoke thus to the king of the earth :
« 18. « I can no longer stay thus miserably shut up in this bowl, prepare for me therefore a bigger dwelling where I may live in comfort. »
« 19. The king took it out and put it in the water contained in a jar ; as soon as the fish was placed therein, it grew three cubits in one hour.
« 20. « This jar, o king, is not big enough for me to live comfortably in it. Get me a vaster place, since I have sought refuge with you. »
« 23. After this, the king took it successively to inexhaustible lakes, and when the fish had filled them completely, *Satyavrata* threw it into the ocean.
« 24. At the moment it was thrown, the fish said to the king : « Here monsters stronger than I will come and devour me, o hero, you must not abandon me here. »
« 25. Thus deceived by the fine speeches of this animal, the king said

Representations of *Matsya* are very rarely found (Fig. 23).

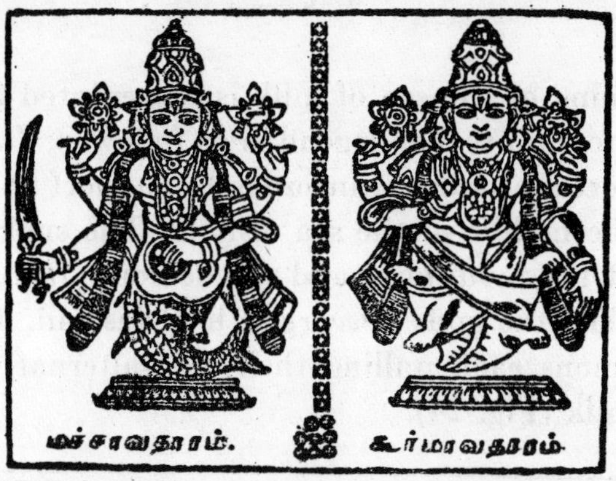

FIG. 23. — *Matsya and Kûrma.*

The upper part of the god's body keeps its usual form, while only the lower part takes the form of a fish.

We have never seen this image in ancient temples.

to it : « Who art thou who so deludest me, in the shape of a fish ?

« 27. Without doubt thou art the ever happy *Hari, Nârâyaṇa.* »

« 32. *Bhagavat* said : « In seven days from today, o king, the three worlds, the earth, the air and the sky will be submerged by the ocean of destruction.

« 33. At the moment when the three worlds shall be covered by the ocean of annihilation, a great vessel sent by me will present itself to receive you.

« 34. Then surrounded by the seven *Ṛishis*, and bringing together the collection of all beings, and taking with you plants and seeds, great and small.

« 35. You will enter the great ship and voyage fearless over the immense dark ocean, guided only by the splendour of the *Ṛishis.*

« 36. When the violent wind shakes your vessel, I shall be near, and you will tie your ship to my horn with the aid of the great serpent (*Vâsuki*). »

« 39. After giving these instructions to the king, *Hari* disappeared. But *Satyavrata* waited the period which had been indicated by *Hṛishîkêśa.*

« 41. Then the ocean burst its bounds, and coming forward covered the whole of the earth.

« 42. Totally occupied with remembering the orders of *Bhagavat, Satyavrata* saw a vessel approaching him, he entered it with the chiefs of the Brahmins after gathering herbs and plants.

« 44. *Vishṇu* appeared in the midst of the great ocean in the form of a golden fish having a single horn (on his head) and being ten thousand *yôjanas* long.

« 45. The king tied his vessel to this horn, using the snake as *Hari* had previously told him, and being satisfied celebrated *Madhuṣûdana.*

« 57. When the end of the cataclysm came, *Hari* killed the *Asura Hayagrîva* and brought back the *Vêdas* to *Brahmâ* who had woken up. »

2. *Kûrma.*

The churning of the sea of milk is represented fairly often in modern iconography. The legend is as follows : *Vishṇu* took the form of a tortoise (*kûrma*) in order to support the hill *Mahêndragiri* in the middle of the sea of milk. The snake *Vâsuki* was rolled round the mountain, and the demons (*Râkshasas*) caught his head, while the gods (*Devargal*) held his tail. Then the gods and the demons each pulling their side alternatively, churned the sea of milk (Fig. 24).

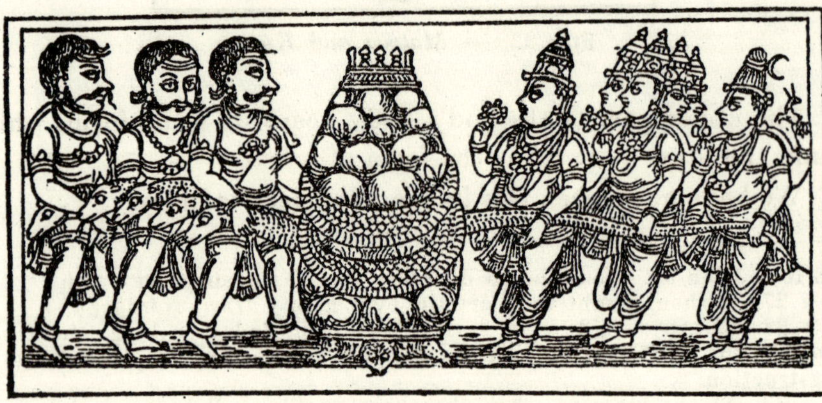

Fig. 24. — *Amurdam kadaigirathu* (*Churning of the sea of milk*).

The churning of the sea of milk is called in Tamil *Amurdam kadaigirathu*. The snake (*Vâsuki*) spat forth so great a quantity of poison that the frightened demons fled, and only came back on condition that the gods pulled on the side of his head. *Vishṇu* ordered the serpent to retain his poison.

From the sea of milk came the desirable cow *Kâmadhenu* which is represented with the head of a woman, wings, three peacock's tails, and suckling a little calf ; the horse *Sabara*, the goddess *Lakshmî*, the elephant *Airapadam* and the tree *Kalpagavrucham* (Sanskrit : *Kalpavṛiksha*).

But *Vâsuki* vomited new poison (*Hâlahala*). *Śiva* drank it up and held it in his throat which became blue, he thus earned the name *Nîlakaṇṭha* (he who has a blue neck). Lastly appeared

the sage *Danuvandri* holding a vase full of *Samudramadam* (1).

(1) *Bhâgavata Purâṇa*, Burnouf's translation, book VIII, chap. v :

« 15. When stricken in the fight by the sharp weapons of the *Asuras,* the gods bereft of life had fallen and were unable to rise.

« 17. *Mahêndra, Varuṇa* and the other gods who witnessed this spectacle held counsel together, but were unable to come to a decision.

« 18. So they betook themselves to the assembly of *Brahmâ.*

« 19. On seeing *Indra, Varuṇa* and the other gods deprived of their strength and splendour, beholding the world full of misery, and the *Asuras* enjoying an undeserved happiness.

« 20. The ever happy and powerful Sovereign spoke thus to the gods :

« 21. « Let us take refuge with Imperishable Being... »

« 26. *Brahmâ* said : « We bow down before the best and most desirable of the gods... »

« 49. As when watering the roots of a tree the boughs and branches are also watered, so in worshipping *Vishṇu* worship is given to others and to one's self.

« Chap. vi. 1. Thus praised by the company of the *Suras*, the ever happy *Hari,* who is the lord, appeared before their eyes.

« 18. *Bhagavat* said :

« 19. « Go and make peace with the sons of *Danu* and *Diti.*

« 21. « Delay not : but make every effort to obtain ambrosia.

« 22. «... take the mountain *Mandara* for churning stick and the snake *Vâsuki* for cord.

« 23. « Then with my aid stir the sea without ceasing. »

« 32. « Then the *Dêvas* and the *Daityas* made friends the one with the other, concluded a treaty, and set about with supreme efforts to get ambrosia for themselves.

« 33. In the pride of their strength they uprooted the mountain *Mandara* ; and with their mighty arms which were like clubs, they bore it with singing, towards the ocean.

« Chap. vii. 1. They invited *Vâsuki*, the king of the serpents, promising him a share of the ambrosia ; the gods full of joy used him as a cord to encircle the mountain.

« 2. Beginning to churn the ocean... *Hari* took first place towards the head, and the *Dêvas* arranged themselves behind him.

« 3. The chiefs of the *Daityas* did not approve of this plan of *Mahâpurusha.* « We will not take » cried they « the tail of the snake, that part of the body is dishonourable. »

« 4. The *Daityas* kept silence, and the best of men looking on them with smiles, abandoned the head of the serpent and seized the tail followed by the Immortals.

« 5. Thus partitioning their places, the sons of *Kaśyapa* began to churn the ocean to obtain ambrosia therefrom.

« 6. But while the sea was thus stirred, the moutain which rested on nothing, sank by its own weight to the bottom of the waters, however much the powerful gods sought to keep it up.

« 8. The Lord assuming the form of a tortoise, marvellous and gigantic, plunged into the sea and upheld the mountain.

« 18. By the movement of the sea was engendered a fearful and irresistible poison called *Hâlahala.*

« 19. Spreading with terrific speed, and intolerable strength, it percolated through all points of space both above and below the world. The frightened and unprotected creatures ran together with their leaders to find a refuge near the beneficent god.

« 42. Then holding the redoubtable and all pervading poison in the

Historical (1). — The churning of the sea of milk is represented at *Kañchîpuram* (Rea, *Pallava Architecture*, Pl. XXXIII, fig. 3, and LXXIV, fig. 2), but the sculptures in the *Kailâsanâtha*

hollow of his hand, *Mahâdêva*, out of pity returning life to all creatures, proceeded to swallow it.

« 43. The poison produced by the water showed its strength on the god himself by blackening his throat, but the beneficent god made an ornament of this stain.

« Chap. viii. 1. When *Vṛishâṅka* (*Śiva*) had drunk the poison, the immortals and the *Dânavas* full of joy, hastened to beat up the ocean. The cow which gave clarified butter, issued from it.

« 2. The *Ṛishis* exercised in the *Vêda* took possession of the cow of *Agnihôtra*, to get the clarified butter which is offered in sacrifice, which is the route to the gods.

« 3. Then appeared the horse *Uchchaiḥśravas*, whose colour was pale as the moon.

« 4. The chief of the elephants *Airâvata* next issued from out of the sea, the glory of his four tusks eclipsed the splendour of the mountain where dwells the happy *Śiva*.

« 5. The jewel called *Kaustubha*, this ruby of the vasty deep, next appeared. *Hari* desired to possess it for an ornament for his breast.

« 6. Then came the *Pârijâta*..., the tree which always showers blessings.

« 7. Next was seen the birth of the *Apsaras*, all dressed alike with the *Nishka* hanging on their necks, the nymphs who charm those dwelling in heaven.

« 8. Then was seen the ever happy *Râmâ*, devoted spouse of *Bhagavat*.

« 30. Then followed the young goddess *Varuṇî* with the lotus eyes, the *Asuras* took possession of her with the consent of *Hari*.

« 31. While the sons of *Kaśyapa* churned the ocean for ambrosia, there appeared a marvellous human form.

« 32. A man with long and rounded arms, he was black, young...

« 34. His arms ornated with bracelets, held up a vase full of ambrosia. This was *Dhanvantari*, the author of the *Ayurvêda*.

« 35. At the sight of the god and the vase full of ambrosia, the *Asuras* greedy to get all blessings, hastily took possession of the cup.

« 36. When the *Asuras* carried off the vase with the ambrosia, the disappointed *Dêvas* sought solace with *Hari*.

« 37. Seeing their distress, *Bhagavat*, who grants the desires of his servants said : « Be not distressed, I assure you of success by sowing discord among them with the aid of illusion, which I possess. »

« 41. At that moment *Vishṇu*, the powerful god to whom no resource is unknown, assumed the form of a marvellous indescribable woman.

« Chap. ix. 11. ... The *Asuras* encouraged by the allurements of this woman, lost their self-control, and gave her the vase which held the ambrosia.

« 20. Disposing the two companies in distinct rank, the sovereign of the Universe caused the gods and the *Asuras* to be placed in the rank to which they belonged.

« 21. With vase in hand he misled the *Asuras* with deceitful advances and gave the far off gods to drink the nectar which does away with old age and death. »

(1) This subject is the theme of two little friezes : one in the cave No. 2 at *Bâdâmi* (6th century) and the other on the pillars of the sanctuary of the *Kailâsa* (8th century).

and *Vaikuṇṭha-Perumal* being covered over with lime and deteriorated, are barely visible.

Perhaps the legend was different in olden times to what it is now, but in any case it is not so important in the iconography of the temples of India as it is in Khmer temples (1).

3. *Varâha.*

The demon *Hiraṇyâksha* (the golden eyed) held the earth prisoner at the bottom of the waters. *Vishṇu* took the form of a boar in order to lift up the earth represented by the goddess *Bhûmidêvî*, and bring it back to the surface (2). In our

(1) It is noteworthy that this churning has a singular resemblance to the method of producing fire for sacrifices. The *areni* (Sanskrit : *araṇi*) is formed of two pieces of wood of the *attimaram* (*Ficus racemosa*, Linné : morée), one of the frames of wood is fixed to the ground and a hole drilled in it, in which the sharpened end of the other beam is placed. A cord wound round the latter allows of a very rapid rotary movement which sets the wood on fire. This way of producing fire is described in the *Vêdas* (*Atharva-vêda*, 111, 29, 1), and is still employed at the present day by Brahmins who offer sacrifices.

(2) *Bhâgavata Purâṇa*, Burnouf's translation, book III, chap. xiii :

« 6. ... When the *Manu Svâyambhuva* was created with his wife, he thus addressed the god who is the fountain of the *Vêdas*, with his hands folded in token of respect, and bowing before him.

« 14. The *Manu* said : « May I, o thou who destroyest sin, never depart from the commandments of *Bhagavat !* Be pleased, however, o lord, to give me a place in this world, wherein I may dwell with all creatures.

« 15. The earth which is the dwelling place of all beings, is submerged beneath the mighty ocean, exert thy strength, o god, that this blessed earth may be liberated from the abyss. »

« 16. ... *Paramêshṭhin* having seen that the earth was really lying in the midst of the waters, meditated long with his spirit saying : « How shall I get it up?

« 17. At the moment when I wish to create, the earth, submerged by the waters lies in the bottom of the abyss, what then am I to do now that I am charged with creation ? »

« 18. While he thus reflected... suddenly a small boar no longer than an inch, issued from his nostril.

« 19. As *Brahmâ* looked at it, the animal held himself suspended in the air, and instantly became as large as an elephant.

« 27. With tail raised, body stiff, shaking its mane, every pointed bristle standing out, trampling the clouds underfoot, showing his white tusks, with blazing eyes he crossed the heaven. Thus appeared *Bhagavat* to raise up the earth.

« 28. This Being, who is himself the body of the sacrifice, in the disguise of a boar, armed with terrible tusks, tracing out the earth by its scent, and turning loving eyes on the singing Brahmins, plunged into the waters...

« 31. There, at the moment when the first of the *Daityas* advanced against him with raised club to obstruct his way, the god... while disporting

days the god with a boar's head (*Adivaragai-Perumal*) holds *Bhûmidêvî* seated on his knee (Pl. XL).

Historical. — One of the most beautiful and most famous low-reliefs of *Mavalipuṛam* (7th century) represents *Varâha* (Pl. XLI). It is noticeable that in all the ancient low-reliefs the god wears a small conical head-dress, and not the large Vishnuvite tiara which is later given to him (see Pl. XL) (1).

Varâha is represented on the *Vaikuṇṭha-Perumal* temple (A. Rea, *Pallava Architecture*, Pl. XXII). One sees him also on the *Kôrâṅganâtha* temples at *Srinivasallallur* (10th century), at *Tanjore* and at *Gaṅgaikondapuram* (11th century).

4. *Narasiṁha.*

King *Hiraṇyakaśipu* (he who is clothed in gold) wished to have himself worshipped. His son *Prahlâda* refused to render him the homage which was due only to *Vishṇu*. The young *Prahlâda* affirmed that *Vishṇu* was present everywhere, even in one of the pillars of the palace, and the angry king struck the pillar. The column suddenly opened and *Vishṇu* appeared in the shape of a terrible giant with a lion's head (*siṁha*). *Hiraṇyakaśipu* was conquered and the god devoured his entrails (2).

himself in the bosom of the waters, slew the giant endued with strength indomitable as the chief of animals slays an elephant. His cheeks and snout were fouled with the blood of *Daitya*, as when the king of elephants, tearing up the ground, is fouled with (reddish) clay.

« 32. Recognizing this animal, blue as the *tamâla*, who sporting as does an elephant, lifted up the earth on the end of his white tusks, the sages with *Viriñchi* at their head, with joined hands celebrated the sovereign lord with sacred hymns. »

(1) It is probable that this is the legend portrayed by the boar of *Eran* (Burgess, *Ancient Monuments of India*, Vol. I, Fig. 216), which is perhaps the oldest Hindu sculpture that is known. However, the boar of *Eran* has only two arms, and it is not certain that at that period (probably the *Gupta* period, 5th century) *Vishṇu* was the hero of the story. From the 6th century onwards, no doubts can be admitted, because *Varâha* with four arms carrying the *Śaṅkha* and the *Chakram* as carved in No. 3 cave at *Bâdâmi*, the date of which is quite certain (578 A. D). Pl. XLII represents the image of *Varâha* in cave No. 2 at *Bâdâmi*. At the feet of the god is found a giant whose body, half man, half snake, represents *Adiśêsha*. The goddess lifted in the hand of the divine boar, lightly balances herself by putting her arm on his snout. The same subject is treated, almost in the same way, in the caves at *Ellora*.

(2) *Bhâgavata Purâṇa*, Burnouf's translation, book VII, chap. vii:

« 2. *Hiraṇyakaśipu* said (to *Prahlâda*):

« 13. « And he whom you call sovereign of the world, o miserable one,

In our days the different episodes of this history are represented (Pl. XLIII) :

1. *Narasiṁha* coming forth from the column.

2. The fight of *Narasiṁha* and *Hiraṇyakaśipu.*

3. *Narasimha* devouring the entrails of the giant (see Pl. XLIV).

4. *Narasiṁha* holding the goddess *Lakshmî*, is worshipped.

The *Narasiṁha* festival, called *Jayanti*, falls on the eve of the new moon in the month of *Vayasi* (May).

Historical. — *Narasiṁha* is often represented on ancient temples (1), but he is never seen in them issuing from the pillar. The fight of *Narasiṁha* and *Hiraṇyakaśipu* is found in the *Pallava* temples at *Kañchîpuram*, in the *Kailâsanâtha* temple

as if there was any other sovereign than I — where is he ? And if he is everywhere why doth he not appear in this column ? »

« 15. After thus insulting again and again with hard words his son the great servant of *Bhagavat*, the raging *Asura*, drawing his dagger, rushed down from his high seat, and with all his force, struck the column with his fist.

« 16. On the instant was heard from therein a terrible roaring.

« 18. Then to justify what his servant had said, and to prove that he really did dwell in the breast of all beings, the god appeared in the assembly from out of the midst of the column, in a miraculous shape which was neither that of a man nor an animal.

« 20. The god in the man lion's shape bounded forth, terrible with red eyes like gold burnished in the fire, with a face on which the thick and bristling hair increased its size.

« 23. The *Asura* said : «Without doubt it is *Hari*. It is the great magician who thinks that thus he will slay me, but his efforts will be in vain. »

« 24. And immediately uttering a yell, the hero of the *Daityas* armed with his club, rushed against *Nrîsiṁha.*

« 29. Like a reptile which seizes a rat, *Hari* pounced on his foe, and turning him over on his thigh, he tore with his talons the skin, which thunderbolts could not penetrate...

« 30. Rolling his eyes of which the wrath which inspired him made the sight unbearable, licking the corners of his wide mouth with his tongue, *Hari*, his head surrounded with a ruddy halo caused by the blood which dropped therefrom, made himself a garland with the entrails.

« 34. The conqueror then entered the assembly, and moderating his splendour as he saw no further enemy, he seated himself on the royal throne.

« 37. *Brahmâ*, *Indra*, *Giriśa* and the other immortals...

« 38. carrying to their foreheads their folded hands in token of respect, came... to worship the hero amongst men, who was seated in the splendour of his glory. »

(1) *Narasiṁha* is figured in cave No. 3 at *Bâdâmi* (6th century) ; see Pl. XLV.

(Pl. XLVI) (1) and in the temple of *Vaikuṇtha-Perumal* (A. Rea, *Pallava Architecture*, Pl. LXXXIII, fig. 4) (2).

In all the ancient reliefs the god with the lion's head has no mane ; it is only later that a mane like a frill or band is seen round the face of *Siṁha*.

5. *Vâmana.*

In our days this incarnation of *Vishṇu* is worshipped in certain temples at *Tirukoilur*. The commemorative festival takes place on the full moon day in the month of *Kartigai*. The legend is well known : *Vishṇu* presents himself before the king *Bali* in the form of a Brahmin dwarf (Fig. 25) carrying an umbrella (*kodai*) and a vase (*chembu*) used by Brahmins for their ablutions (*saṅkalppa*), and asked him as a boon the amount of land he could cover in three paces. The king agreed and as is the custom, poured some water on the palm of the right hand of the Brahmin. The latter, as soon as the compact was made, transformed himself suddenly into a giant, and with one stride, the god *Padiyalandan* (he who traversed the universe in three strides) bestrode the space from the earth to the sky (3).

(1) There is a great likeness between this low-relief and one seen at *Ellora* (Pl. XLVII) in the cave of the *Avatârs*.

(2) And also in the *Kailâsa* at *Ellora* (8th century).

(3) *Bhâgavata Purâṇa*, book VIII, chap. xviii (Burnouf's translation) :

« 12. ...The god whose way is supernatural changed himself... into a Brahmin dwarf...

« 20. When he heard that *Bali* owed his greatness to the *Aśvamêdha* whom he worshipped under the orders of the *Bhṛigu*, he approached this prince...

« 23. ... he entered the enclosure where the horse sacrifice was held, with his staff, his umbrella, and his pot full of water.

« 24. On seeing the Brahmin dwarf, who was none other than *Hari* in disguise, entering with a belt made of the *muñja* herbe, the cord, the skin of an antelope over his shoulders, and his hair falling in locks,

« 26. ... the sacrifice offering king joyfully offered him a seat.

« 29. *Bali* said : « Be welcome, worship to thee, o Brahmin, what can I do for thee ?

« 32. Receive from me, young Brahmin, all that thou desirest. »

« Chap. xix. 1. Hearing this kind speech, true and conforming with the justice of the son of *Virôchana*, *Bhagavat* was pleased and approvingly replied :

« 16. « I ask then of thee, chief among generous men, a little ground, only three paces, o prince of the *Daityas*, measured with my own strides. »

« 28. At these words, *Bali* laughingly replied : « Receive what thou

This giant is called *Tri-vikrama* (three strides).

Plate XLVIII represents the scene : in it is seen the little Brahmin carrying a sunshade (Tamil : *kodai* ; Sanskrit : *kuḍai*) ; the king *Bali*, his head adorned with a tiara and holding a copper cruise for pouring water, the giant *Trivikrama* whose foot touches the clouds, and in the heavens, *Brahmâ*, pouring a little lustral water on the divine foot.

Historical. — The subject is frequently represented in ancient sculptures, and with little difference from the modern manner (1). Plate L shows the celebrated low-relief at *Mavalipuram* (7th century). Near the god's head, at his left, is *Jâmbavat*, the bear king, beating a drum. The same subject is seen on the *Kailâsanâtha* and *Vaikuṇṭha-Perumal* temples at *Kañchîpuram*

desirest » ; and to grant this portion of ground to the dwarf, he took a pot full of water.

« Chap. xx. 16. He gave to the dwarf the ground he asked for, after honouring him, and accomplishing the ceremony of the water.

« 21. Immediately the dwarf grew in a miraculous way...

« 30. The *chakra Sudarśana*, of which the splendour is irresistible and the bow *Śârṅga*, the noise of which is like thunder.

« 31. The conch *Pâñchajanya*, the sound of which is like a cloud, *Kaumôdaki*, the swift club of *Vishṇu*, *Vidyâdhara* the sword bedecked with a hundred moons, the two fine quivers with inexhaustible arrows and the troop of servitors of whom *Sunanda* is the chief, also the guardians of the worlds gathered respectively round the lord.

« 32. Adorned with an aigrette, with bracelets and earrings made like shining fishes, bearing the *Śrîvatsa* (breast ornament) and precious jewels, a belt and rich clothing encircled with flowers from trees frequented by bees, *Bhagavat* was seen in his glory, the god of great strides.

« 33. With one pace he cleared the earth which *Bali* possessed, filling the atmosphere with his body and touching the limits of the horizon with his arms ; with the second step he overran the sky, at the third step there did not remain an atom for him to occupy ; still raising himself upwards, the feet of the great striding god touched the spaces beyond *Mahas*, *Janas* and *Tapas*.

« Chap. xxi. 1. ... the god born of the lotus came before him.

« 3. *Brahmâ* presented the water of hospitality to the foot of *Vishṇu*, which was raised up so high, and having honoured him with worship, the god whose glory is pure, sang of him whose navel had produced the lotus whence he himself was born.

« 8. *Jâmbavat*, the king of the bears, as swift as thought, proclaimed a great festival to the sound of his drum, in honour of *Vishṇu* who had always conquered all the points of space. »

(1) Plate XLIX depicts a low-relief in cave No. 2 at *Bâdâmi* (6th century). The god *Brahmâ* holds a sunshade in his hand, which proves that Brahmins used sunshades at that period.

(A. Rea, *Pallava Architecture*, Pl. CXXIII, fig. 7, and LXXXI, fig. 1 and 2).

6. *Paraśurâma* (*Râma* with the axe).

A Brahmin, the *Ṛishi Jamadagni*, one day was visited by the king *Kârtavîrya*, who wished to get hold of the cow *Kâmadhenu* which Indra had entrusted to *Jamadagni*, as she was an inexhaustible source of riches. *Paraśurâma*, son of *Jamadagni* and *Rêṇukâ*, cut off king *Kârtavîrya*'s head and destroyed the caste of warrior (Sanskrit : *Kshatriya*).

Paraśurâma defiled by all these murders, retired to mount *Gôkarṇa*.

Varuṇa the god of the ocean conceded to him the amount of land which he could cover with the flight of an arrow. The ascetic

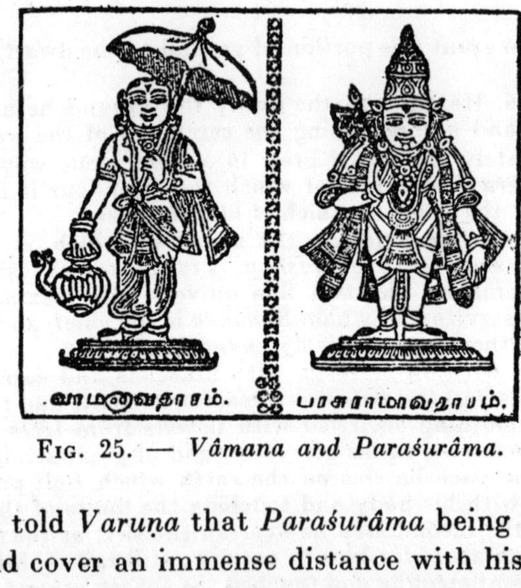

Fig. 25. — *Vâmana and Paraśurâma.*

Narada then told *Varuṇa* that *Paraśurâma* being no other than *Vishṇu*, could cover an immense distance with his arrow.

Varuṇa was frightened and implored *Yama* for help, who transformed himself into a termite (white-ant) and gnawed through the bowstring, so that it only had enough strength to hold the bow taught. The territory covered forms *Malayalam* (the coast of Malabar).

The chief of the Briguides, *Râma* of the axe (*Paraśu*), carrying also a fan of palm leaves called *visiri* (Fig. 25), is rarely seen in modern and never in ancient temples.

7. *Râmachandra.*

The story of *Râma-chandra* (*Râma*, like the moon) (1), the *Râghavide* (*Râghava*, grandson of *Raghu*), is well known. *Daśaratha*, who reigned at *Ayôdhyâ*, had three sons by his first wife *Kauśalyâ* : *Râma*, *Lakshmaṇa* and *Śatrughna* (2). The second wife, named *Kaikêyî*, had only one son *Bharata*. She obtained from *Daśaratha* who had become old and blind, a decree that this last child should take the place of *Râma* the eldest, as heir to the throne. Further she exacted that *Râma* should be banished and exiled to the forests. This exile lasted twelve years. *Râma* begged his wife *Sîtâ* not to accompany him, but she declined to leave him. *Lakshmaṇa* the king's second son went with them, and all three took refuge in a cave.

The demons (*Râkshasas*) infested this forest of *Daṇḍaka* ; *Râma* slew fourteen thousand of them. *Râvaṇa*, king of *Laṅkâ* the country of demons, furious at the massacre, resolved on vengeance by carrying off *Sîtâ*. He employed a ruse to get *Râma* out of the way. One of his companions, *Mârîcha* took the form of flame-coloured gazelle which excited *Sîtâ*'s desire. *Râma*, urged on by his wife, bounded after the animal and pierced it with an arrow. *Mârîcha* wounded to death, regained his human form and called aloud for *Lakshmaṇa* who, believing his brother was in danger, instantly went to his help. *Sîtâ* was therefore alone in the cave. *Râvaṇa* disguised as an ascetic came to her and vainly tried to seduce her. Then in a rage he assumed a demon's form, and carried her off in his aerial chariot.

A vulture called *Jaṭâyu*, a friend of *Râma*, swooped down on the ravisher to stop him, but *Râvaṇa* mortally wounded it. Meanwhile *Lakshmaṇa* and *Râma* not finding *Sîtâ*, became anxious, and started out to search for her in the forest. They found the dying vulture who told them of *Râvaṇa*'s crime, and the direction he had taken. The two brothers hurried way in chase of their enemy. They soon made the acquaintance of *Hanumân*, the general of

(1) *Râmachandra* was of solar race and not of lunar race as might be expected from his name.

(2) This is a mistake. King *Daśaratha* had a third wife, *Sumitrâ* by name. *Lakshmaṇa* and *Śatrughna* were her sons. *Râma* was *Kauśalyâ*'s only son. (Tr.)

the monkey armies of *Sugrîva*, the monkey prince who had been dethroned by his brother *Vâli*. *Râma* wishing to take them to fight against *Râvaṇa*, first helped them against *Vâli*, who was killed by an arrow, shot by *Râma*.

Sugrîva in gratitude joined in the campaign against *Râvaṇa*, with all his monkey army. First *Hanumân* was ordered to make sure that the king of *Laṅkâ* had really taken his captive to his palace. With one jump the son of the wind cleared the arm of the sea which separated India from the island of *Laṅkâ*. He met *Sîtâ* by night in the gardens, and giving her a ring from *Râma*, told her that they were coming to deliver her.

He then bounded through the streets of the capital with a burning torch tied to his tail, and set fire to all the houses. With a single spring to India he returned, appeared before *Râma* and said : « I have seen *Sîtâ*. » — *Râma*, *Lakshmaṇa*, *Sugrîva* and *Hanumân* then prepared to attack *Laṅkâ*. With blocks of rock the monkey army made a bridge over the straits. Several battles were fought between the monkeys and the *Râkshasas*. In the end *Râma* in single combat vanquished *Râvaṇa*, the ten headed giant.

Râma's birthday is commemorated by the festival *Śrî-Râma-Navami*, and he is represented (Pl. LI) as a warrior. He holds a bow (Tamil : *villu*), called *Sâraṅga* (Sanskrit : *Śârṅga*) or *Kôdaṇḍa* (thus the god is called *Śârṅgapâṇi* and *Kôdaṇḍarâma*) in his left hand, while his right hand holds an arrow (*ambu*) ; a quiver (*amuratoni*) crosses over his right shoulder ; a tiara (*kriḍam*) is on his head, and his feet are shod with sandals of wood. His colour is always green. At his side his wife *Sîtâ* is found, holding a lotus flower in her hand, *Lakshmaṇa* his brother, carrying a bow and arrow, and the monkey *Hanumân*.

Hanumân also is green in colour. This son of *Pavana* (the wind) is represented sometimes with joined hands (*kummudugirathu*, *añjali*), sometimes seated on his tail which is rolled in a spiral (*kodikamban*), sometimes carrying *Sañjîvi* to cure *Râma* and *Lakshmaṇa*. The legend is as follows :

The plant *mulligai* has the property of curing illness and raising the dead to life. It grows on the mountain *Imayagiri*. *Hanumân* not being able to identify this plant among all the others, carried away the whole mountain (Pl. LII).

Many incidents of the *Râmâyaṇa* are trated in modern iconography. The principal ones are :

Sîtâ-kalyâṇa : the marriage of *Sîtâ* and *Râma* (1).

Râma-sêtubandha : *Hanumân* and the army of monkeys constructing the bridge of *Râma* (Adam's bridge between India and Ceylon).

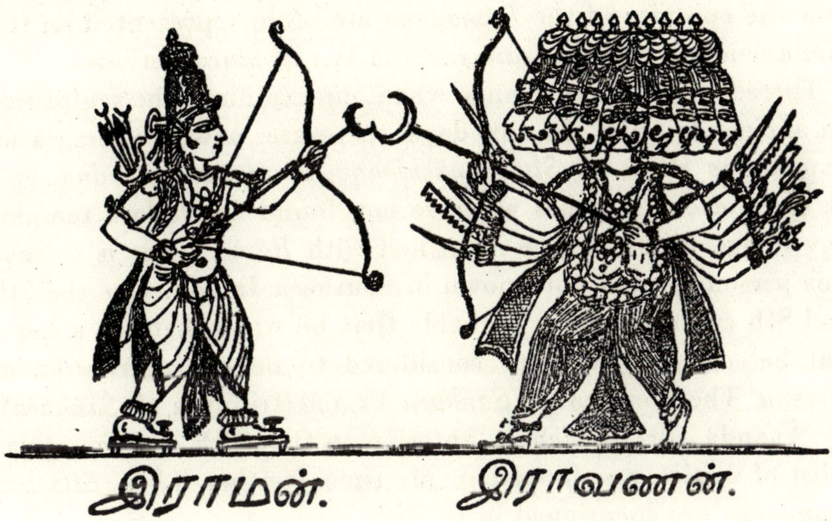

FIG. 26. — *Fight of Râma and Râvaṇa.*

Râvaṇa-yuddham : the combat of *Râma* and *Râvaṇa* (Fig. 26). *Daśagrîva*, surnamed *Râvaṇa*, king of the *Râkshasas* of *Laṅkâ*, is represented with ten heads and twenty arms carrying formidable weapons. His colour is red, and on his ten foreheads the three white horizontal stripes of Sivaites are marked.

Râma-Liṅgam : of which we have already spoken.

Râma-paṭṭâbhishêkam: coronation of *Râma* at *Ayôthi* (*Ayôdhyâ*) (Pl. LIII). *Râma* is seated and making the gesture *abhaya-hastam*. *Sîtâ* seated at his left, holds a lotus flower. *Hanumân* supports *Râma*'s foot. To the side of the god stands *Śatrughna*, holding a sun-shade (*kodai*) over the head of the god, while *Laksh-*

(1) Every time a marriage is represented, plantain trees bearing fruit are seen on the image. This is indeed the usual custom in Southern India where plantain trees in fruit are cut to decorate the *pandal* (canopy made of sticks, twigs, leaves etc.), under which the marriage ceremony takes place. (See Pl. XXII.)

maṇa and *Bharata* fan *Râma* with fly-whisks (chowry). At the feet of the god is seen *Vibhîshana* (recognizable from his moustache) who had just been crowned king of *Laṅkâ* in place of his brother *Râvaṇa* (1).

Historical. — The iconographical history of the legend of *Râma* is a question as interesting as it is important. We know how the episodes of the *Râmâyaṇa* are often represented on the monuments of the *Bijayanagar* and the *Madura* periods.

There is a complete change when one examines the sculptures on ancient temples. In our days there are nowhere images as popular as those of *Sîtâ*, *Lakshmaṇa*, *Hanumân*, *Râvaṇa*, etc. In spite of our searches we have not found in *Pallava* temples any image which can be identified with *Râma*. That is to say, this personage was not known in Southern India before the 7th and 8th centuries. It is probable that he was taken for a hero, but he certainly was not considered to be an incarnation of *Vishṇu*. The book called *Śaṅkara-Vijaya* (triumph of *Śaṅkara*), by Ânanda Giri, which is anterior to the 10th century, gives a list of deities worshipped in his time. Neither *Râma*, *Sîtâ* nor *Hanumân* are mentioned in it (2).

It seems that the cult of *Râma* spread in Southern India in the

(1) The description in the *Râmâyaṇa* is slightly different. *Śatrughna* himself carried the splendid white sun-shade. *Sugrîva*, king of the apes, held the white fly-switch and the white fan. The sovereign of the *Râkshasas*, *Vibhîshana* joyfully took another beautiful fly-switch, with an incomparable fan, like the star of the nights, to fan *Râma*. (*Vâlmîki Râmâyaṇa*, translated by Fauche, Vol. IX, p. 414.)

(2) In the *Kailâsa* at *Ellora* (second half of the 8th century) there is a long gallery entirely given up to Vishnuvite low-reliefs. It is indubitable that the sculptures would have shown *Râma* among the incarnations of *Vishṇu* if it had been in conformity with religion at that time.

It is proved however that the *Râmâyaṇa* was known at that period. On the Southern face of the *Kailâsa*, are seen two low-reliefs the meaning of which is clear. One represents the fight of the monkeys in which the struggle of the two brothers *Vâli* and *Sugrîva* can be seen. Below is the death of *Vâli*, and two figures which can be identified with *Râma* and *Lakshmaṇa*. *Râma* does not seem here to be only a simple hero. The other has for its subject the rape of *Sîtâ* : *Râvaṇa* carries a wagon in space, with *Sîtâ* in it. The vulture (*Jaṭâyu*) is starting in pursuit and the giant turns round to deal a mortal blow to the bird (Pl. LIV).

This low-relief is very remarkable owing to the following particularity : the giant who takes away *Sîtâ* in an air-car has only one head. Can it be said then, that this is the same personage who, when under *Kailâsa* (Pl. XXI), is always shown with ten heads and twenty arms ?

Bijayanagar period, perhaps under the influence of the princes of that realm. The monkey god to this day is still the protecting dèity of the city of *Bijayanagar*.

8. *Balarâma* (or *Balabhadra*).

Vishṇu incarnated himself simultaneously in both sons of *Vasudêva* and *Dêvakî*. *Balarâma* was the senior and *Kṛishṇa* the junior. *Balarâma* is therefore only a part (*aṁśa*) of the deity. His principal exploit was the vanquishing of the giant *Vṛitrâsura*.

We have never met with this image in ancient temples.

The distinctive emblem of this god is the plough (Tamil: *kalapai*) (Fig. 27). Consequently *Balarâma* has the titles *Râma-*

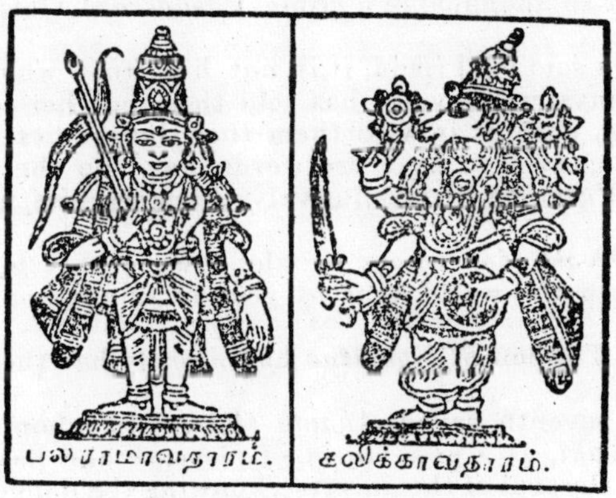

Fig. 27. — *Balarâma and Kalki.*

lâṅgalî (he who holds the plough), *Haladhara* (he who carries the plough share), *Halâyudha* (he who makes a weapon of the plough share), *Saṅkarshaṇa* (he who ploughs through armies).

In place of *Balabhadra* the 8th incarnation of *Vishṇu* is sometimes said to be *Bapuda* (none other than *Gautama*).

9. *Kṛishṇa*.

The heroes of the *Mahâbhârata* are not less known than those of the *Râmâyaṇa*. *Kṛishṇa* (the Black) of the *Yâdava* race (descendant of *Yadu*) was the son of *Vasudêva* and his wife *Dêvakî*. His uncle *Kaṁśa* wished to make away with him, but he was miraculously saved, and his foster-mother *Yaśôdâ* (1) was

(1) *Bhâgavata Purâṇa* (BURNOUF's translation), book X, chap. I:
« 27. Once upon a time there was a chief of the *Yâdavas* at *Mathurâ* called *Śûrasêna*, who lived in that town and ruled over the *Mathurâ* and *Śûrasêna* countries.

« 29. Now it came to pass that *Vasudêva*, son of *Sûra*, came there to get a wife. He had mounted his chariot and was about to start with his new wife *Dêvakî*,

« 30. When *Kaṁśa*, son of *Ugrasêna*, wishing to be polite to his sister took the reins in hand in the midst of an escort of several hundred chariots of gold.

« 34. On the way while *Kaṁśa* held the reins, he heard a mysterious voice which said to him : « The eighth child of her whom you drive, will put you to death, o fool ! »

« 35. Thus spake the voice, and the wicked perverse *Kaṁśa*, he who brought shame to the family of *Bhôjas*, brandishing his sword in one hand while he grasped her hair with the other, sprang upon his sister to slay her.

« 36. In order to appease the pitiless and shameless prince who was ready to commit so abominable a crime, *Vasudêva* the fortunate addressed him thus :

« 54. *Vasudêva* said : « Friend, it is not her from whom thou hast to fear what that mysterious voice has told thee, but her sons. I shall give them up to thee, since it is with them that danger lies for thee. »

« 55. *Kaṁśa*, convinced by these words, gave up the design of killing his sister, and *Vasudêva* after effusively thanking him, proceeded to his dwelling.

« 56. Then *Dêvakî*, for whom he alone was everything, in fact was god, brought into the world year by year in due season, eight sons and one daughter.

« Chap. II. 4. The son of *Ugrasêna* had already had the first six children of *Dêvakî* slain,

« 5. When a seventh called *Ananta* (*Râma*) in whom *Vishṇu* resides, was born to *Dêvakî*, as a new object of pleasure and pain.

« 6. *Bhagavat*, the soul of the universe, knowing the danger to the *Yâdavas* his faithful servants, of which *Kaṁśa* was the cause, said to the *Mâyâ* of the *Yôga* :

« 7. « Blissful goddess ! go to the park where live the herdsmen and their cattle. There, in the cow-shed of *Nanda* dwells the wife of *Vasudêva* (named) *Rôhiṇî*, others living in caves for dread of *Kaṁśa*.

« 8. *Dêvakî* carries at her bosom a fruit called *Śêsha* (*Râma*), in which I reside, take it away and put it ot the breast of *Rôhiṇi*. »

« 14. Thus adjured by *Bhagavat*, the goddess accepting his order exclaimed : « Yes, I salute thee ! » and having walked round him, went to the earth and did as she had been instructed.

« Chap. III. 1. Then came the time when all the propitious conditions brilliant with supreme beauty, were united : the constellation of *Ajana*'s son (the constellation of *Rôhiṇî*) eclipsed all constellations, planets and stars ;

« 8. And for the birth of *Janârddana*, the midnight hour enveloped in darkness, when in the bosom of *Dêvakî* of beauty divine, was born *Vishṇu* who lives in all hearts, as in the East rises the glorious star of the night.

« 47. At the moment when *Śûra*'s son inspired by *Bhagavat*, made ready to take his son and leave the room of the youthful mother, the *Mâyâ* exchanged in his place. *Yaśôdâ* was the wife of the shepherd *Nanda*. (See Pl. LV.)

The exploits of *Kṛishṇa* in his infancy are numerous :

1. He killed *Pûtanâ*, the murderess of small infants, who came to suckle him and make him drink milk that was poisoned.

2. He overturned a chariot with his foot.

3. He strangled *Triṇâvarta*, who wanted to carry him off in the air.

4. Tied to a mortar, he stole some butter and uprooted the *arjuna* trees.

5. He killed a demon (in Tamil : *Richabasuram*) who had changed himself into a calf, by hurling him against a tree.

6. He slew the bird *Baka*.

7. He overcame the python *Agha*.

8. He threw the ass *Dhenuka* on to the top of a tree.

9. He overcame the serpent *Kâliya*.

10. He killed the demon *Pralamba*, who wished to carry him off on his shoulders, in pretence of play.

11. He ate fire from the burning.

12. He took away the clothing of the maiden cowherds.

13. He held up the mountain *Gôvardhana*.

14. He gave himself up to the games of *Râsa*.

15. He vanquished the serpent *Śaṅkhacchûḍa*.

16. He killed successively : the buffalo *Arishṭa*,

17. The winged-horse *Kêśin*,

18. The magician *Vyôma*,

of the *Yôga*, *Aja* (the Uncreated) was born in the bosom of *Nanda*'s spouse.

« 48. When she had taken from the wardens of the doors all feeling of perception and plunged all dwellers of the town in sleep profound, all doors which were shut with huge bolts, iron bars and with chains,

« 49. opened of themselves for the passing of *Vasudêva*, holding *Kṛishṇa* in his arms : just as darkness (melting away at the approach) of sleep. The clouds poured forth their water with a dull roar, while *Śêsha* (*a*) coming behind them, protected them under his hoods.

« 51. On coming to the park of *Nanda*, the son of *Śûra* found the herdsmen unconscious under the influence of *Nidrâ* (goddess of mystic slumber) ; he put his son on the couch of *Yaśôdâ* and taking her daughter he returned to his home.

« 52. On *Dêvakî*'s bed he placed the baby girl, and himself putting back the shackles on his feet, became a prisoner as before. »

(*a*) Commonly called *Ain-talai-pambu*, the five-headed cobra. (Tr.)

19. The elephant *Kuvalayâpîḍa*,

20. *Kaṁśa*, king of *Mathurâ*.

It is necessary to study particularly some of the episodes more often represented.

Kattunda-kaṇṇan (*Kṛishṇa* tied) (Fig. 28, A). — We borrow from Burnouf's translation of the *Bhâgavata Purâṇa*, the following legend :

« Chap. ix. 1. One day while the servants were occupied with household work, *Nanda*'s wife *Yaśôdâ* churned the butter herself ;

« 5. She took him on her knees, and exposing her breasts, which flowed with milk under the influence of motherly tenderness, she looked upon his smiling face, but suddenly put him away before he was satisfied, and ran to the milk which was boiling over on the fire.

« 6. The child bit his ruddy quivering lips with rage, broke the churn with a stone pestle while pretending to cry, and stole away to eat the fresh butter, hiding himself in the house.

« 7. Once the milk had boiled and was taken off the fire, the lady came back, and guessing by the sight of the broken churn, that it was the work of her son, as she still did not see him there, she burst out laughing.

« 8. Perched on the base of a mortar, he gorged himself like a monkey with the fresh butter which hung like a thread, all the while betraying by his look the fear of being surprised. As soon as she saw her son, she came up quietly behind him.

« 9. *Kṛishṇa* saw her coming with a switch in her hand, got down in haste and ran away as if he was frightened ; the shepherdess set herself to run after him whom the *Yôgis* do not catch, even when by penitence their hearts have become capable of reuniting with him.

« 10. His mother ran after him, and although hampered by the weight of her supple hips, whose breadth enhanced the slimness of her waist, and (by her anxiety) while still running she picked up the flowers which fell from her hair, she at last put her hand on him.

« 11. The culprit, crying and rubbing his eyes, smearing his hand with the black eye-salve, cast timid glances at his mother while she, holding him by the arm, scolded him in threatening tones.

« 12. She left her switch there ; when she saw her son was frightened, the tender mother wanted at least to tie him up with cord, not knowing the power which he had.

« 15. The cord with which the lady had tied the little culprit her son, being short by two fingers she added a second bit.

« 16. The new string was also too short, and she tied on yet another, but each bit she took to tie him up, was always too short by two fingers.

« 18. The sweat ran down her limbs ; the tresses of her hair and her garland flowed outspread. *Kṛishṇa* seeing his mother at the end of her strength, took pity on her, and tied himself up.

« 22. While his mother was busy with the affairs of her household, the vigorous *Kṛishṇa* saw two *arjuna* trees, two old *Guhyakas*, sons of the god of wealth,

« 23. Whom *Narada* had aforetime cursed and changed into trees, as a punishment for their drunkeness ; they were called *Nalakûbara* and *Maṇigrîva*, both dazzling in their beauty.

« Chap. x. 26. *Kṛishṇa* advanced between the twin *arjunas*, and He who is the universal soul had hardly passed between them, when the mortar turned obliquely.

« 27. By the efforts of the child who dragged it, the mortar followed straight. The two trees suddenly struck by *Dâmôdara* (*Kṛishṇa*) from the trammels in which their feet were tied, fell with violent shaking from the contact with the power of the Most High, — trunks, branches and twigs with a fearful sound. »

Fig. 28. A. shows *Dâmôdara* tied by a cord to the mortar and delivering the *arjuna* trees.

Kṛishṇa stealing the butter (*Navanida-kaṇṇan*) is very often represented (Pl. LVI). The god as a little child is naked, with his head decorated with peacock plumes ; in one hand he holds a pot (vase) full of butter while the other hand carries butter to his mouth (1).

(1) Mr. Guimet has noticed a great resemblance between the Hindu image

Vêṇu-gôpâla (the shepherd with the bamboo) (Pl. LVII). — *Kṛishṇa* is often represented in the attitude of a herdsman (*gôpâla*) playing the flute under a tree in the midst of his herds.

Bagachuren-vadei (the slaying of *Baka*) (Fig. 28. B). — *Bhâgavata Purâṇa* (Burnouf's translation):

« Chap. XI. 35. One day all the young herdsmen wanting to water their herds went to the banks of a pond. There they made their calves drink, and then drank themselves.

« 36. Then seeing in front of them a gigantic animal which did not move, like the peak of a mountain detached by a thunderbolt, the children took fright and fled.

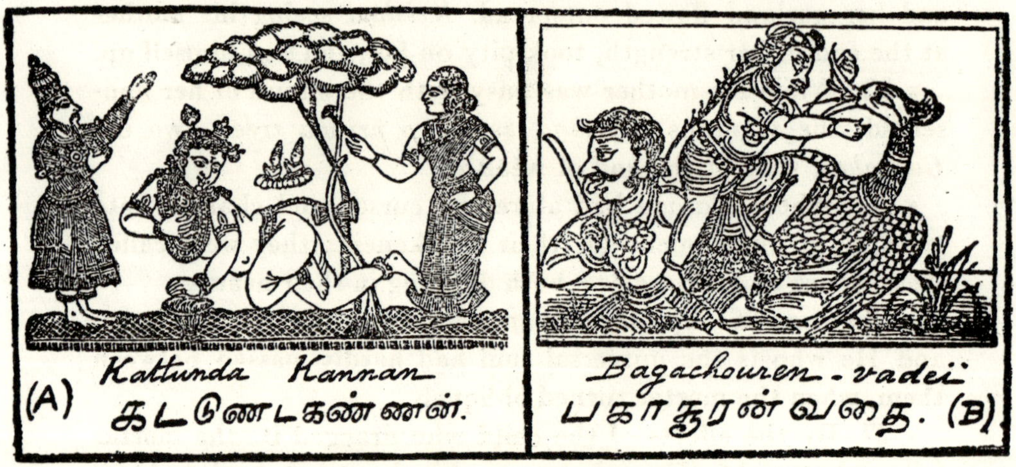

Fig. 28. — *Exploits of Kṛishṇa.*

« 37. It was the great *Asura* called *Baka* (crane) appearing in the shape of the bird of the same name. It suddenly swooped upon *Kṛishṇa* and gulped him violently into his sharp beak.

« 38. On seeing *Kṛishṇa* devoured by this monstrous crane, *Râma* and the other boys were struck with stupor, as are the senses when life leaves them.

« 39. *Baka* feeling that the son of the shepherd, the father of the *guru* of the worlds (*Brahmâ*) was burning his palate at its root like a devouring fire, threw him up suddenly with fury,

of *Kṛishṇa* eating butter and the Egyptian statues of *Chons* with the buds. Mr. Flinders Petrie has also pointed out the resemblance between the images of *Horus* and of *Kṛishṇa*.

without having hurt him and came at him anew to peck at him with his beak.

« 40. At the moment when *Baka*, the friend of *Kaṁśa*, flung himself at him, he who makes happy those who are good, caught him by the two mandibles, and rent him in two, as if in play, like a plant with a knot-less stem, before the eyes of his young companions, and filled the inhabitants of heaven with joy. »

Kâliyâhi-mardaka (the crushing of *Kâliya*) (Fig. 29). — This scene recalls the legend of Hercules and the Lernean Hydra.

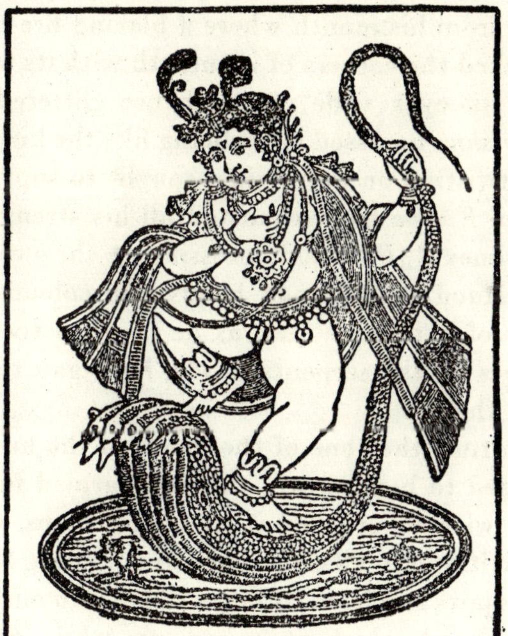

Fig. 29. — *Kâliya-mardaka.*

Bhâgavata Purâṇa (Burnouf's translation) :

« Chap. xvi. 4. *Kâliya* lived in the *Kâlindî* (the *Yamunâ*), in a lake, the water of which boiled with fire of his poison, wherein fell the birds which ventured over it.

« 6. *Kṛishṇa* who went down below to punish the wicked, seeing the force, and the irresistible thunderbolt effects, of the poison with which the serpent fouled the stream, mounted a very high *kadamba* tree, and therefrom defying the monster and girding his loins, he plunged into the poisoned water.

« 9. While the young and handsome hero, as gracious as the clouds, like some *Śrîvatsa*, garbed in yellow robe, whose face beamed with a smile, played with indifference, shaking his lotuslike feet, the serpent in a rage bit him at the sources of life, and covered him with his coils.

« 24. *Kṛishṇa*'s body as it swelled caused horrible agony to the serpent which held him in his coils, so it let go and raising its hoods with fury, began to hiss and directed on *Hari* the poisoned fluid from its nostrils, from its glassy eyes like the holes in a grid and from his mouth where a blazing fire-brand burned.

« 25. It licked the corners of its mouth with its forked tongue, still keeping its eyes wide open whence glittered a poisonous fire, while *Kṛishṇa* harassed it, frolicing like the king of the birds. The serpent twisting on every side, sought to suprise him.

« 26. When *Kâliya* had exhausted all his strength in turning thus, the primeval (*Purusha*), pressing on the swelling necks of the monster, stood on his broad hoods, and colouring a burning red the lotus of his divine feet, as he touched the innumerable precious stones on the serpents heads, he began to dance like a master of all the arts.

« 28. Each time that one of the heads of the hundred-headed monster refused to bend down, the hero, armed for the punishment of the wicked, crushed it under his leaps, o king, while the serpent writhing in all directions, and pouring forth floods of blood from its jaws and from its nostrils, fell into misery profound.

« 29. Each head which it raised up while darting poison from its eyes, and wrathfully hissing sharply, *Kṛishṇa* made to bend, mastered it and crushed it under the rythmic movement of his feet. Such is the age-long *Purusha*, whom men here below honour with a rain of flowers.

« 30. While under the fantastic bounds of his marvellous dance, he had broken in pieces the crests of the serpent, which were like a sunshade, and shattered its limbs, the latter, o king, remembered the preceptor of the movable and immovable worlds, the age-long *Purusha*, *Nârâyaṇa*, and came back to him in thought.

« 66. After thus honouring the master of the worlds, and becoming reconciled with the god whose symbolic name is *Garuḍa*, he turned around him, and joyfully saluted him.

« 67. And, followed by his wives and his children, he went with permission to the isle of *Ramaṇaka*. On the instant the waters of the *Yamunâ* ceased to be poisonous, and acquired ambrosial sweetness. » (See Pl. LVIII.)

Gôpikâ-vastrâpaharaṇa (the rape of the milkmaids clothes) (1). — The episode is also called *jala-krîḍâ* (the water games) (Pl. LIX).

Bhâgavata Purâṇa (Burnouf's translation) :

« Chap. XXII. 1. *Śuka* said : During the first month of winter, the young women of the park of *Nanda* celebrate pious observances in honour of *Kâtyâyanî* (*Durgâ*) during which time they live on nothing but wild grain.

« 2. They bathe in the water of *Kâlindî* (the *Yamunâ*), and at the first rays of the sun, make an image of the goddess with river sand, and worship it, o king.

« 8. The ever happy *Kṛishṇa*, the Master of the masters of the *Yôga*, approved of their thoughts, and whishing to assure to them the fruit of their sacrifice, he repaired to the place with his companions.

« 9. He took away the clothes of the young women, hastily climbed a *nîpa* tree, and exchanging smiles with his camrades, jokingly said :

« 10. « Ladies, come hither, and each one take as she wishes, the clothes which are hers. Seriously I speak, and not in jest, for you are reduced by your fast. »

« 12. At these mockeries of *Kṛishṇa*, the shepherdesses with hearts overflowing with love, felt shy, and glanced at each other, without coming out of the water.

« 13. When *Gôvinda* thus spake, the young women, whose hearts were ravished by his pleasantries, immersed in cold water to their necks while shivering said :

« 14. « Come now, no nonsense ! o child, we know whom thou

(1) Commonly called : *Kṛishṇa* and the *gôpikâs*. (Tr.)

art, dear son of *Nanda* the shepherd, thy praises all sing in the park, our clothes give to us, here we freeze.

« 15. O thou, whose rich colour enhances thy beauty, thy slaves we all are, and as thou hast said, so wish we to do. Give us our clothing, or else we must take our plaint to the king. »

« 16. *Bhagavat* said : « If you are my slaves, and will do all I say, come take your clothing, o beauties with smile so pure. »

« 17. Then all the young women, shivering with cold, came out of the water covering their nudeness with both hands, and crouching together because of the cold.

« 18. The Ever-happy seeing that their feelings were hurt, was won by the purity of their thoughts, and putting their cloths on a branch, said with affectionate smile :

« 19. « You have offended the gods bathing quite naked in the water during the time of your pious observances, to wipe out your sins ; put your hands on your head, and bowing low, take all your clothes. »

« 21. Then seeing them bowed down before him, the ever-happy son of *Dêvakî*, touched by this mark of submission, graciously returned their garments. »

« 22. He had grievously teased them, and despoiled them of all modesty, had toyed with them, making them move like puppets, and taken away their cloths. But they bore him no grudge, so great was their joy to be so near their loved one.

« 23. They put on their cloths, ready to unite with the object of their love, with hearts filled by him alone, they moved not, and modestly fixed their eyes on him. »

Gôvardhana-dhara (*Kṛishṇa* supporting mount *Gôvardhana*). — *Bhâgavata Purâṇa* (Burnouf's translation) :

« Chap. XXIV. 1. While *Bhagavat* lived in the park with *Baladêva*, he saw the herdsmen busy one day preparing a sacrifice in honour of *Indra*.

« 2. *Bhagavat*, who knew well what they were doing, since he is the Universal Soul, and He who sees everything, respectfully bowing before *Nanda* and the other elders, asked them the following question :

« 3. « Tell me, father, why the turmoil which reigns among

you ? What result do you expect ? What orders do you obey ? With what do you celebrate this sacrifice ? »

« 8. *Nanda* said : « The ever-happy *Indra* is god of the storms, with clouds for his visible signs, these are they which spread over creation the water which makes it live and breathe. »

« 12. So spake *Nanda* and the other dwellers in the park. On hearing them *Kêśava* who wished to drive *Indra* to the extreme, said to his father :

« 15. « What has *Indra* to do with earthly beings, since each of them is subject to the influence of what he himself does, and *Indra* cannot change at all the fate which nature assigns to men.

« 17. If a being unites with the body of a superior or inferior order or if it leaves them, it is by virtue of action. Acts are its enemy ; abstension is its friend, it is the *guru*, it is *Îśvara !*

« 18. So it is acts which ought to be honoured by the being which makes its own destiny in obedience to Nature. The true deity of the Sacrifice for him is that which makes him live.

« 25. Therefore one should offer sacrifices to cows, to Brahmins and to the mountain, and for this, the preparation for *Indra*'s sacrifice should be used. »

« 38. He spoke, and the herdsmen made sacrifice in honour of the mountain, the cows and the Brahmins as the son of *Vasudêva* advised, and returned to the park with *Kṛishṇa.*

« Chap. xxv. 1. Then *Indra* seeing his honours abolished, turned his anger against *Nanda* and the herdsmen who had taken *Kṛishṇa* as protector.

« 2. The clouds ordained to put an end to the world, formed battalions to the order of him who is called the Destroyer. Wounded in his pride as sovereign master, furious *Indra* encouraging their zeal, spoke to the clouds in these words :

« 5. « By putting their trust in a babbling, foolish, ignorant and presumptuous child, in *Kṛishṇa*, a mortal, the herdsmen have cut me to the quick.

« 6. Since prosperity has made them so proud and the support of *Kṛishṇa* so confident in themselves, strike down the blind drunkeness with which prosperity fills them, and destroy their herds.

« 7. I myself riding my elephant *Airâvata* shall proceed against the park ; with the powerful legion of the winds, shall I overthrow the byres of *Nanda.* »

« 8. At this order of *Maghavân*, the clouds released, beat with torrential rain upon *Nanda*'s park, and bore down violently upon it.

« 9. Flashing with the fire of lightenings, roaring with the claps of thunder, and driven on by the frenzied bands of *Maruts* (the winds), they poured upon it avalanches of water and gravel.

« 11. The domestic animals shuddering under the beating rain and blasts of wind, with the shepherds and shepherdesses shivering with cold, all ran to the protection of *Gôvinda.*

« 14. Seeing the rain of gravel which drove violently down on the dwellers of the park, and drove them wild, the beneficient *Hari* recognized the work of the wrath of *Indra.*

« 15. « This unseasonable and violent storm (said he to himself), these blasts of wind, this rain of sand, are sent by Indra to destroy us, since we have abolished his cult. »

« 19. Thus said *Kṛishṇa*, and with one hand only he lifted up the *Gôvardhana* mountain from its base, and supported it in the air as easily as a child holds up a mushroom.

« 20. *Bhagavat* said to the herdsmen : « Mother, Father, and you dwellers in the park, enter as you will under the mountain you and your herds. »

« 22. Reassured by the encouraging words of *Kṛishṇa*, they went under the mountain and settled themselves as well as they could, with all they had, their herds and their servants.

« 23. Without feeling the pangs of hunger and thirst, caring not for his own well being, he held up the mountain for seven days under the eyes of the dwellers of the park, without moving from his place.

« 24. *Indra* witnessed the mysterious power of *Kṛishṇa*, and was astonished ; at the end of his resources and giving up his plans, he called away his servants the clouds. »

Rukmiṇî-kalyâṇa. — This is the marriage of *Kṛishṇa* and *Rukmiṇî*, daughter of the king of *Vidarbha* (*Dvârakâ*).

Kṛishṇa is also represented (Pl. LX) with his wife *Rukmiṇî* and his favourite mistress *Râdhâ*, in his palace at *Dvârakâ.*

Historical. — One fact can be established in the history of the iconography of *Kṛishṇa.* Two legends are often found in ancient temples :

1. The hero crushing the serpent *Kâliya* ;
2. Holding up the *Gôvardhana* mountain.

None of the other legends of *Kṛishṇa*'s life seem to have been known to the sculptors of the 7th and 8th centuries.

Kṛishṇa conquering the snake *Kâliya* is represented in the *Dharmarâja* at *Mavalipuram* (1st story, South side) (it is noticeable that the upper part of the snake's body is human) and on the *Vaikuṇṭha-Perumal* at *Kañchîpuram* (A. Rea, *Pallava Architecture*, Pl. LXXXIII, fig. 3) (1).

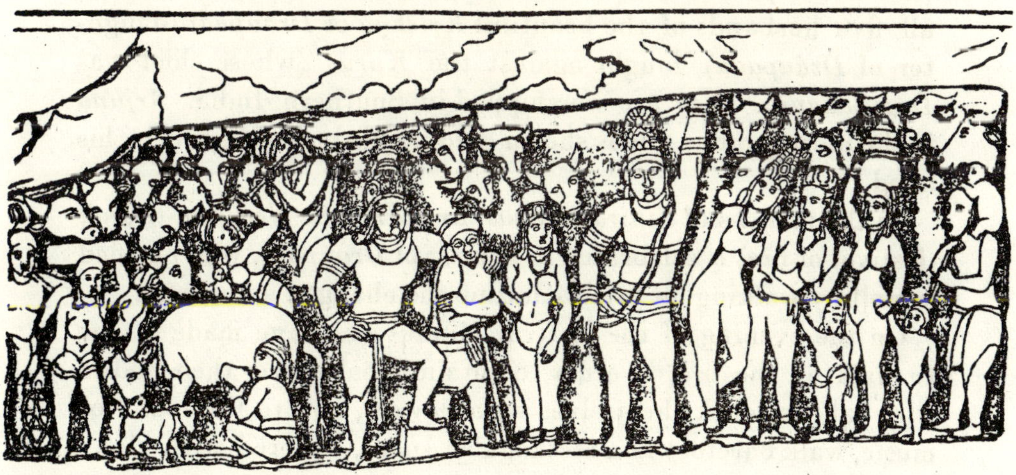

Fig. 30. — *Relief at Mavalipuram (7th century) representing Kṛishṇa supporting mount Gôvardhana* (Babington's drawing).

A large low-relief at *Mavalipuram* represents *Kṛishṇa* holding up the mountain *Gôvardhana* above the herdsmen, their families and their herds (Fig. 30) (2).

(1) It is in this way too, that the subject is treated in the *Kailâsa* at *Ellora* (see Pl. LVIII) ; but in this place the hero has four arms, one carrying the *Śaṅkha*, which proves that at that period (8th century) he was identified with Vishnu.

(2) *Kṛishṇa* is ordinarily represented playing the flute, and charming

The same subject is found in the *Vaikuṇṭha-Perumal* temple, at *Kañchîpuram* (A. Rea, *Pallava Architecture*, Pl. LXXVIII, fig. 3) (1).

We are tempted to believe that in the 7th century the two exploits about the snake *Kâliya* and the mountain *Gôvardhana* were not yet attributed to the hero of the *Mahâbhârata* (2).

One fact is clear, which is, that the poetical and pretty stories of the young *Kṛishṇa* (*Kṛishṇa* stealing the butter, *Kṛishṇa* and the *Gôpikâs*, *Kṛishṇa* the flutist, *Kṛishṇa* and his wives) are altogether absent from Hindu iconography before the 12th century.

Draupadî and the Pâṇḍavas. — The five *Pâṇḍava* brothers (*pañcha Pâṇḍava*) : 1. *Dharmarâja* or *Yudhishṭhira* ; 2. *Bhîma* (the terrible) ; 3. *Arjuna* (the white) ; 4. *Nakula* ; 5. *Sahadêva*, all five husbands of the beautiful *Kṛishṇâ* or *Draupadî* (daughter of *Drâupada*), fought against the *Kurus* (whose chief was *Duryôdhana*). They are worshipped in Southern India. *Arjuna* is the most famous ; he is shown holding his bow *Gâṇḍîva* in his hand.

In the months of *Sittirai*, *Vayasi* and *Ani*, the *Neruppu-tirunâḷ* (festival of fire) is celebrated in honour of *Draupadî*, who purified herself by walking on fire, each time she changed a husband.

On the evening of the festival, Hindus who have made a vow to walk on the fire, in order to obtain boons, cover their bodies with saffron, deck themselves with flowers, and to the sound of music, walk barefoot in a rectangular space, covered with glowing charcoal.

Historical. — The episode of *Śiva* in the form of a hunter following a wild boar in order to prove the courage of *Arjuna*

all creation with his divine music. As one of the personages is figured with this instrument at his lips, it would be necessary to suppose that the god is represented twice in the same tableau. It is easier to think that the player of the flute whom we see is some herdsman or other. (*Le Tour du monde, Eight days in India*, by Emile Guimet, 1889, Vol. LVI, 1440th part, p. 96.)

(1) And also in the *Kailâsa* at *Ellora*.

(2) *Kṛishṇa* the Yâdavide is identified with *Gôvinda*, the pastoral god ; *Râma* the Râghavide is identified with a popular god, the conqueror of the demons, *Râma* (Chantepie de La Saussaye, *Histoire des religions*, p. 404).

(*Mahâbhârata : Vana-Parva*, 1616-1713) is shown on the *Kailâsanâtha* temple at *Kañchîpuram* (A. Rea, *Pallava Architecture*, Pl. XXXIV, image on the right).

10. *Kalki.*

The incarnation of *Vishṇu* as a giant with a white horse's head, bearing a sword and shield has not yet taken place. It will occur at the end of the world. It is rarely represented and then only in modern temples. This *avatâr*, the tenth and last, bears the name of *Kalki* (Fig. 27) (1).

Môhenî or Môhinî.

When quoting the translation of the *Bhâgavata Purâṇa* about the churning of the sea of milk, it was stated that *Vishṇu* took the form of a beautiful woman in order to seduce the giants and take the *amurdam* (Sanskrit : *amṛita*) (Pl. LXI) away from them. This image is only seen in mordern temples.

Vênkaṭêśa Perumal.

Certain Vishnuvite sages are thought to be incarnations of *Vishṇu*, the most famous being *Vênkaṭêśa* (*Vênkaṭâchala-mûrti* or *Vênkaṭêśvara-Perumal*), god of *Vênkaḍa* (*Tirupati*). He is generally represented as in Fig. 20, between *Śrîdêvî* and *Bhûmi-ḍêvî.*

§ 2. — *Lakshmî.*

The wife of *Vishṇu* (who is called *Lakshmî-pati*, husband of *Lakshmî*) was born out of the sea of milk (whence her name *Jaladhi-jâ*). She is also called *Śrîdêvî*, and considered to be the goddess of the sky and of fortune. She stands at *Vishṇu*'s right hand and carries in her left hand a lotus flower (*padma*, *kamala* or *tâmarasa*).

(1) According to Lassen, the idea of an incarnation of *Vishṇu* in the form of a horse, only appeared in India after Mahmoud of Gazni had overcome the Hindus with the aid of his cavalry.

When *Vishṇu* incarnated himself in *Râma*, *Lakshmî* was incarnated in *Sîtâ*, and when *Vishṇu* was incarnated in *Kṛishṇa*, *Lakshmî* was incarnated in *Rukmiṇî*.

Gaja-Lakshmî.

In modern iconography the goddess *Lakshmî* is often represented (Pl. LXII) seated with legs crossed, on a lotus throne. She has four arms. Two of her hands are in the attitude *abhaya-hastam*. The two hands behind these, each carry a lotus. On each side of *Lakshmî* an elephant holds up a vessel with his trunk, and with it waters the flower which the goddess holds.

Historical. — This subject is extremely ancient. Two hundred years before our era, the Buddhists represented a goddess between two elephants.

At *Mavalipuram* (7th century) in the *Varâha* cave, a low-relief (Pl. LXIII) shows how this scene was treated by the *Pallavas* (1). It is to be found in the *Kailâsanâtha* temple at *Kañchîpuram* (A. Rea, *Pallava Architecture*, Pl. XXX).

If the old designs are compared with those of modern iconography it is noticeable that in olden days the subject represented the bath of the goddess. She was seated in a very simple costume in the middle of a pool, and it was on her person that the elephants poured water.

Now-a-days the goddess, magnificently arrayed and decked with jewels, does not bathe, and the elephants no longer pour water on her shoulders, but on the flowers she holds in her hands.

§ 3. — *Manmadan* (*Manmatha*).

Manmatha (he who stirs the heart), also called *Kâma* (desire), *Abhi-rûpa* (the Pretty), son of *Vishṇu* and *Lakshmî*, is the Eros of the Hindus (2).

(1) Two similar low-rèliefs exist in the *Kailâsa* at *Ellora*. One of the two is at the entrance of this temple, and it is the first thing the visitor sees on entering the monument.

(2) *Kâma* is represented in the *Kailâsa* at *Ellora*. He holds his bow of sugar cane. He is without his parrot, and he has a *makara* for his emblem.

Manmadan having struck *Śiva* when he was engaged in his austerities, with his arrows, the latter burnt up his body with a glance. Hence *Manmadan* got the name of *Anaṅga* : the Incorporeal. This event is commemorated by the festival *Kâmadahanam* which takes place during the month of *Phâlguna* (March).

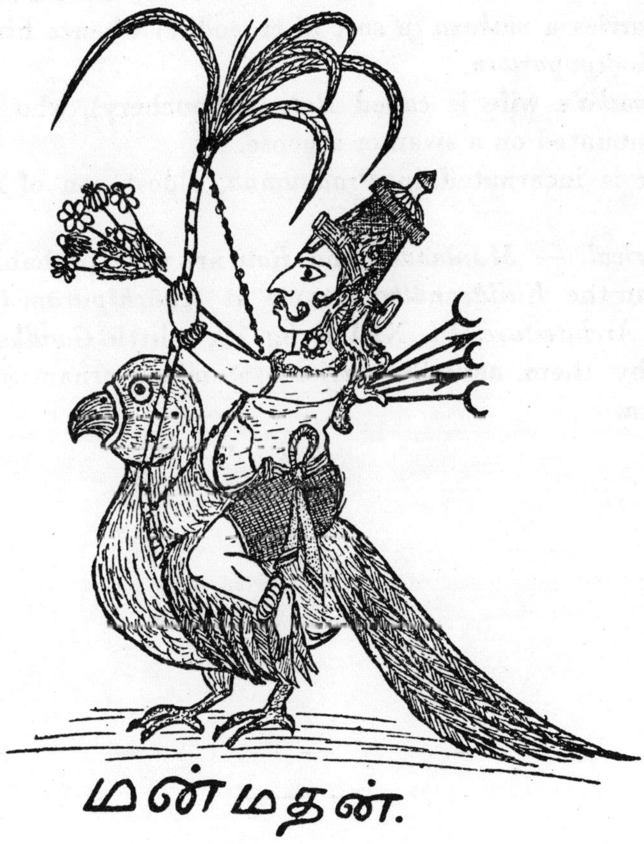

Fig. 31. — *Manmadan.*

Kâma (Fig. 31) is represented riding a parrot. His arrows are flowers ; his quiver contains five arrows (the number is characteristic), each of which represents a passion the magical charm of which provokes love. Each arrow is a flower, of lotus, mango, jasmine, *aśoka* and blue lily : *Amra* (the mango blossom), *Nagatêshara* (*Mesua ferrea*), *Champaka* (*Michelia champaka*), *Kêtaka* (*Pandanus adoratissimus*) and *Malura* (*Egle marmelos*). To *Kâma* also are applied the epithets *Pañchâsana* (he of the five arrows),

Kusumâyudha (armed with flowers), *Aindhunaikijavan* (master of five arrows), and *Pushpa-kêtana* (adorned with flowers).

Manmatha's bow is a stalk of sugar cane (whence *Kâma*'s name *Karuthiyakaruppu-villi*) and the bow-string is formed of bees holding each other's feet. *Kâma*'s dart is called *Kamabuna* (from the Sanskrit *Kâmabâṇa*, arrow of love). On his standards *Kâma* carries a *makara* (a sort of crocodile) whence his name : *Minurokoḍiyuyarttan.*

Manmatha's wife is called *Rati* (debauchery), who is represented mounted on a swan or a goose.

Kâma is incarnated in *Pradyumna*, eldest son of *Kṛishṇa.*

Historical. — *Manmadan* and *Rati* are very probably represented on the *Kailâsanâtha* temple at *Kañchîpuram* (A. Rea, *Pallava Architecture*, Pl. XLIII, fig. 1) ; a little *Gandharva* who stands by them, actually carries a standard ornamented with a *makara.*

CHAPTER III

BRAHMÂ AND SECONDARY DIVINITIES

§ 1. — *Brahmâ* (Tamil : *Biraman*).

Brahmâ is the Brahmin god, and the author of the *Vêdas* We have seen him celebrating the marriage of *Śiva* and *Pârvatî*, and pouring lustral water on the foot of *Vishṇu-Trivikrama.* In his honour the Brahmins perform the *Sandhyâvandana* ceremony, but he has no special temples.

Brahmâ occupies an important place in iconography. We have already seen him in the *Trimûrti.* He is who drives *Śiva*'s chariot (*Tripurasaṁhari*). We have spoken of his efforts to reach the top of the flaming column at *Tiruvanamallai.*

He is seated on the lotus flower which issues from the stomach of *Vishṇu* lying on the snake (*Raṅganâtha*). With the other gods he holds the tail of the serpent at the churning of the sea of milk. He is easily recognized by his four faces (*Chatur-mukha, Chatur-ânana, Nâlu-mukha*), of which three only are visible in pictures and reliefs, the fourth looking backwards.

According to one legend these four heads arise from the fact that there are four *Vêdas*, and each *Vêda* came from one of the four mouths. It is said that once there were five heads, but that *Śiva* cut off the fifth. When speaking of *Bhairava*, we have given the first legend, the second is as follows :

Overcome by a culpable passion *Brahmâ* wished to seduce his own daughter *Sandhyâ*. She vainly tried to escape him by hiding in the most secret retreats. At each attempt she made to fly, a new head with a new face grew on *Brahmâ*, the penetrating looks of which followed and discovered his daughter. In the end *Śiva* was roused, and cut off one of the heads, and placed it in his head-dress as a trophy.

Brahmâ does not wear the cylindrical tiara of the Vishnuvite divinities on his head ; his plaited hair is gathered into a conical knot (*mukuṭa*) (Fig. 32). He is red, or more exactly rose coloured.

He has four arms, and the back ones carry emblems. The back right hand holds an oval disk bordered with pearls called *Brahmâtandram.* It is said that he uses this instrument to mark their fate on the brows of men, but originally it may have been a sacrificial spoon. In the second right hand he holds a chaplet (*jata-*

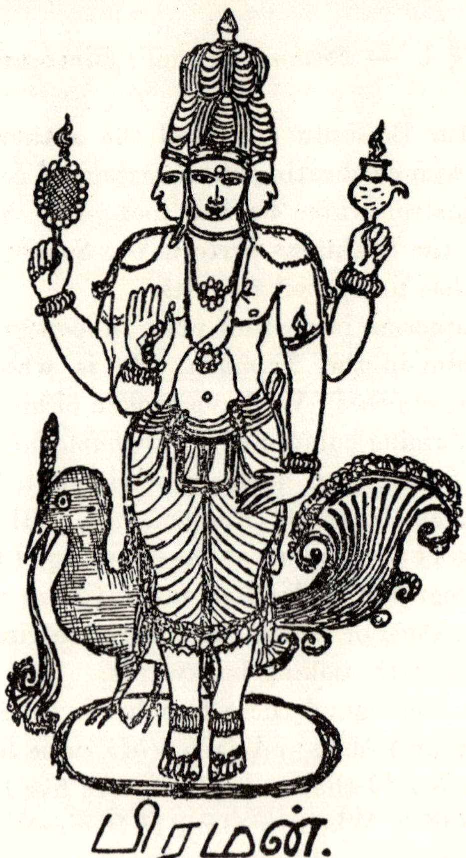

Fig. 32. — *Brahmâ.*

malai) made with *rudrâksha* beads. The left hand at the back carries an emblem called *Kamandalam* (Sanskrit : *Kamaṇḍalu*) which is a vessel used for ablutions.

His riding animal (in Sanskrit : *vâhana*) is a kind of swan called in Sanskrit *haṁsa* and in Tamil *annam*, whence *Brahmâ*'s epithet : *Annavûrti.*

Historical. — *Brahmâ* is very often represented on the *Pallava* monuments, very little differently from the fashion of today. Plate LXIV is a reproduction of an image of *Brahmâ* in the cave without inscriptions at *Trichinopoly* (7th century).

In the *Kailâsanâtha* at *Kañchîpuram*, a low-relief shows *Śiva* cutting off the fifth head of *Brahmâ* (A. Rea, *Pallava Architecture*, Pl. XXXIV, figure on the left).

We have never seen the bird of *Brahmâ* in *Pallava* temples (1). In all ancient Sivaite temples, a sanctuary consecrated to *Brahmâ* is found on the left hand side of the building. (It has been mentioned that the right hand side is consecrated to Vishnu.)

§ 2. — *Sarasvatî.*

She is the wife of *Brahmâ*, and the goddess on the arts (2). She is represented sitting and playing an instrument of music called the *vîṇâ* (Pl. LXV). The other hands (she has four) hold a book and a style. It is a fact that Hindus write on palm leaves called *ollai* with a point of iron called *jezhutheny*.

History. — In *Pallava* temples, *Brahmâ* is generally alone; however in the *Kailâsanâtha* at *Kañchîpuram* he sits beside his wife (Rea, *Pallava Architecture*, Pl. XXXVI, fig. 2), but she has no *vîṇâ*, and there is nothing to prove that at that period *Brahmâ*'s wife was identified with *Sarasvatî*, the divinity of rivers.

§ 3. — *The Devargal.*

We have mentioned that *Śiva* and his family lived in *Kailâsa* and that the paradise of *Vishṇu* is *Vaikuṇṭha*. There is another celestial abode called *Sargan* (*Svarga*), which is inhabited by the *Devargal*. Among the first of these due to be noted, are the eight

(1) At *Ellora*, in the gallery at the back of the *Kailâsa*, the bird *Annam* is at his feet, and in some low-reliefs *Brahmâ* is shown riding his swan in the midst of the Vêdic gods.

(2) In the *Ellora* caves, *Sarasvatî* is often represented not as the wife of *Brahmâ* but as a fluvial deity, and stands on a tortoise.

gods called *Tigupâlagar,* from the Sanskrit *Ashṭadikpâlaka,* who rule the eight regions of the heavens.

These gods correspond to the cardinal points, and their portraits are used to illustrate Hindu compass cards (Fig. 33).

The following are the eight guardians of the sky :

1. *Devandiren* (in Sanskrit, *Indra*) ; he is also called *Mayêndiran* (Sanskrit : *Mahêndra*). He is the son of *Kassipar* (Sanskrit : *Kaśyapa*) and *Aditi.* — *Indra*'s wife's name is *Sachî,* daughter of *Pulôman* (she is sometimes called *Indrâṇî*).

Indra annihilated *Pulôman* in order to carry off his daughter *Sachî.* So he is called *Pulômâri* (destroyer of *Pulôman*) or *Sachîpati* (husband of *Sachî*). The result of their union was a son called *Jayanta.*

Indra's capital *is Amarâravatî.* He is the god of the sky and carries in his left hand a double trident (like the *Triśûla* of *Subrahmaṇiar*), an emblem of the thunder (*Vajrâyudha*). In his right hand he carries a sort of flower.

Indra's body is covered with a thousand eyes, whence his name *Ayiraṅkannan.* His *vâhana* is a white elephant called *Airâvata* (beautiful elephant) which came out of the sea of milk. From his *Indra* got the name *Karivâhana.*

2. *Akkini* (Sanskrit : *Agni*) who governs the South-East is the god of fire. In our days he is considered to be god of the kitchen, so he carries in his four hands a porringer, a spoon, a torch and a fan with which to flow the fire. He has two hands adorned with flames (Pl. LXVI).

He is sometimes represented with three legs and seven arms. He lives in the South-East into the town of *Têchôbadipatnam* (Sanskrit : *Tejôvati*). He is the son of *Aṅgiras,* and married *Suvagay* (Sanskrit : *Svâhâ*) and had three sons : *Pavanema* (*Pâvaka*), *Pavemanam* (*Pavamâna*) and *Sussi* (*Śuchi*).

3. *Heman* or *Yaman* (Sanskrit : *Yama*), also called *Dharma* (the just) and *Tendisaikan* (because he governed the South), is god of the nether world. He lives in *Pâtâla* (under the earth). His town is *Emapuram.* He rides on a buffalo and carries a club.

His sister *Yamî* is goddess of the river *Yamunâ* (Jamna). We have already told how *Yama,* god of the infernal regions,

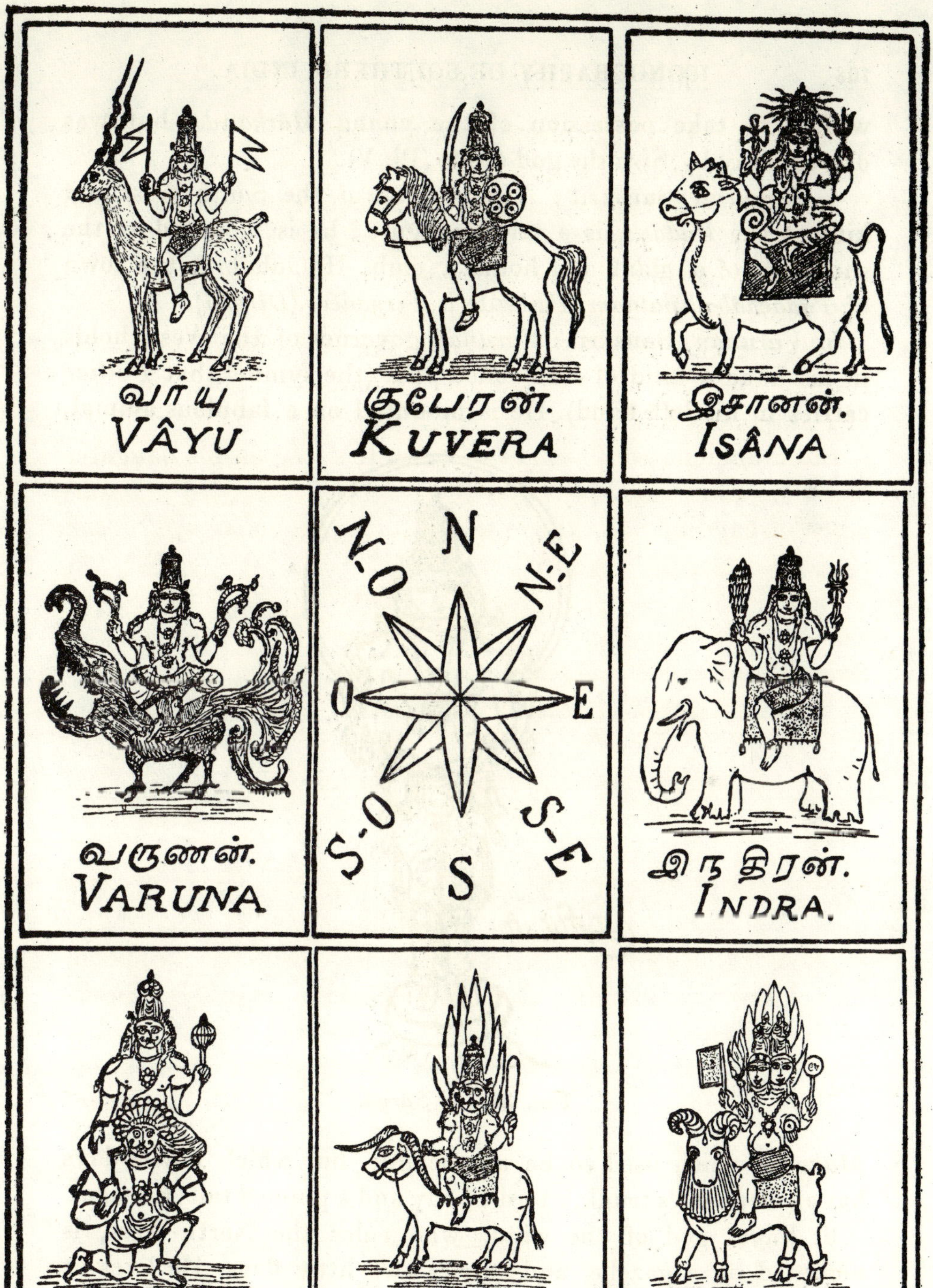

FIG. 33. — *Ashṭadikpâlaka.*

wished to take possession of the young *Mârkaṇḍa*, but was driven away by *Śiva* the god of life (Pl. V).

4. *Nayuruti* (Sanskrit : *Nirṛiti*), god of the South-West and king of the *Budans*, is a terrible figure ; he is mounted on the shoulders of a giant and holds a club. He inhabits the town of *Tadachâbadipatnam.* His wife is *Tirgadêvi* (*Dîrghâ*).

5. *Varunan* (Sanskrit : *Varuṇa*), governor of the West, holds in his hand a kind of cord called *pâśa* (the symbol that *Pulliar* carries in his left hand). He is mounted on a fabulous animal,

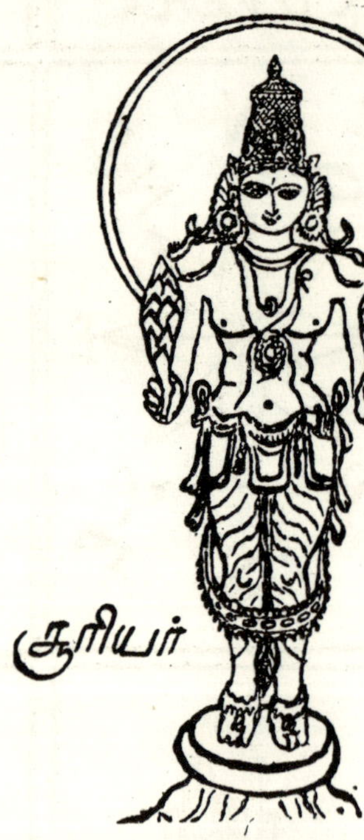

Fig. 34. — *Sûrya.*

Makara, which used to be a crocodile, but which now-a-days has an elephant's trunk, a bird's body and a plumed tail (*Karuku*).

6. *Vayu*, god of the wind, who rules the North-West, is mounted on a gazelle, and carries two little flags. He lives at *Tuchabadipatnam.*

7. *Kuberan* (Sanskrit : *Kuvêra*), son of *Viśravas*, lives in the North, in the city of *Alakâ* (*Vasu-sthalî* or *Prabhâ*). His chariot's name is *Pushpaka.* He is mounted on a white horse, and holds a sword and buckler (*parisai*).

8. *Isanian* (Sanskrit : *Îśânâ*) rides an ox, and is represented just like *Śiva*, thus he has for insignia the trident (*śula*) and the drum (*uḍukkai*). He governs the North-East.

Besides these eight *Devargal* there are others of whom *Sûrya*, god of the sun, is most famous and very frequently represented. He is known by his holding one flower in each hand, and especially because there is a large circle at the back of his head, representing the solar disk. He is often mounted in a chariot drawn by seven horses. His sons the two *Aśvins* (horsemen) are the physician gods (See Fig. 34.)

The chariot of *Sûrya* is driven by *Aruṇa* ; his capital is *Vivasvatî*. The prayer (*mantra*) called *Gâyatrî*, which Brahmins daily recite is addressed to him. The festival *Nâyittukizhamavrata*, or simply *Nâyiru* (sun or Sunday) is also celebrated in his honour.

The god of the moon is *Chandran* whose head is ornamented with a crescent, the antelope being his emblem. *Aruṇa*, half man half bird and *Viśvakarman*, the architect god, are also to be noted.

Historical (1). — *Indra* is represented (Pl. LXVIII) on the Eastern *gôpuram* at *Chidambaram ;* he is mounted on an elephant and carries the symbols (triple shining squares and double trident) representing thunderbolt (*Vadjra*), which today are the characteristics of *Subrahmaṇiar*.

Sûrya is often shown in ancient temples, with but little difference to the modern style. He is to be seen on the last story on the North side of the *Dharmarâja-ratha* at *Mavalipuram* and in the cave without inscriptions at *Trichinopoly* (7th century) (Pl. LXIX).

One point is to be noted here : The gods which appear on ancient temples outside the Dravidian country, at *Bâdâmi*, *Ellora*, etc., have their heads surrounded with an elliptic halo

(1) In the caves at *Ellora* these gods are represented in nearly all the great low-reliefs. They appear in the sky under the clouds, riding on their respective *vâhanas*, and respectfully worshipping, are present at the exploits of *Śiva*. On the exterior facade of the *Kailâsa*, on each side of the entrance door a row of niches are consecrated to them. For example *Agni* and his ram is seen (Pl. LXVII). He has only one head and two arms which do not bear emblems.

(*prabhâ*). This sign of divinity is of Greco-Buddhist origin. In Southern India, at *Mavalipuram* and *Kañchîpuram*, the gods have no halo. Only *Sûrya* has his head surrounded with a circle by which he is recognized in the low-reliefs of the *Penance of Arjuna* and in that of *Varâha.*

§ 4. — *The Kurus of the Devargal.*

The *Kurus*, sons of *Kasibar* (Sanskrit : *Kaśyapa*) and *Aditai*, are celestial Spirits similar to angels. They are : the *Vasugal*, the *Charana*, the *Marut ;* the *Kinarar* (Sanskrit : *Kinnara*), musicians who have horses heads, of whom the chief is *Tomburu*, adept at playing the *vînâ ;* the *Kimburudar* (*Kimpurusha*), singers with human heads and bodies of birds ; the *Chiddar* (*Siddha*), who have wings and fly in the air; the *Vitiadar* (*Vidyâdhara*), knowing in arts and science ; the *Gerudar* (*Garuḍa*), a kind of eagles ; the *Panaga*, snake charmers, the *Pidurdevadegal* (genii of the dead), the *Gananâtha* or *Duta*, and lastly the famous *Gandruvar* (*Gandharva*) who are wedded to the *Apsara*. *Dêvadâsîs* (dancing girls) also adorn the celestial abodes, of whom the principal ones are : *Urvasî*, *Rambhâ* and *Tilottamâ.*

Historical. — Ever after the Buddhist period, secondary spirits which too often look like little demons, appear on sculptures. In cave XXIV at *Ajanṭa* (Burgess, *Cave temples of India*, p. 157) little musicians with animals feet are to be seen, very like those which are found in the low-reliefs of the *Penance of Arjuna* at *Mavalipuram ;* especially at *Bâdâmi* (see for example the lower part of Plate XLIX) where friezes show little *Gandharvas* who amuse themselves, play tricks and fight.

The same friezes are often seen in the *Pallava* temples at *Kañchîpuram*. These little *genii* correspond to Cupids in the friezes of Western art. They wear garlands of flowers, and are chubby and naked. A characteristic of the *Gandharvas* of the 6th, 7th and 8th centuries is that they have plaited hair which hangs down on their shoulders like a pig-tail. At *Chidambaram* (Eastern *gôpuram*, 13th century) one sees friezes in which Cupids play about, but the design entirely disappears in the *Bijayanagar* period.

The friezes then display animals (elephants, horses, etc.) and dancing girls. In Hindu paintings of our days, *Kurus* figure in the sky below the gods.

§ 5. — *Demons* (*Peygal*).

Giants and monsters of terrible aspect are often to be seen represented, with scattered hair, strong moustaches, pointed teeth (*pallu*) and pot bellies. They are armed with clubs and snakes. These are the *Achurar* (*Asuras*), *Rachadar* (*Râkshasas*) and *Budan* (*Bhûtas*).

§ 6. — *Dvarabalagar* (Sanskrit : *Dvârapâlaka*).

Temple doors are protected by giant guardians of the threshold armed with clubs. They are called *Dvarabalagar*, and have four arms and carry the emblems of the gods whose sanctuaries they protect. Another name for them is *Munadiyâr*.

Historical. — In monuments of the Buddhist period, *Chaityas* are placed at each side of entrances. Archaeologists think that these heroes represent Hindu chiefs who protected Buddhism, but it is probable that these statues (at *Karli*, *Nasik* and *Kandheri*, etc.) represent guardians and protective spirits, prototypes of the modern *Dvarabalagar*.

These last are often very artistically presented at *Mavalipuram*, *Trichinopoly* (7th century), and *Kañchîpuram* (8th century). At *Tanjore* and at *Gaṅgaikondapuram* (11th century) they have already assumed a move terrible aspect. Plates LXX and LXXI show their evolution.

§ 7. — *Nâgas*.

Snakes have been venerated in India from all time, and particularly the cobra (*Cobra Capello*), called *Nâga*. Their worship is displayed in Buddhist sculptures (FERGUSON, *Tree and Serpent Worship*). Now-a-days sacred trees enclosed with a paling are found everywhere, and shelter images of snakes (*Nâgas*).

The trees are of two species of which the *Arasu* is considered the male and the *Margosa* the female. The snakes are carved on tall stones stuck in the ground. Nearly always they are inter-

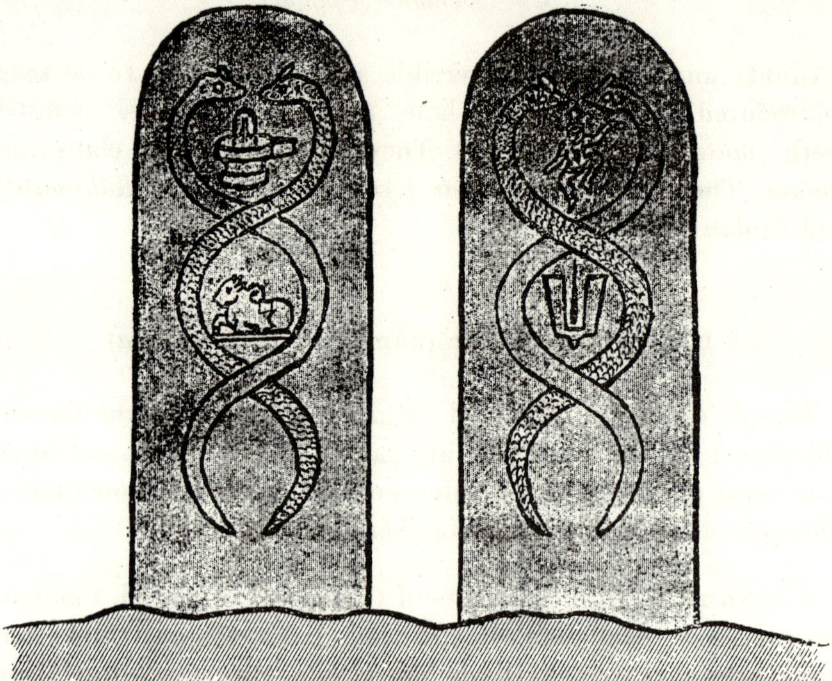

FIG. 35. — *Nâgas.*

twined as in Mercury's caduceus (Fig. 35). Women perform the office of *Nâgapûjâ* before them (See Pl. LXXII.)

§ 8. — *Grâma-Dêvatâs.*

This is the name given to village deities such as *Ellammal*, *Ankâlamman*, *Bhadrakâlî*, *Pidari*, etc. ; *Châmundî*, the goddess who conquered *Mahishâsura*, is also a *Grâma-dêvatâ*. We shall make particular mention of four other of these deities : *Ayanar*, *Mâriatâl*, *Maduraivirappan* and *Manarsvâmi*.

Ayanar. — Probably an indigenous and local deity. He is attached to Hinduism by the following legend : *Śiva* who was of the number of Giants and *Ṛishis*, was seduced by *Mogheni*

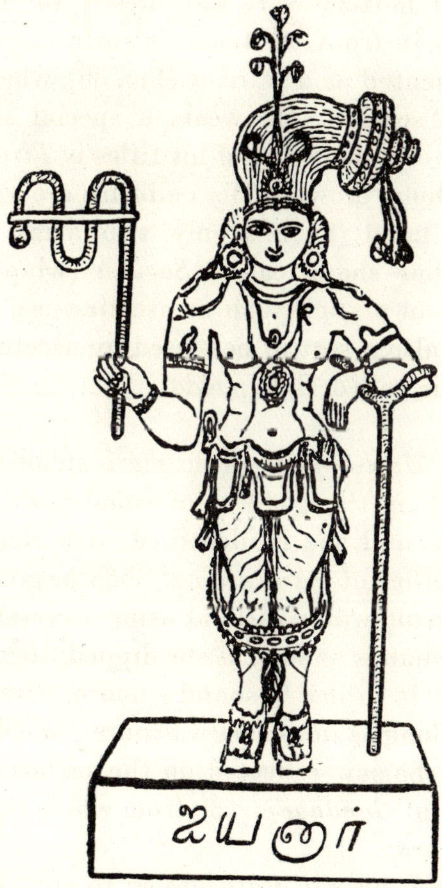

Fig. 36. — *Ayanar*.

(*Môhinî*) who accorded her favours to him. She became the mother of *Ayanar* who is thus the son of *Śiva* and of *Vishṇu* (whence the Tamil name *Hariharaputiran*, Sanskrit : *Hari-Hara-putra*, son of *Vishṇu* and *Śiva*).

The two wives of *Ayanar* are *Pûranai* and *Pudkali*. He rides on a white elephant, whence his title : *Vellayânaimurti*. In his temple one often sees seven mothers who are : *Trikara-sûri*, *Muyakara-sûri*, *Rakta-châmundî*, *Kâttêri*, *Bhagavatî*, *Bâlasakti* and *Bhuvana-sakti*.

Ayanar is the god of the field watchmen. He protects gardens and chastises thieves and is then called *Purattavan* (the watchman). His generals are the *Pâlaiyakarar*. They ride on horses, so horses made of pottery-ware are offered to them, and are arranged in troops in front of *Ayanar*'s shrines.

Ayanar is represented as a warrior (Fig. 36), whence his name *Nallasêvaga* (good soldier). He wears a special sort of crown which lops over to one side. One of his titles is *Tirumudi-Śêvaga* (the soldier of the holy crown). His emblems are very charateristic. In his right hand (he has only two arms) he holds a sceptre of a peculiar shape called *Savuku* (whip) or *Koradâ*. His left arm rests on a stick such as ascetics use, called *Yôgatandam*. He wears also a sort of belt used by ascetics when they are seated, which is called *Bâhupaddai*.

Mâri-atâl (1) or *Mâri-ammai* (from *mâri*, small-pox, and *atâl* or *ammai*, mother), is the goddess of small-pox (2). Only her head is worshipped and she is identified with *Rêṇukâ*, wife of *Jamadagni* and mother of *Paraśurâma*. She was given the miraculous power of drawing water without using a vessel. The liquid became solid in her hands as soon as she dipped them in the tank, and so she brought it to her husband's house. She was to keep this power only as long as her heart was pure ; one day when she was taking water, she saw reflected on the surface of the tank the forms of beautiful *Gandharvas* (3), from which time the liquid became solid no more.

Jamadagni ordered his son *Paraśurâma* to cut off her wicked head, which was done. *Mâriatâl* obtained the favour of having her head put on her body again, but by mistake it was put on to the body of a Pariah woman (*Paraichi*). This legend explains

(1) In Northern India, *Śîtalâ*, cold.

(2) On the subject of *Mâriatâl*, goddess of small-pox, consult the excellent work of Dr. Paramananda Mariadassou, *Mœurs médicales de l'Inde*, Pondicherry, 1906, pp. 116, 119.

(3) A variation is that she saw *Chitraratra*, prince of *Mrittikâvati*, sporting with his wife.

why *Mâriatâl* is a deity whose head only is worshipped (Fig. 37).

Uttukâdu, *Kannapuram* and *Periyapalayam* are the places of pilgrimage for *Mâriatâl*. In her shrines images of *Mâtaṅgî* (the Pariah woman whose body she got), of the demon *Kâttân*, with *Pâppâti* and *Chettipen* his mistresses, are also to be seen, and other demons : *Periyatambiram* (the big god) *Irulan* (the wild),

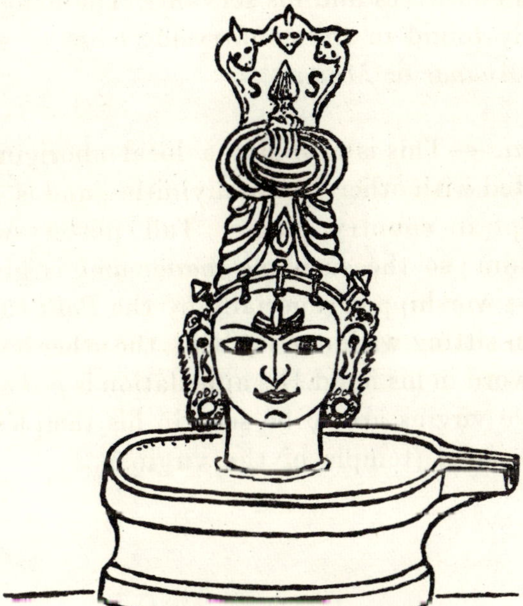

மாரியாத்தா.

FIG. 37. — *Mâriatâl.*

Ranavira, *Pâvâdaivirei* or *Pâvâdairayer*, *Uyirtundilkarar*, and the goddess *Kâttêri*.

Maduraivirappan. — *Virappan*, son of *Kâśî-râja* (king of *Kâśî*, Benares), was born under an unlucky star, so his father handed him over to the executioners, who being moved by the child's beauty, slew an animal in his place and abandoned him in the forest. He was brought up as a leather worker in the realm of king *Pomainayakan*. The king's daughter fell in love with him and he fled with her to *Madura*, where he became king, and after conquering the troops of *Pomainayakan*, he reigned as *Madurai-Virappan*.

As the god of wine he is held above all in veneration by sellers of *kallu* (palm juice which is drunk) who worship his image by the side of *Kâlî*'s. He is represented dressed as a *râja*, sword in hand, and carrying a shield. He always rides a horse. His moustaches are large and thick, and on his forehead are the three white horizontal stripes of the Sivaites. He is often accompanied by his two wives and his servants. The image of this god is usually only found in the countryside close to small shrines dedicated to *Ayanar* or *Manar*.

Manarsvâmi. — This is probably a local aboriginal god who is not connected with other Hindu divinities, and is hardly worshipped except in country places. Tall pottery-ware statues are raised to him ; so the surname *manarsami* is given to very tall men. He is worshipped especially by the *Palli* caste.

He is shown sitting with one leg bent, the other hanging down, and holds a sword in his hand. His appellation is *god of the virgins*, because twelve virgins are to be seen in his temples, which are called *Kanniarkovil* (temple of the virgins).

CHAPTER IV

HISTORY OF THE RELIGION
ACCORDING TO ICONOGRAPHY

There are no images known in the Tamil country which are of earlier date than the 7th century. It is therefore impossible to know what was the religion of the land before that period (1).

(1) The Vêdic gods are the only Brahminical deities found represented on the monuments of the *Aśoka* and *Kanishka* periods.

Sûrya, the sun-god, is carved in the small *vihâra* of *Bâjha* (3rd century B. C.) (Fig. 34) in the peristyle of the *Ananta-Gumpha* cave at *Khandagiri* (Orissa) and on the balustrade of *Bodh-Gaya* (see also Burgess, *Archaeological Survey of Western India*, 1883, Fig. 5 on page 6).

On the ancient Buddhist monuments, the gods of *Svarga* are frequently represented jointly in their paradise. At *Barhut* and on the Northern door-post of the Eastern door at *Sanchi*, the thirty three gods of which *Indra* is the chief one, are seen, also those of the kingdoms of *Brahmâ* and *Yama*, etc. Besides these, the goddess *Śrîdêvî* sprayed by the elephants, perhaps appears in sculpture at *Sanchi* and *Barhut*.

Indra is represented very clearly in several Greco-Buddhist carvings at *Gandhâra* (Visit of Indra, Photo 1058, I. M. List). He wears the characteristic cylindrical tiara, and has only two arms.

It is admitted that the most ancient iconographical documents known of a purely Hindu deity are the coins of Kadphises II (Ferguson and Burgess, *History of Indian Architecture*, 1910, Vol. I, p. 42 : « The earliest engraved representations of this god (*Śiva*) seem to be those on the coins of Kadphises II (about 80 to 90 A. D.) where the figure with the trident and the bull certainly prefigure the principal personage in his religion »). Cf. Wilson, *Ariana Antiqua*, Pl. 10 and 11 ; P. Gardner, *Cat. Coins of Greek and Scythic Kings of Bactria and India*, pp. 124-128, Pl. XXV, and Introd., p. 50 ; Vincent A. Smith, *The early History of India*, 1908, p. 285 : « Kadphises II, the Justran conqueror, was himself conquered by captive India, and adopted with such zeal the worship of Siva as practised by his new subjects, that he constantly placed the image of that Indian god upon his coins, and described himself as his devotee. »

If we examine one of the coins of the king Kadphises II, it will be noted that it bears a figure of a personage seated on a bull and holding a trident (P. Gardner, *Cat. Coins of Greek and Scythic Kings of Bactria and India*, Pl. XXV, 7).

The monuments of the *Gupta* period are rare, and are nearly all dedicated to Buddhism. It is probable however that the wild boar of Eran represents *Vishṇu* in an archaic form of *Varâha* (he has only two arms and the goddess is supported by a lotus flower), and dates from this period.

The religion of the Chalukyas in the 6th century. — It is in the 6th century

The religion of the Pallavas in the 7th century. — If the *Pallava* carvings of the 7th century (*rathas* and caves at *Mavalipuram* and cave at *Trichinopoly*) are compared with those of the 8th century (*Kailâsanâtha* and *Vaikuṇṭha-Perumal* at *Kañchîpuram*),

that the history of Hindu iconography really begins : the Vishnuvite cave No. 3, at *Bâdâmi*, bears an inscription which shows that the carving in that cave dates from the twelfth year of the reign of *Kirtivarman* I in the year 500 of the *Śaka* era, that is 578 A.D. Besides, it is extremely probable that the two other caves Nos. 1 and 2 at *Bâdâmi* belong to the same century as cave No. 3.

The three caves give an idea of the state of religion of the *Chalukyas* at *Bâdâmi* in the 6th century. The principal subjects are : 1. *Vâmana* (incarnation of *Vishṇu* in the giant *Trivikrama*) shown three times ; 2. *Varâha* (incarnation in the wild boar) shown twice ; 3. *Hari-Hara* (*Vishṇu-Śiva*) shown twice ; 4. *Vishṇu* seated on the serpent, represented once ; 5. *Narasiṁha* (incarnation in the man-lion) once ; 6. *Ardhanâri* (*Śiva-Pârvatî*) once, and 7. *Nadêsa* (*Śiva* dancing) once. Such is the catalogue of the large low-reliefs.

There are other small friezes, of which one shows the churning of the sea of milk (cave No. 2), and carvings representing *Garuḍa* (at the entrance of cave No. 3). The *Ashṭadikpâlaka*, the guardians of the quarters of the sky, ornament the ceilings. One also sees *Subrahmaṇiar*, *Pulliar* and *Kâlî*. The *Liṅgam* occupies the sanctuary of cave No. 1, and before it is *Nandi* (*Ṛishabha*).

Hinduism of the ancient Brahminical caves at Ellora. — Cave No. 3 at *Bâdâmi* (date 578 A.D.) has a facade of very special style : the pillars are ornated with statues of men and women which form brackets and caryatids. The cave called *Raṃêśvaram* at *Ellora* has a facade with much the same sort of pillars. Moreover the same cave seems to be one of the most ancient of the Brahminical caves of *Ellora*, so we think it must date from the 6th century. It is probable that the cave of the *Avatârs* and the cave of the *Ashes of Râvaṇa* (*Ravan-ka-khai*) were sculptured during the same period.

The low-reliefs of *Ellora* permit us to know fairly accurately the state of Hinduism at that period. As a matter of fact there are some subjects which are repeated to satiety. The piety of the sculptor destroyed his desire for variety. Thus it becomes easy to find out the fundamental legends.

At *Ellora* Sivaism preponderates : the *Liṅgam* occupies nearly all the sanctuaries. The great themes at *Ellora* consist of the four following subjects : *Śiva* in *Kailâsa* under which is *Râvaṇa* ; the marriage of *Śiva* and *Pârvatî* ; *Śiva* investing himself with the elephant's skin, and *Śiva* dancing.

The mothers are often seen seated in a long row, also *Bhṛiṅgi-Maharuchi* with his wife,and *Pulliar* bearing an axe and a flower, and more rarely the following themes : *Śiva* coming out of the column, *Śiva* issuing from the *Liṅgam*, *Śiva* in his chariot, *Śiva* and *Gaṅgâ*, lastly *Kâlî* and *Mahishâsura*. Certain Sivaite subjects which are usual in *Pallava* temples are nowhere to be seen at *Ellora*, for instance, *Sômaskanda* and *Pichandi* (*Śiva* begging).

No. 27 is the only cave dedicated to *Vishṇu*, and it is of little importance, though some Vishnuvite legends are represented in Sivaite caves. These subjects are as follows : *Varâha*, *Vâmana*, *Narasiṁha*, *Raṅganâtha*, *Vishṇu* riding on *Garuḍa*, and *Kṛishṇa* only in the two legends of mount *Gôvardhana* and of the serpent *Kâliya*. These are the only subjects of *Vishṇu* legends. It seems therefore that the other Vishnuvite subjects were unknown or considered to be of secondary importance.

an appreciable difference will be noticed. It is therefore best to study them separately.

Firstly an important fact is to be noted; iconography proves that in the 7th century in Southern India, Hinduism was a single religion. For example it may be thought that in the *Pallava* period the religion was exclusively Sivaite, and that Vishnuvism was only later introduced.

On the other hand it must be admitted that for fourteen centuries Hindus while showing in some cases a preference for some particular deity or other, still worship all the gods. It is true that in Vishnuvite temples, Sivaite images are fairly rare, and *vice versa*, but this refers to a matter of precedence and priestcraft, and only concerns the issue as to whether *Vishṇu* or *Śiva* is to be deemed the supreme god.

Iconography shows us that since the 7th century, images of

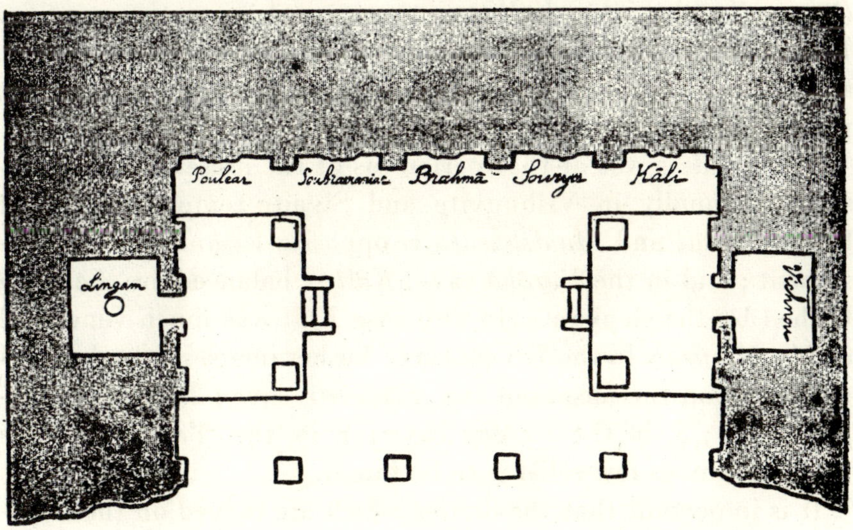

FIG. 38. — *Plan of the cave without inscriptions at Trichinopoly.*

Śiva, *Vishṇu*, *Indra*, *Brahmâ*, etc., are found not only in the same monument, but in the same low-relief. The positions of the sculptures in the « cave without inscriptions » at *Trichinopoly*, in our opinion gives an idea of the state of the religion in the Carnatic in the 7th century. Figure 38 gives the plan of this cave.

On each side of the entrance are two sanctuaries opposite each other and each with a small peristyle in front of it. The left hand sanctuary is dedicated to *Śiva*, and the right hand one to *Vishṇu*. It seems that both were equal as deities and both objects of worship.

On the wall which forms the back of the cave, there are deities who are not objects of worship but are only venerated : in the centre *Brahmâ* ; to his right, that is to say on *Siva*'s of the sanctuary, are *Subrahmaṇiar* and *Pulliar*. On *Brahmâ*'s left are *Sûrya* and *Kâlî*.

The *Śiva* cult seems to have prevailed subsequently, for the cave No. 2 at *Trichinopoly*, which is covered with inscriptions, and seems to be more recent than the other, is dedicated to *Śiva*. A beautiful low-relief shows *Śiva* drawing *Gaṅgâ* out of his hair. The carvings at *Mavalipuram* are also divided between Vishnuvism and Sivaism, the latter slightly preponderant.

It is noteworthy that *Kâlî* is the object of a special cult. The *Draupadî-ratha* is a *Kâlî* sanctuary, and near the cave of *Trimûrti* there is a cave consecrated exclusively to this goddess, as is proved by the presence of warrior maidens who occupy the place of *dvarabalagar* at the entrance of the central niche.

This goddess was at that period (as at the present time) worshipped equally in Vishnuvite and Sivaite temples. The fight between *Kâlî* and *Mahishâsura* is opposite *Vishṇu* lying on the serpent ; and in the *Varâha* cave, *Kâlî* is balanced by *Lakshmî* bathed by the elephants. In any case *Kâlî* was much venerated at *Mavalipuram* in the 7th century, for her image is found everywhere : 1. on the facade of the *Trimûrti* cave ; 2. on the *Draupadî-ratha* ; 3. in the *Varâha* cave ; 4. in the *Yamapuri* cave where a famous low-relief is to be found.

It is important that the deities which are carved on the *Dharmarâja-ratha* at *Mavalipuram* should be noticed. *Narasiṁha* and *Varâha* are nowhere to be seen there. Mr. Burgess is therefore wrong in writing : « The *Ardhanâri*, a favourite form of *Śiva*, as half-male and half-female, occurs several times, and *Vishṇu* as *Narasiṁha* or the boar avatar. » (*The Cave temples of India*, p. 126.) (1).

(1) This same erroneous statement has been repeated in the *History of Indian Architecture*, by FERGUSON and BURGESS, 1910, Vol. I, p. 332.

In Fig. 39 we have given the names and respective positions of the different images.

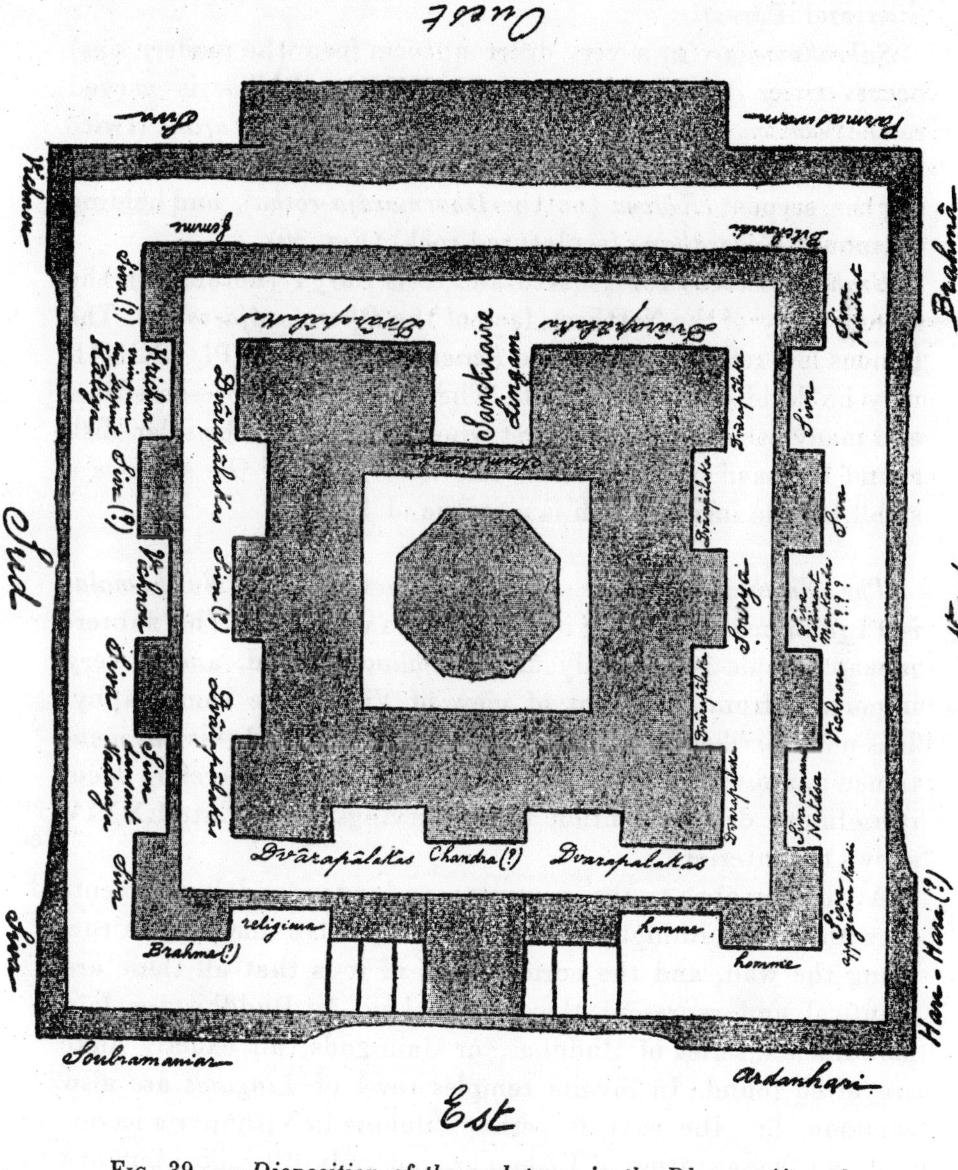

Fig. 39. — *Disposition of the sculptures in the Dharmarâja-ratha at Mavalipuram.*

The *Liṅgam* is found in nearly all sanctuaries. In *Pallava* temples there are often rows of five or seven cells, each of which contains a *Liṅgam*. The subjects so often repeated at *Ellora*, are nowhere to be seen; such as *Śiva* in *Kailâsa* under which is *Râvaṇa*, *Śiva* donning the elephant's hide, and the marriage of *Śiva* and *Pârvatî*.

Subrahmaṇiar (in a very different form from the modern one) occurs twice at *Mavalipuram* (Pl. XXXI). *Pulliar* is carved in the *Vallam* cave. The Vishnuvite subjects are: *Varâha* (twice at *Mavalipuram*), *Vamâna*, *Raṅganâtha* and *Kṛishṇa* overcoming the serpent *Kâliya* (on the *Dharmarâja-ratha*), and holding up mount *Gôvardhana* (sculptured rock) (Fig. 30).

Brahmâ is often represented and so is *Sûrya* (notably on the second story of the Northern face of the *Dharmarâja-ratha*). The famous low-relief known as the *Penance of Arjuna* (Pl. LXXIII) may be divided into two parts. The upper part represents *Śiva* and many other deities amongst whom *Sûrya* with the solar disk round his head is discernable. The lower part of the scene is a small temple inside which is a statue of *Vishṇu*.

The Narthamalai Cave. — Near the village of *Narthamalai* is a Brahminical cave dug in the side of a rocky hill. This subterranean temple is certainly of the *Pallava* period, and is very important from the point of view of Vishnuvite iconography. It is not described in any work, and to our knowledge is not mentioned in any list of South Indian antiquities. We therefore deem it useful to draw attention to the carvings in it. Plate LXXIV shows the interior.

At the entrance to the sanctuary is a long verandah ornamented with statues in high relief. There are twelve images in a row along the wall, and the curious part of it is that all these are identical and represent the god *Vishṇu*. In Buddhist or Jain monuments, series of Buddhas, or Jain gods, all exactly alike are often found. In Sivaite temples rows of *Liṅgams* are also common, but the cave is perhaps unique in Vishnuvite iconography. These statues of *Vishṇu* are not only all alike, but are very beautiful. The shape of the tiara, emblems and dress indicates the *Pallava* period.

Pallava religion in the 8th century. — The *Pallava* temples at *Kañchîpuram* (*Kailâsanâtha*, *Vaikuṇṭha-Perumal*, *Mataṅgêśvara*.

Muktêśvara, *Tripurântakêśvara* and *Airavatêśvara*) are covered with sculptures. The *Kailâsanâtha* temple especially is a veritable museum. So it is not difficult to envisage the state of religion in the 8th century at *Kañchîpuram*.

Sivaism seems predominant. The *Liṅgam* is the great object of worship. The facade of the *Kailâsanâtha* temple is ornamented with seven rows of cells containing prism shaped *Liṅgams*. Statues of *Nandi* are innumerable. Some religious subjects are multiplied to excess, others on the contrary are quite rare.

Among the most often repeated images, the principal is *Sômaskanda* (Pl. XIX). The god *Śiva* is seated beside *Pârvatî* who holds a small child in her lap. This subject so constantly repeated in the Sivaite temples gives a good notion of the fundamental idea of *Pallava* religion. *Śiva* as the supreme god, appears between *Brahmâ* and *Vishṇu*. He is propitious and good ; *Pârvatî* holding a little child is full of graciousness and motherly love. The moral and social ideas of the *Pallava* people may be imagined, as the Supreme God is represented as a father, by the side of his wife and child. The *Śiva* of the *Pallavas* is not a terrible and cruel god, he does not inspire fear and terror, but shows an example of family life.

Another very common subject is *Śiva* dancing, but never in the *Chidambaram* style. *Kâli* is represented as often as *Nadarâja* and *Sômaskanda*. Her image may be seen everywhere. She is generally seen standing beside her lion. The following *Śiva* legends are often represented : *Śiva* drawing the *Gaṅgâ* out of his hair, *Śiva* issuing from the column, and *Pichandi*.

Others such as *Śiva* and *Pârvatî* in *Kailâsa* under which is *Râvaṇa*, *Śiva* clothing himself in the elephant's hide, the marriage of *Śiva* and *Pârvatî*, and *Śiva* in his chariot driven by *Brahmâ*, are less frequent.

Pulliar's place does not seem important. He is seen in the South-Eastern corner of the court in the *Kailâsanâtha* temple in quite an inconspicuous place in the midst of various ornamental designs. As for *Subrahmaṇiar*, he is not to be found anyhwere.

The worship of *Vishṇu* was important, for the great *Vaikuṇṭha-Perumal* temple is dedicated to him. The Vishnuvite subjects at *Kañchîpuram* are the usual ones seen on monuments of the period : *Narasiṁha*, *Varâha*, *Vishṇu* on *Garuḍa*, *Raṅganâtha*, *Kṛishṇa* and the serpent *Kâliya*, and *Kṛishṇa* supporting the *Gôvardhana* mountain.

Conclusion : *Hinduism before the* 10*th century.* — To recapitulate, the greater part of Sivaite legends before the 10th century seem to be much the same as now. This is not the case with Vishnuvite legends.

Iconography of monuments before the 10th century shows a complete absence of the following subjects : *Râma* and all that belongs to his legend ; *Sîtâ*, *Lakshmaṇa*, *Hanumân*, the marriage of *Râma* and *Sîtâ*, the fight of *Râma* and *Râvaṇa*, *Râmaliṅgam*, *Râma*'s coronation, etc. Some *Kṛishṇa* legends : *Kṛishṇa* stealing the butter, *Kṛishṇa* and the bathing girls, *Kṛishṇa* playing the flute, *Kṛishṇa* with his wives *Radhâ* and *Rukmiṇî*. The other incarnations of *Vishṇu* such as : *Matsya*, *Paraśurâma*, *Balarâma*, *Kalki*, *Môhenî*, etc., are all absent.

It seems that it was about the 14th century that the success of certain Vishnuvite sages such as *Râmanuja*, and doubtless also the protection of the *Bijayanagar* princes, produced a reawakening in Vishnuvite worship, and that at this period new religious ideas inspired a new iconography.

CHAPTER V

COSTUMES, STATUES, CARS, ETC.

§ 1. — *The Brahminical Thread.*

In our days Brahmins and the greater part of « caste » Hindus wear over the shoulder a thread made of several strands, which goes round the body. It goes over the left shoulder and hangs above the right hip. This thread is made of several strands (before marriage it is made of three threads each made of nine strands, and after marriage nine threads each of nine strands) which for Brahmins are hand spun cotton threads.

At the height of the heart a knot is made called *Brahmâmudi* (*Brahmâ*'s knot). In Tamil it is called *punul ;* in Sanskrit, *upavîta.* What is the meaning of the *punul ?* Abbé Dubois wrote : « The Brahmins and other persons who have the right to wear this thread attach much value to it, and are prouder of it than the great ones of Europe are of decorations of a similar generical name, to wear which their birth or services entitle them. »

The *punul* is conferred on boys of 7 to 9 years of age. The ceremony of investiture of the triple thread called *Upanayana* is described at length in the work of Abbé J. A. Dubois (*Mœurs des peuples de l'Inde*, Part II, Chap. 1).

It may be asked what is the history of the Brahminical thread according to ancient Hindu sculptures. An attentive examination of the low-reliefs of the *Madura*, *Bijayanagar*, *Pâṇḍya* and *Chôḷa* periods, allows a fixed principle to be enunciated. From the 10th century onwards, the Brahminical deities which are represented on temples, all wear a *punul* of a kind practically the same as at present. It is a cord over the left shoulder, hanging to the right hip. At the height of the heart is the knot of *Brahmâ*.

It is enough to examine the statues which ornament the *Chôḷa* temples (*Tanjore* and *Gaṅgaikondapuram*) to make sure that in the 10th and 11th centuries the *punul* was not very different from what it is now. (See Pl. LXXV.)

This is not so in the *Pallava* temples of the 7th century, at *Trichinopoly* and *Mavalipuram.* The *punul* which for ten centuries of iconography, that is from the 10th century till today, is a cord, a simple thread, is nowhere to be seen. Sometimes the cord is shown as a broad ribbon or a scarf, but most usually as a roll sometimes fairly thick, placed on the left shoulder and falling towards the right, sometimes on the hip, but more often on the right arm at the height of the elbow.

Plate LXXVI, shows an example of the last position, which is very frequent in the carvings of the 7 th century. The person shown in the figure has his arm raised, and it is clearly seen that the rooll falls on the arm, and not on the hip.

We assert as follows : « This roll is none other than the *punul*, and to prove it we point out that the roll always shows a compression at the height of the heart in exactly the same place as *Brahmâ*'s knot. The roll is worn by princes and by gods and appears to be a sign of nobility. Ascetics and religious men wear a scarf which forms a buckle on the left shoulder. Shepherds, servants and women wear nothing of this sort.

It would be interesting to explore the origin of the Brahminical thread with the aid of iconography in carvings previous to the 7th century, which lie beyond the Tamil country ; but we are bound down here to the study of iconography in Southern India, and we know of no carvings in this region before the 7th century.

We shall content ourselves with the enunciation of the following principles which in our opinion may be admitted without rashness : The *punul* is seen in carvings of the 7th century in Southern India, but it is never a simple thread as it is now. Almost always it is a roll placed on the left shoulder and falling, not on the hip, but on the right arm at the height of the elbow. This roll has always a compression at the height of the heart.

§ 2. — *Costumes.*

Male attire. — All parts of the costume of divinities have evolved from the 7th century, to the present time. We have already demonstrated the evolution of the Vishnuvite tiara (Fig. 15). It would take too long to review all the details ; we shall be content with the three principal ones.

1. At the present time the chests of the gods have as ornaments three large jewels which hang from the neck. Beginning from the uppermost they are called : *Magarakandi*, *Magarapadakam* and *Kamalapadakam*. Nothing of this kind existed in the *Pallava* period. The first of these jewels only made its appearence in the middle ages. It was only after some centuries that all the breast was covered with jewels.

2. Only since the 15th century is the scarf called *Vastram* represented. This is passed round the neck and hangs down on each side below the arms.

3. Epaulettes of the sort called *bujakirudu* are worn by deities in our day. Before the 12th century nothing like this is to be seen, the shoulders being quite bare. At the end of the middle ages a small ornament appeared which has gradually grown bigger and bigger.

Female attire. — In olden days feminine deities were almost entirely naked, but the breasts were covered with a ribbon (*kachu* or *kañjugam*), their arms being covered with bracelets from the wrist to the elbow. Now-a-days the goddesses are nearly completely covered with clothing. Their legs are concealed by a cloth. Their bosom is enclosed in a small sort of bodice of Mussulman origin called *ravukai* leaving the waist bare. Then the end of the cloth is passed like a scarf from left to right. They wear rings in their noses (*natu*, *pilaku*) and anklets on their feet (*padagam*).

Multiple arms. — Numerous arms are perhaps the most remarkable peculiarity of Hindu iconography. From the artistic point of view this is not always ungraceful, as the sculptor can thus increase the number of gestures and give more life and movement to his characters. It does not detract much from physical reality. The movement of one arm in a series of rapid and violent gestures, gives an impression of many arms by reason of the successive luminous impressions on the retina.

Let us however remark that the Brahminical deities have only four arms when they are in repose, in that case the two extra arms are only there to express the force of the deity as well as to carry the distinctive emblems of the god. The number of arms is only more than four when the deity is represented in move-ement (*Śiva* dancing or hurling himself at an enemy, *Trivikrama*, *Durgâ* fighting against *Mahishâsura*, *Râvaṇa* fighting *Râma*, etc.). It is a kind of cinematography, and this idea is not devoid of interest from the point of view of the philosophy of art.

Mr. Burgess thought he found in the number of arms a chronological character. According to him the number of arms in excess of four, is not found in the most ancient temples : « We have in this *rath* (the *Dharmarâja-ratha* at the Seven Pagodas) many of the gods of the Hindu pantheon, but in forms more subdued than are to be found elsewhere. The one extravagance is that they generally have four arms — never more, to distinguish them from mortals ; but none of those combinations or extravagances are found in the caves at *Ellora*, *Elephanta* and elsewhere. It is the soberest and most reasonable version of the Pantheon yet discovered, and consequently, one of the most interesting, as well as probably the earliest. »

We do not share the opinion of Mr. Burgess. It is true that the divinities carved on the *Dharmarâja-ratha* have never more than four arms, but the famous low-reliefs of *Vâmana*, *Trivikrama* and of *Durgâ* fighting *Mahishâsura* are surely of the same period and the deities have many more than four arms. The carvings at *Mavalipuram* date from about 650 A. D.

Our conclusion on the other hand is that since the earliest period (7th century) of South Indian iconography, the Brahminical deities are represented with a number of arms, often considerable.

The two front arms are called *kayi* (hand), the arms behind these have no special name, but take those of the emblems they carry. The front arms usually perform very special gestures. The hand is open showing the palm in the gesture called *abhaya-hastam*, which is always made with the right hand, the finger tips pointing upwards. The gesture seems to mean : « Do not come near », but Hindus on the contrary interpret it as meaning :

« Have no fear, I shall protect you » (*a-bhaya*, that is : not-fear). The gesture called *varada-hastam* is always made with the left hand the ends of the fingers being downwards. The word *varada* signifies the act of giving favours.

§ 3. — *Statues.*

The statues at the back of the sanctuaries are of stone ; but those which are carried round during festivals are of copper.

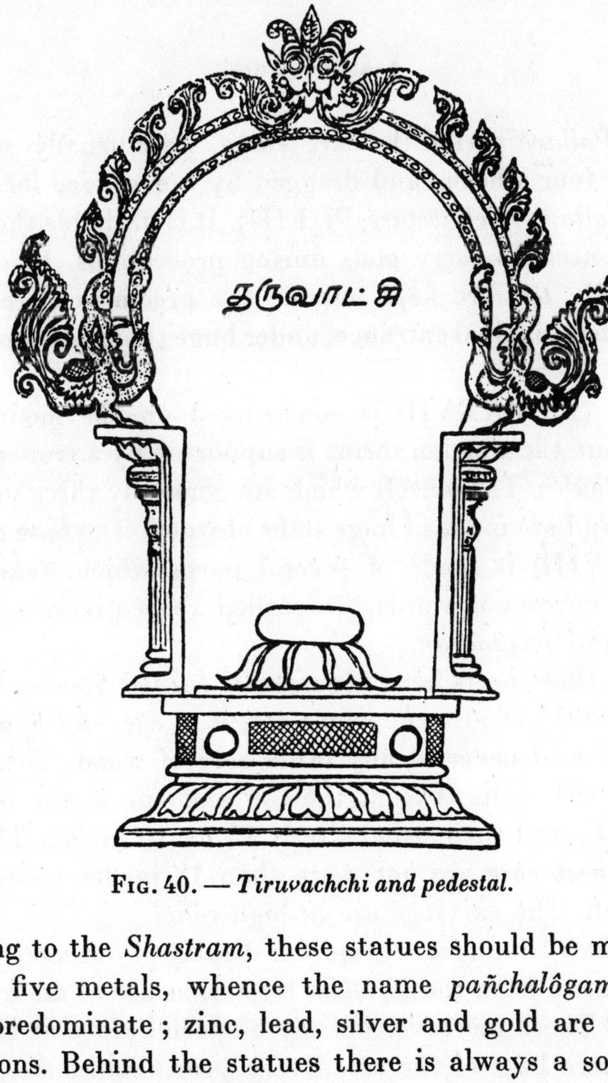

Fig. 40. — *Tiruvachchi and pedestal.*

According to the *Shastram*, these statues should be made of an alloy of five metals, whence the name *pañchalôgam*. Copper should predominate ; zinc, lead, silver and gold are in smaller proportions. Behind the statues there is always a sort of halo called *tiruvachchi* (Fig. 40).

The origin of this ornament is clear : the *tiruvachchi* is only the architectural ornament called *kudu,* which originated with the Buddhist « horse-shoe ». At the top of the *tiruvachchi* a lion's head (*simha-mukha*), and at each side *makaras* with long plumed tails called *karuku,* can be seen. The pedestal of the statues is like the base of monuments.

It is pierced with two holes in which iron bars are inserted to lift the statue without touching it. Rings are fitted to ancient statues, obviously for the same purpose.

§ 4. — *Cars.*

In the *Pallava* period the cars (*ratha*) were usually supported by two or four wheels, and dragged by horses (see for example A. Rea, *Pallava Architecture,* Pl. LIII). It is probable that similar cars were used to carry gods during processions. In our days, cars (Tamil : *têr*) are kept outside the precincts of the temple opposite the principal entrance, under huge thatched cone-shaped roofs.

The car (Pl. LXXVII) is constructed on the model of the *vimâna,* but the wooden shrine is supported by a truncated cone placed on axles. The wheels which are generally three yards high are plain and are made of huge slabs of wood. The base of the car (Pl. LXXVIII) is made of several parts which, taking them from the bottom upwards, are called respectively : *pudapar*, *nagapar* and *pusandran.*

Each of these parts have ornamental carved panels. The wood of these panels, as also the whole car, is of carved *ilupai* (*Bassia sapotaceae*) and never of any other sort of wood. These panels are fixed with bolts (two at the top and one at the bottom of each panel), and their usual size is 12 by 16 inches. The panels of the largest cars are not more than 18 inches broad and 36 inches high. The carvings are in high relief.

All modern Hindu iconography is displayed in these, even such subjects taken from the *Kṛishṇa* legend, as are of most doubtful propriety. These moreover occupy a special place at the angles of the square base of the car. Every year, before the festival, this base is coated with oil, and as no trouble is taken to wipe off the dust first, in time there is formed such a thick layer of the mixed oil and dirt, that the carvings almost completely disappear under it.

The shrine in which the god is placed during the procession is a square pavilion with four openings (one on each face). *Dvârapâla* and rampant lions are used by way of decorating it. A simple cone of painted cloth is usually built up above the dome. Theoretically it is supposed to be an imitation of the *vimâna* and to be ornamented with small separate and superimposed pavilions. It is in this way that the *Conjeevaram* car is constructed. The point of the cone is finished off by a stubi, but strange to say it is placed inside the central axis, and in order to protect it, a small parasol (*pusakara kodai*) is placed over it.

Lastly, around the car decorative cylinders of cloth (*tombai*) are hung, and in front of it supported on springs are painted wooden horses, which seem to prance as they drag the car along. Their reins are held by a richly bedecked personage. This coachman's place is taken by *Brahmâ* in Sivaite cars, and by *Râvaṇa*, when the car is Vishnuvite. A whole crowd of worshippers of the god when taken in procession, take hold of stout ropes and drag the car along much more rapidly than would be expected when the huge mass of this wooden edifice is taken into consideration.

LIST OF PLATES

Pl. XXV. — *Châmundî. Modern image.*

Pl. XXVI. — *Châmundî standing on the head of Mahisha (7th century).*

Pl. XXVII. — *Combat of Châmundî and Mahishâsura the giant, at Mavalipuram (7th century).*

Pl. XXVIII. — *Pulliar at Vallam (7th century).*

Pl. XXIX. — *Subrahmaṇiar on the peacock. Modern image.*

Pl. XXX. — *Arumugam (Subrahmaṇiar). Modern image.*

Pl. XXXI. — *Subrahmaṇiar at Mavalipuram (7th century). On the right of the Dharmarâja-ratha ; on the left in the Trimûrti cave.*

Pl. XXXII. — *Palani-Andavar. Modern image.*

Pl. XXXIII. — *The great Sivaites Saints : Appar, Sundarar, Sambandar, Mâṇikkavâchakar. Modern image.*

Pl. XXXIV. — *Vishṇu (Varadarâja) at Chidambaram (13th century) (Note the form of the disk).*

Pl. XXXV. — *Odeyavar. Modern image.*

Pl. XXXVI. — *Śrî-Raṅganâtha. Modern image.*

Pl. XXXVII. — *Raṅganâtha at Mavalipuram (7th century).*

Pl. XXXVIII. — *Nârâyaṇa. Modern image.*

Pl. XXXIX. — *Vishṇu seated on the serpent in cave No. 3 at Bâdâmi (6th century).*

Pl. XL. — *Varâha. Panel of car (17th century).*

Pl. XLI. — *Varâha at Mavalipuram (7th century).*

Pl. XLII. — *Varâha. Cave No. 2 at Bâdâmi (6th century).*

Pl. XLIII. — *Story of Narasiṁha : Coming out of the pillar ; Fight with Hiraṇya ; Worship.*

Pl. XLIV. — *Narasiṁha tearing out the entrails of Hiraṇya. Modern image.*

Pl. XLV. — *Narasiṁha at Bâdâmi, cave No. 3 (6th century).*

Pl. XLVI. — *Fight between Narasiṁha and Hiraṇya. Kailâsanâtha temple at Kañchîpuram (8th century).*

Pl. XLVII. — *Same subject at Ellora, cave of the Avatârs (6th century).*

Pl. XLVIII. — *Vâmana-avatâram. Panel of car (17th century).*

Pl. XLIX. — *Vâmana-Trivikrama at Bâdâmi, cave No. 2 (6th century).*

Pl. L. — *Same subject at Mavalipuram (7th century).*

Pl. LI. — *Śrî-Râma-avatâram. Modern image : Râma, Sîtâ, Lakshmaṇa and Hanumân.*

Pl. LII. — *Hanumân. Modern image.*

Pl. LIII. — *Śrî-Râma-paṭṭâbhishêkam (Consecration of Râma).*

Pl. LIV. — *Rape of Śitâ. Kailâsa of Ellora (8th century).*

Pl. LV. — *Kṛishṇa-avatâram. Modern image.*

Pl. LVI. — *Navanida-kaṇṇan (Kṛishṇa stealing the butter). Modern image.*

PLATES

ICONOGRAPHY OF SOUTHERN INDIA

PLATE I

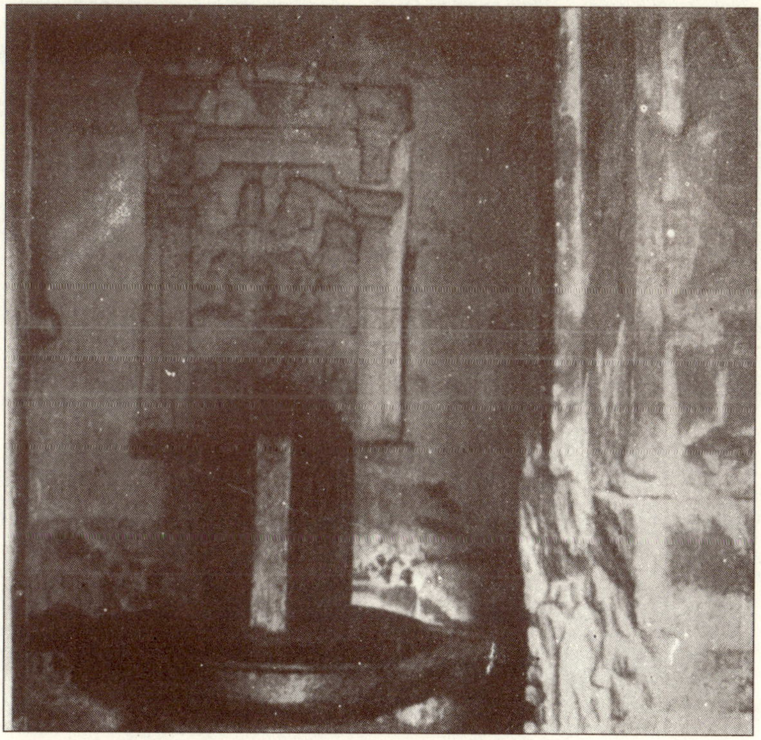

Lingam in the sanctuary of Mahendravarmesvara.
(Kailasanatha temple of Kanchipuram, 8th century)

PLATE II

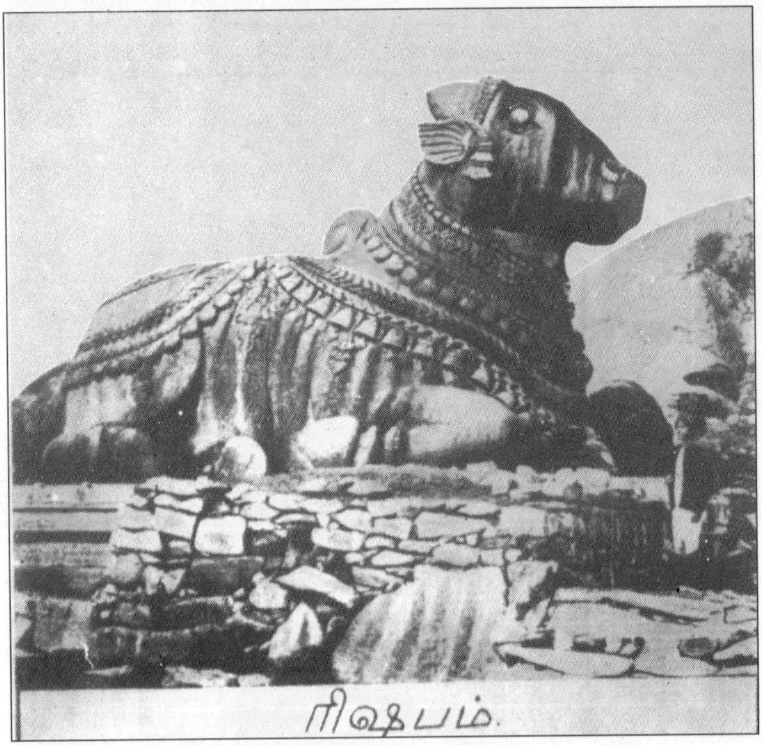

Rishabha (Nandi)

PLATE III

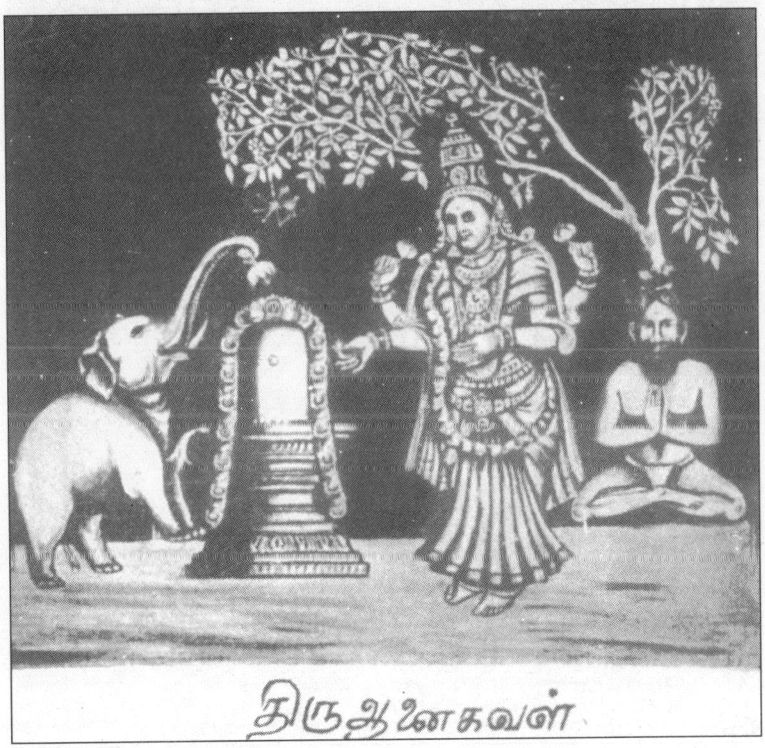

Tiruvanaikaval (Jambukesvara) Modern image.

PLATE IV

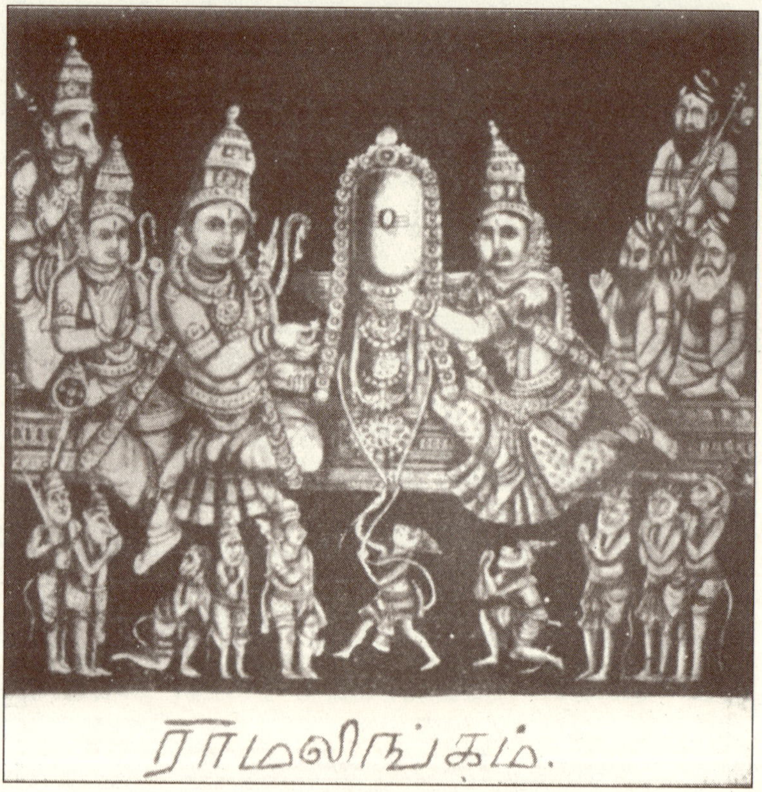

Râma-Liṅgam. Modern image

PLATE V

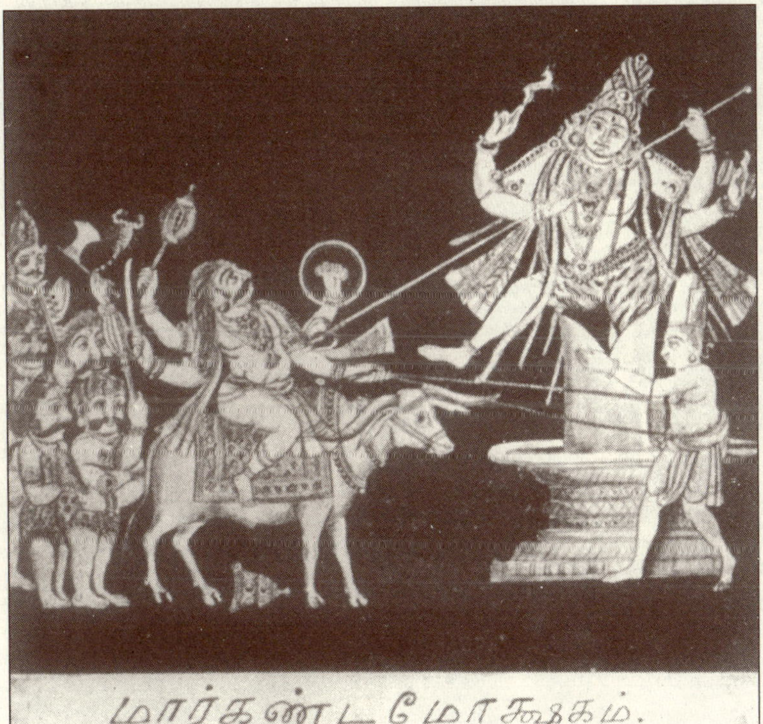

Mârkanda-môksham (Deliverance of Mârkanda). Modern image.

PLATE VI

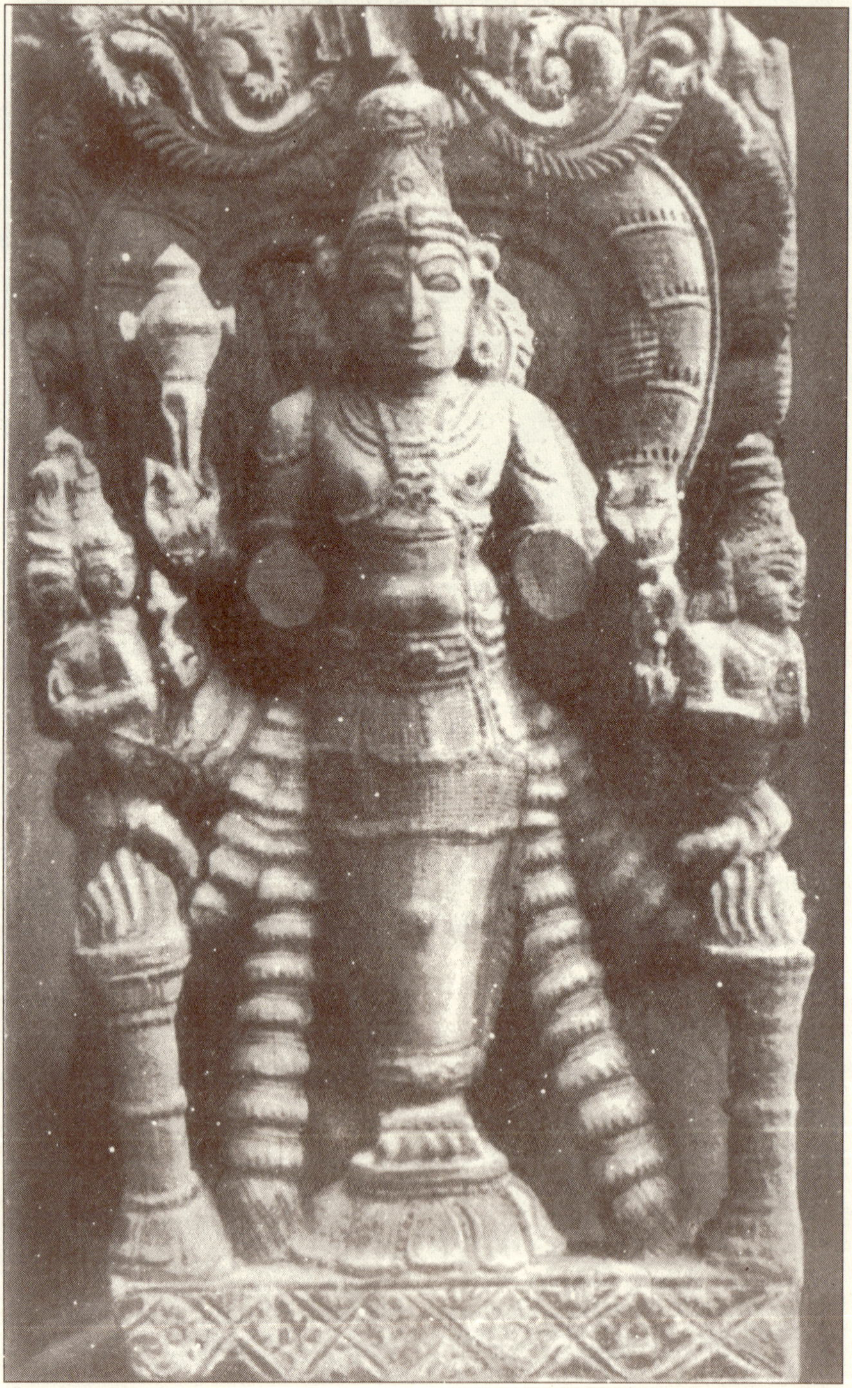

Trimurti. Panel on modern car.

PLATE VII

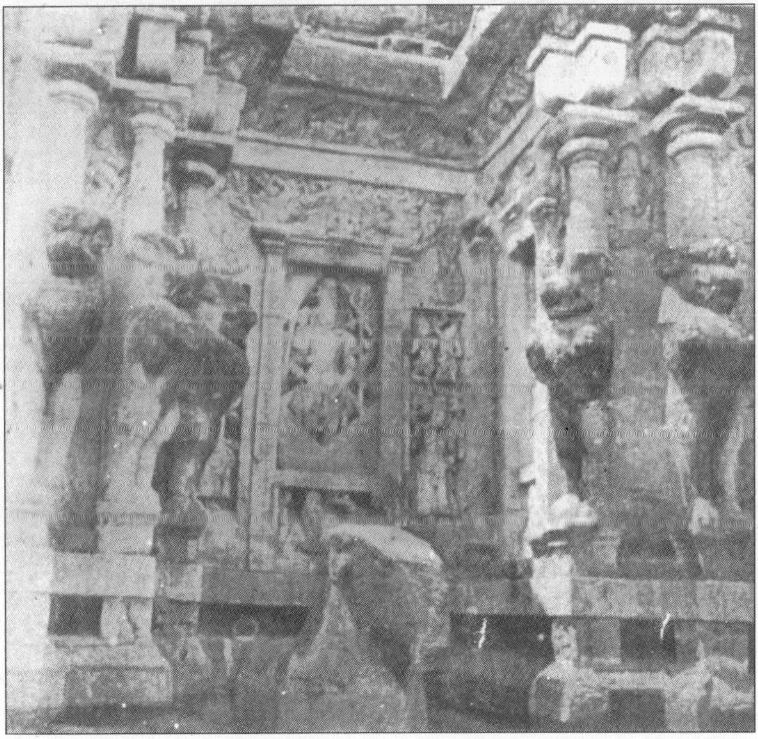

Siva issuing from the pillar.
(Relief in the Kailasanatha temple at Kanchipuram, 8th Century.)

PLATE VIII

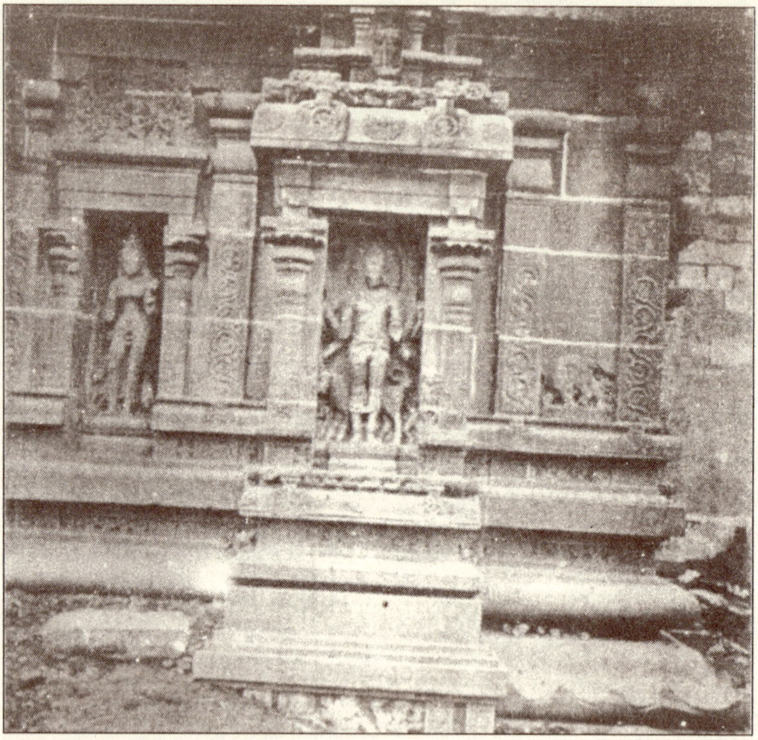

Bhairava at Chidambaram (13th century)

PLATE IX

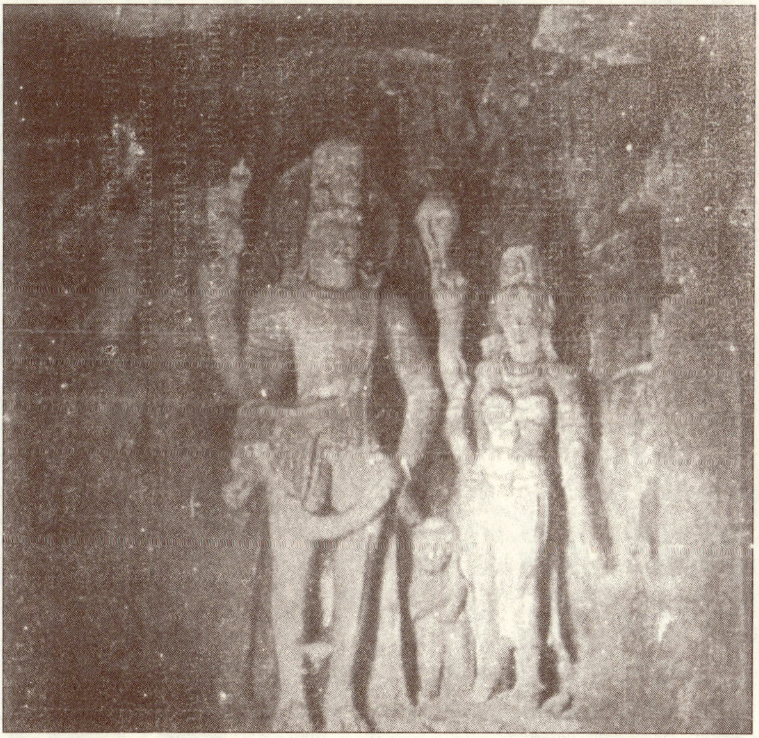

Hari-Hara in Cave No. 1 at Badami (6th century).

PLATE X

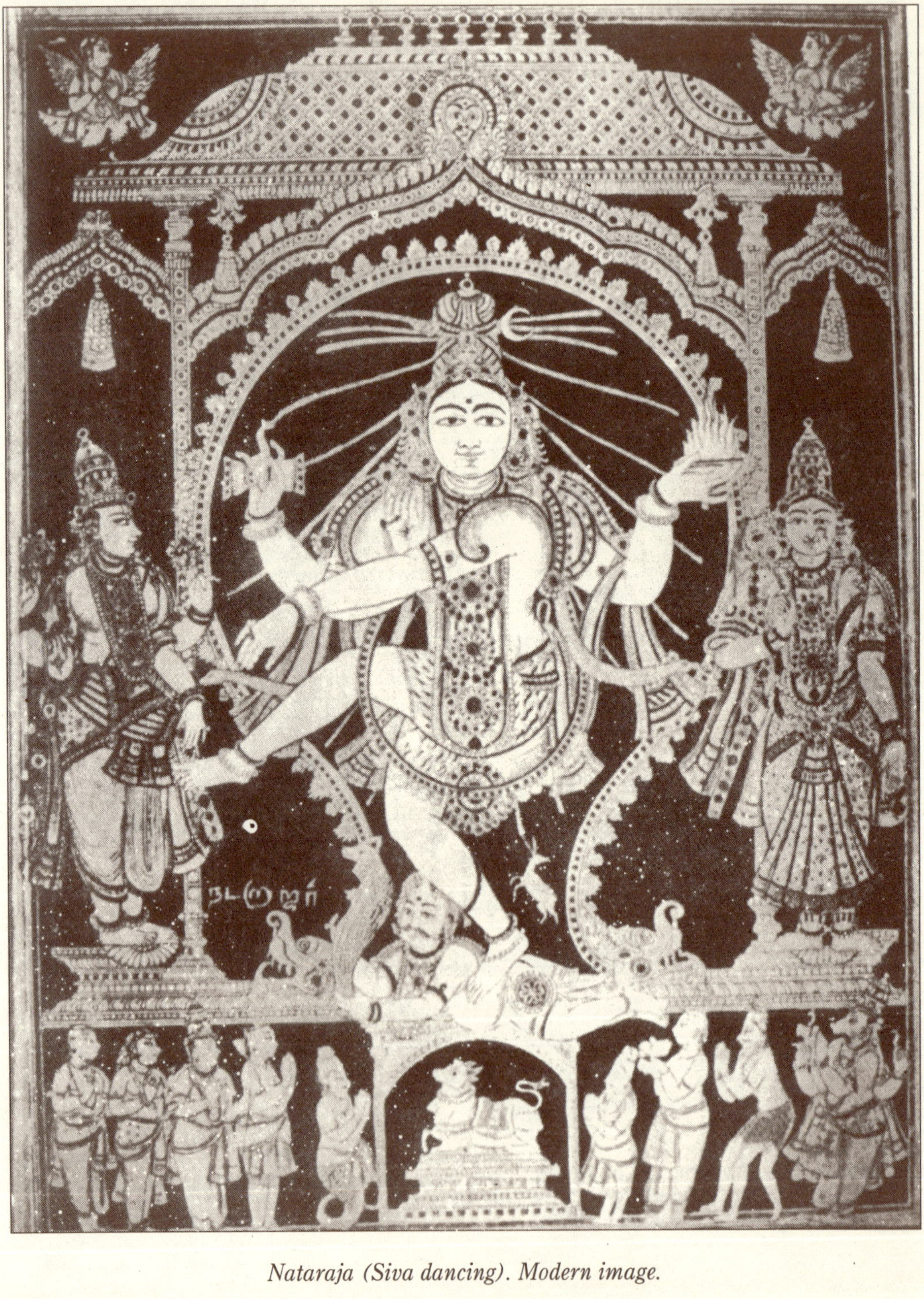

Nataraja (Siva dancing). Modern image.

PLATE XI

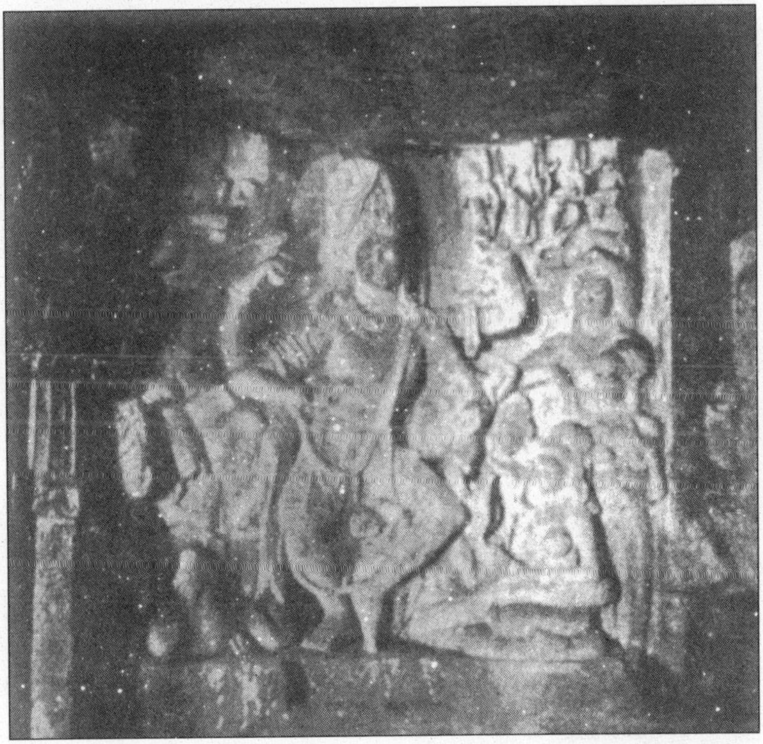

Siva dancing. (Ramesvaram cave at Ellora, 6th century.)

PLATE XII

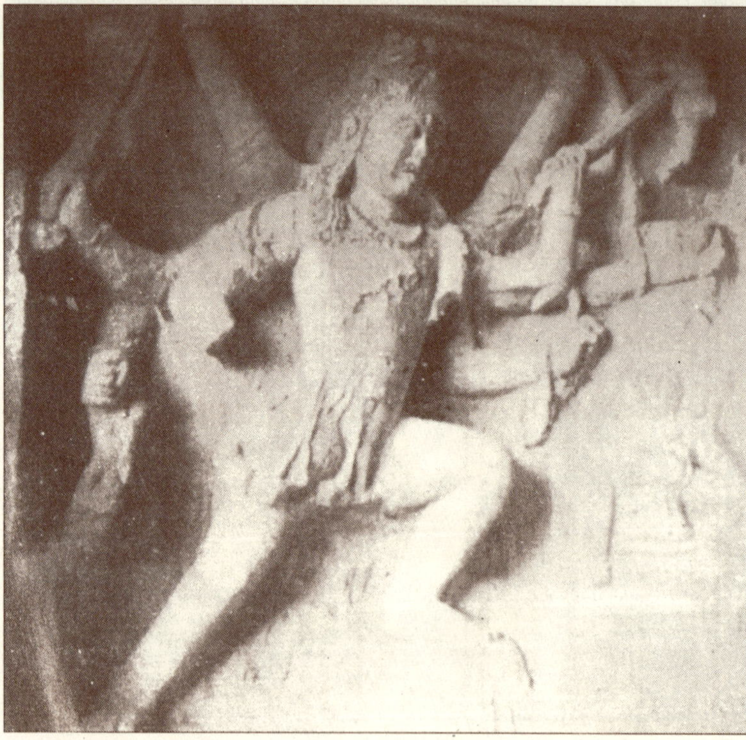

Siva flaying the elephant. (Dhumar-Lena cave at Ellora, 9th century.)

PLATE XIII

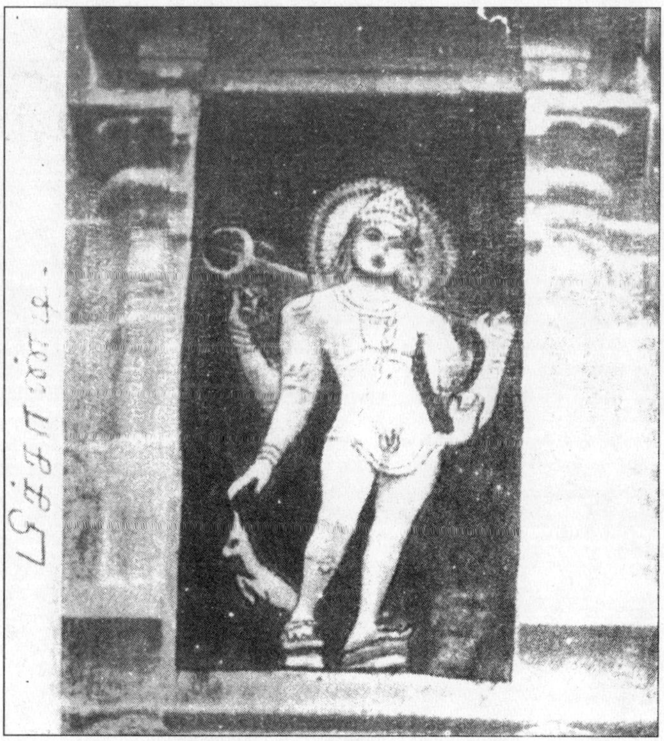

Pichandi at Chidambaram (13th century).

PLATE XIV

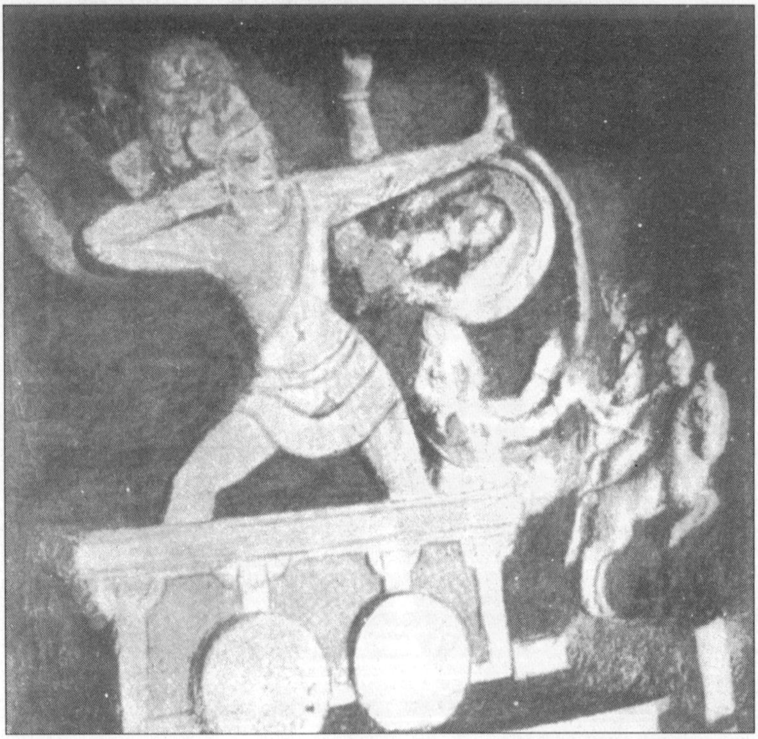

Siva on his chariot in the cave of the Avatars at Ellora (6th century).

PLATE XV

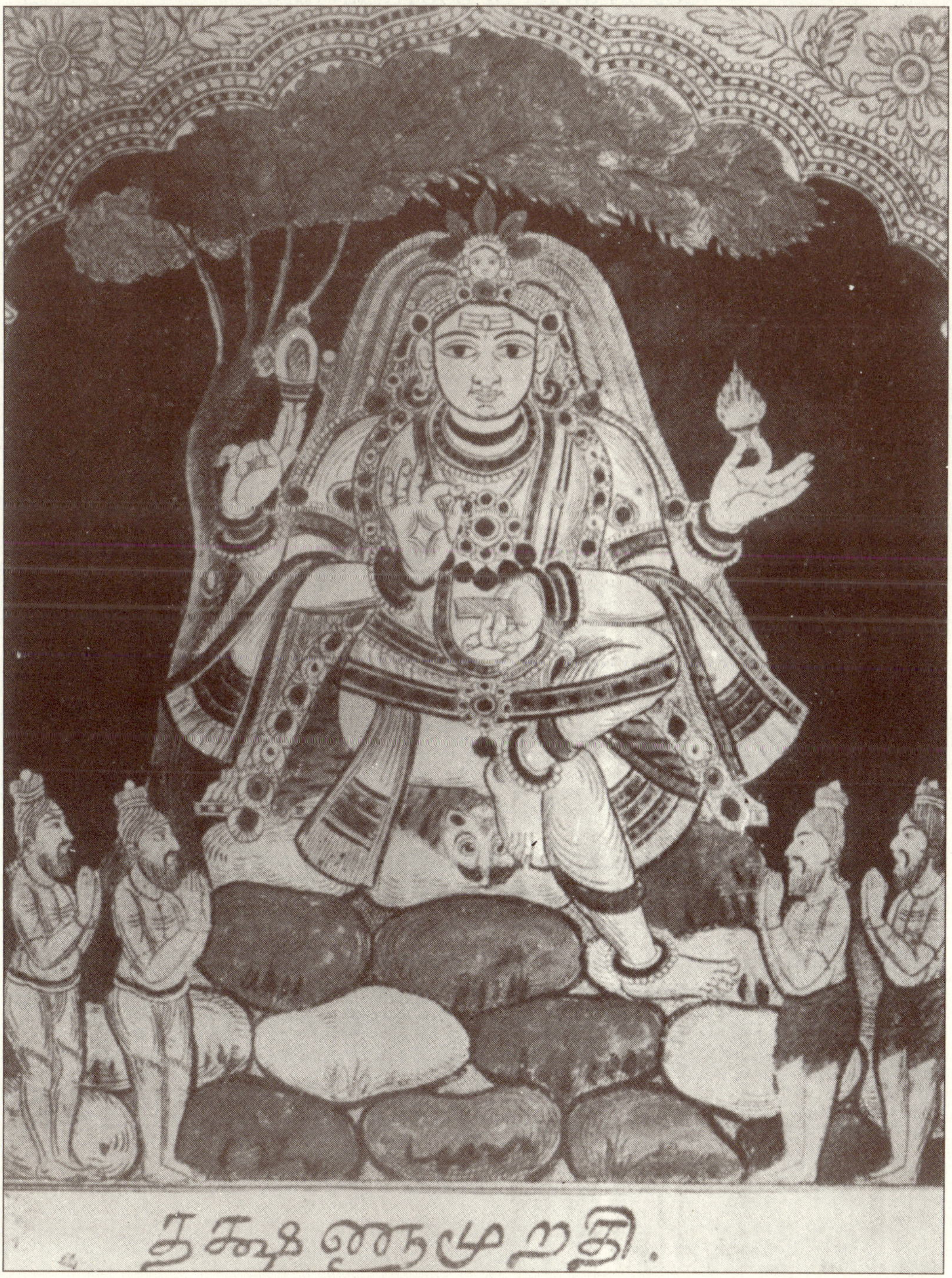

Dakshinamurti. Modern image.

PLATE XVI

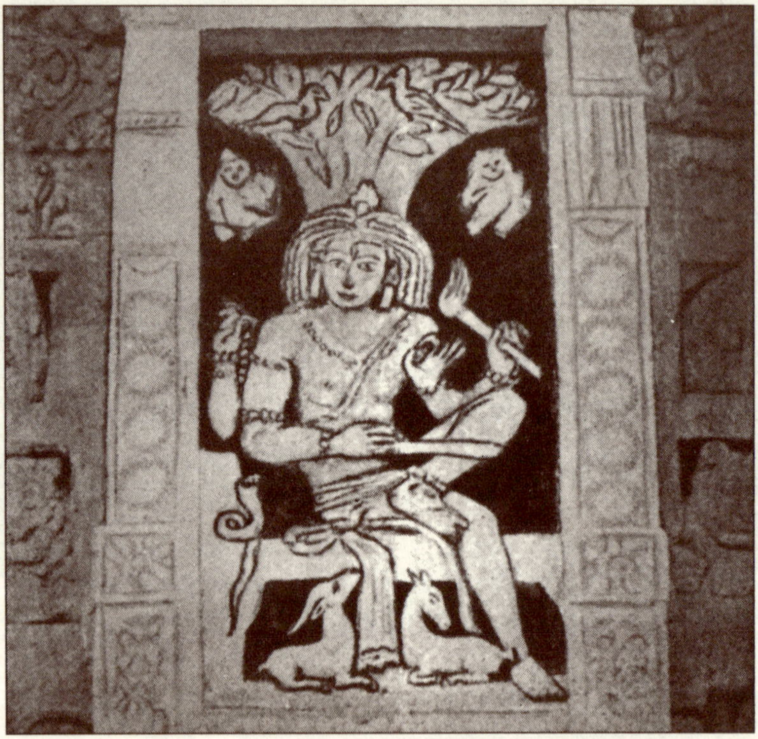

Dakshinamurti in the Pallava temple Kailasanatha at Kanchipuram (8th century).

PLATE XVII

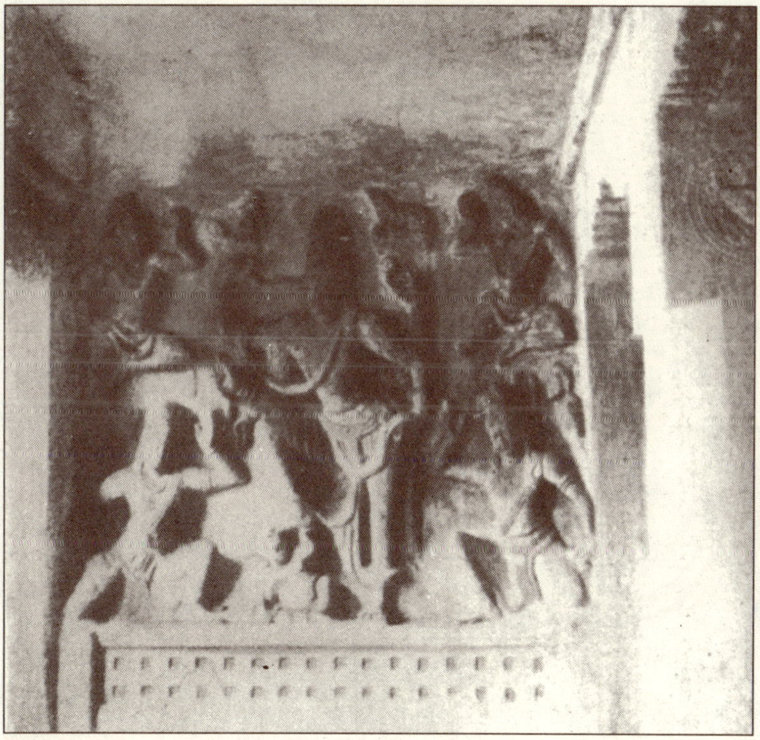

Gangadaram (Siva drawing the goddess Ganga (Ganges) out of his hair). Cave of Trichinopoly, 7th century.

PLATE XVIII

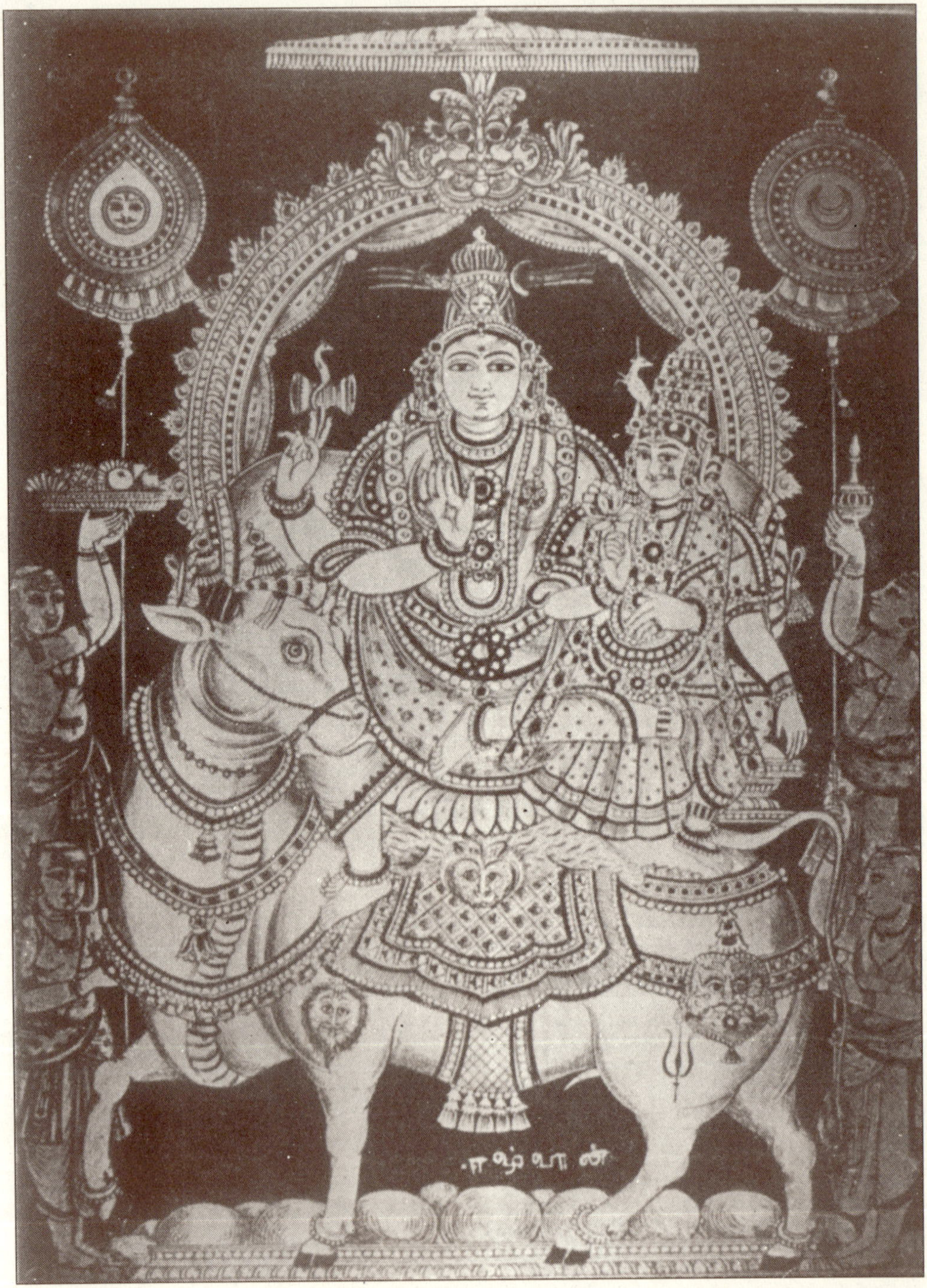

Siva and Parvati riding on Nandi. Modern image.

PLATE XIX

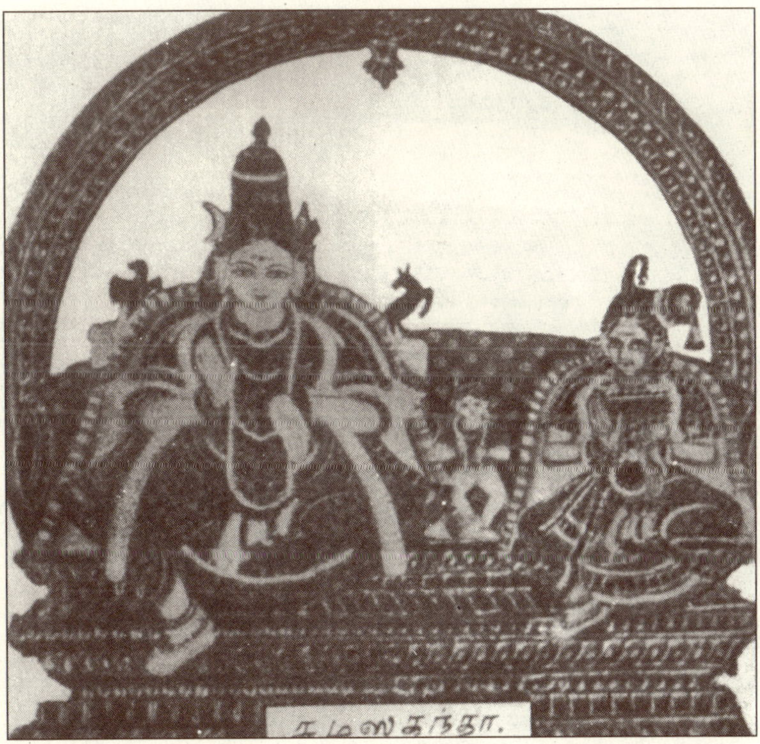

Somaskanda. Modern image.

PLATE XX

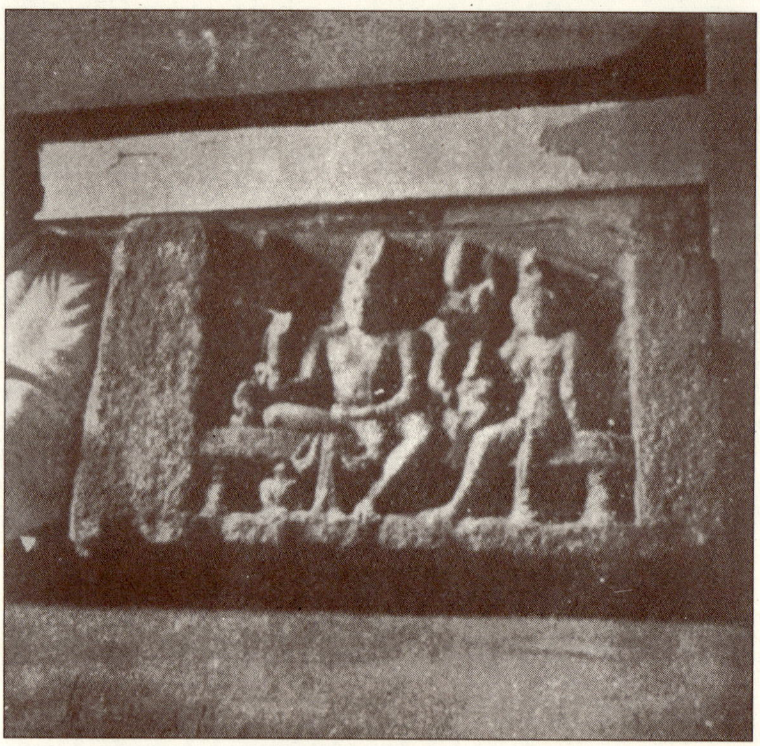

Somaskanda. (Pallava, 7th century.)

PLATE XXI

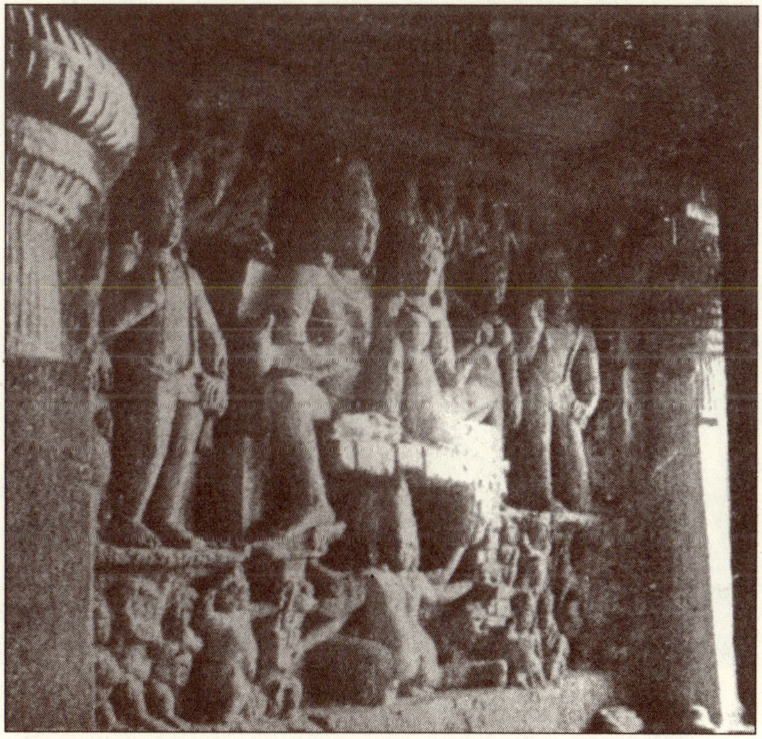

Ravana under Kailasa
Relief in the cave Dhumar-Lena at Ellora (9th century).

PLATE XXII

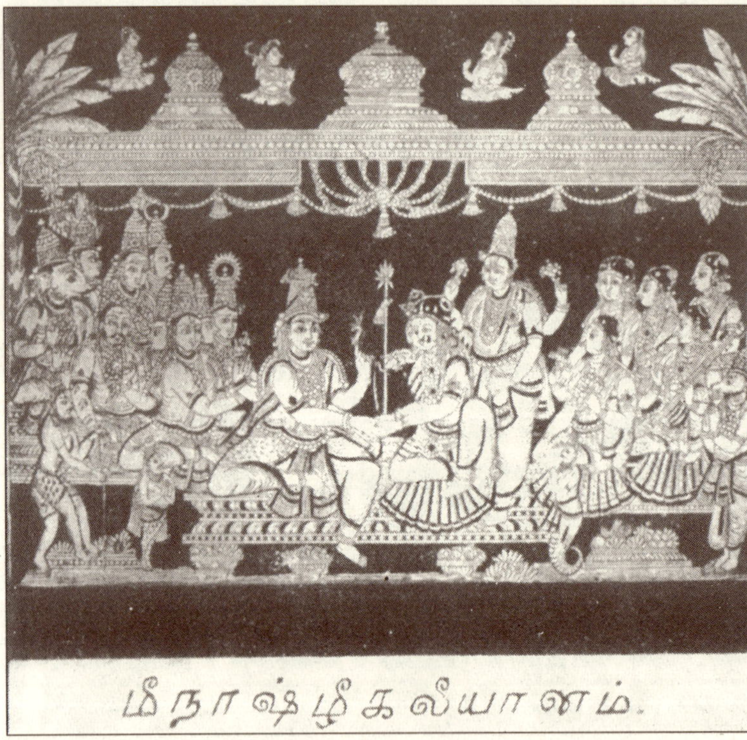

Minakshi-Kalyana.
Marriage of Siva and Minakshi. Modern image.

PLATE XXIII

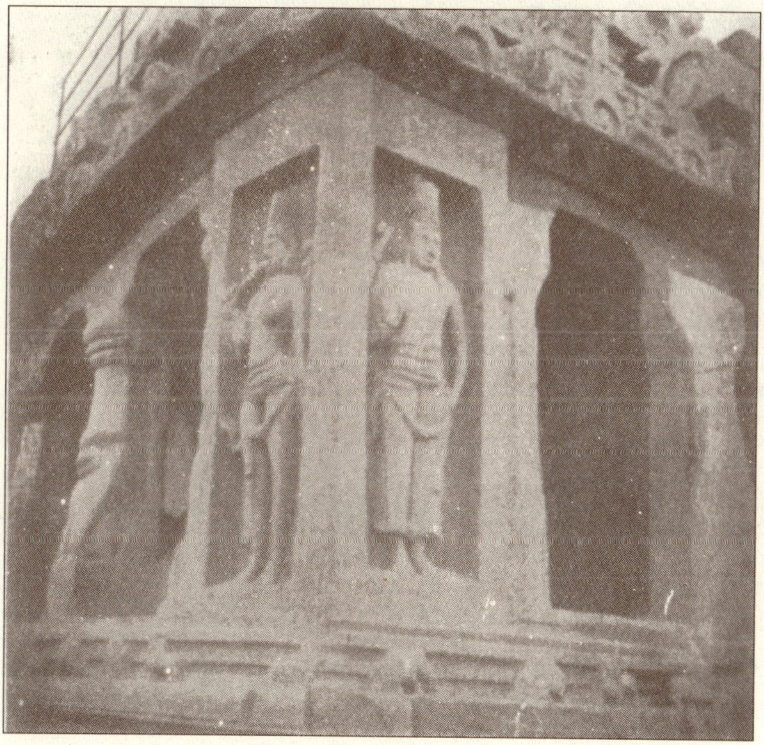

Ardhanari (Left) and Hari-Hara (right) at Mavalipuram.
(Dharmaraja-ratha, 7th century.)

PLATE XXIV

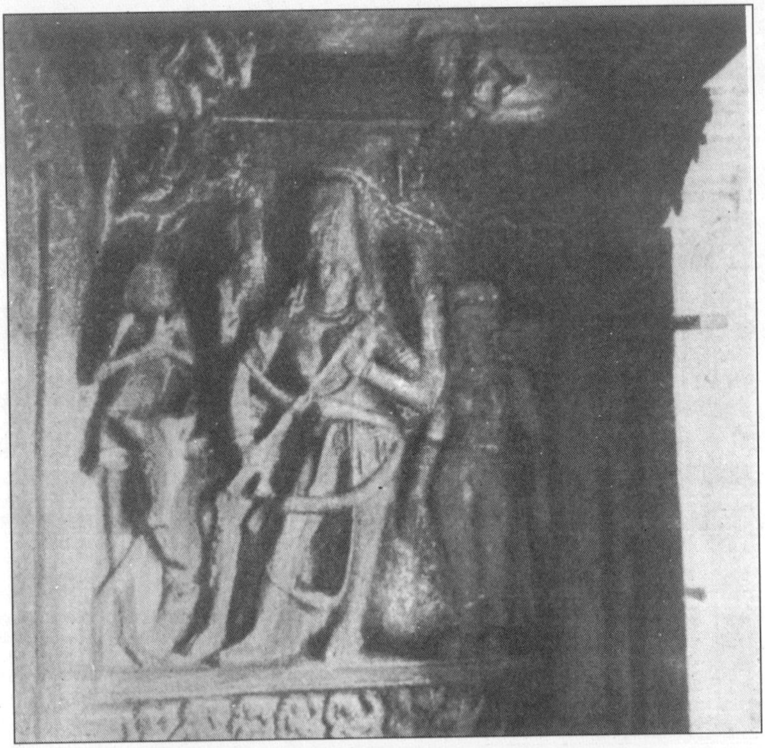

Ardhanari at Badami, Cave No.1 (6th century).

PLATE XXV

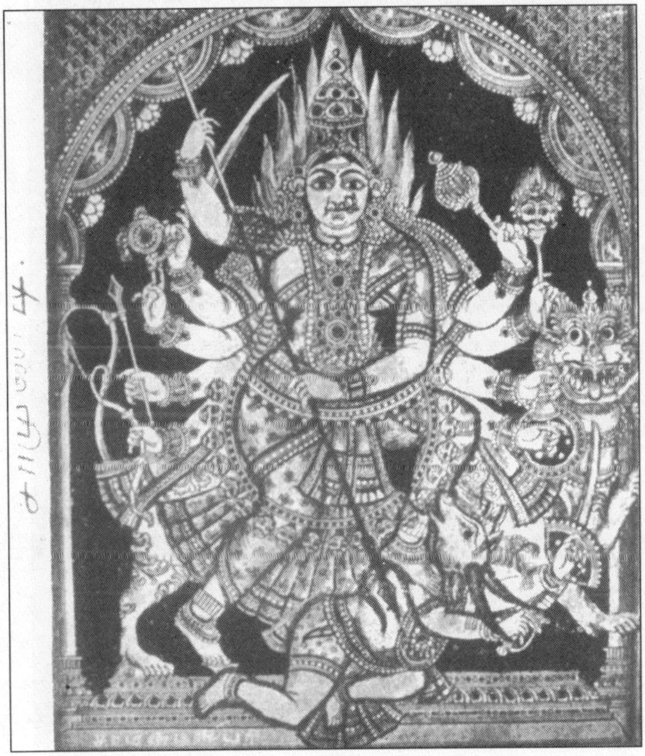

Chamundi, Modern image.

PLATE XXVI

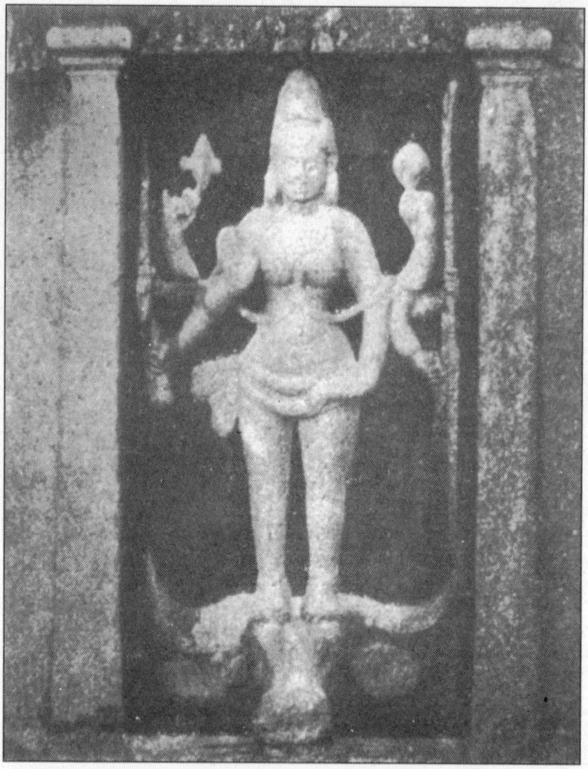

Chamundi standing on the head of Mahisha (7th century).

PLATE XXVII

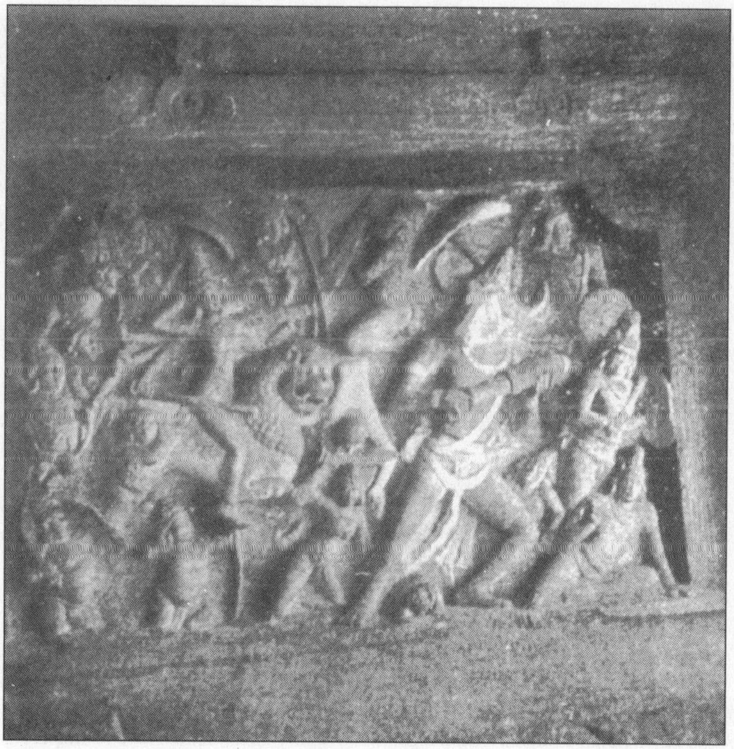

Combat of Chamundi and Mahishasura the giant, at Mavalipuram (7th century).

PLATE XXVIII

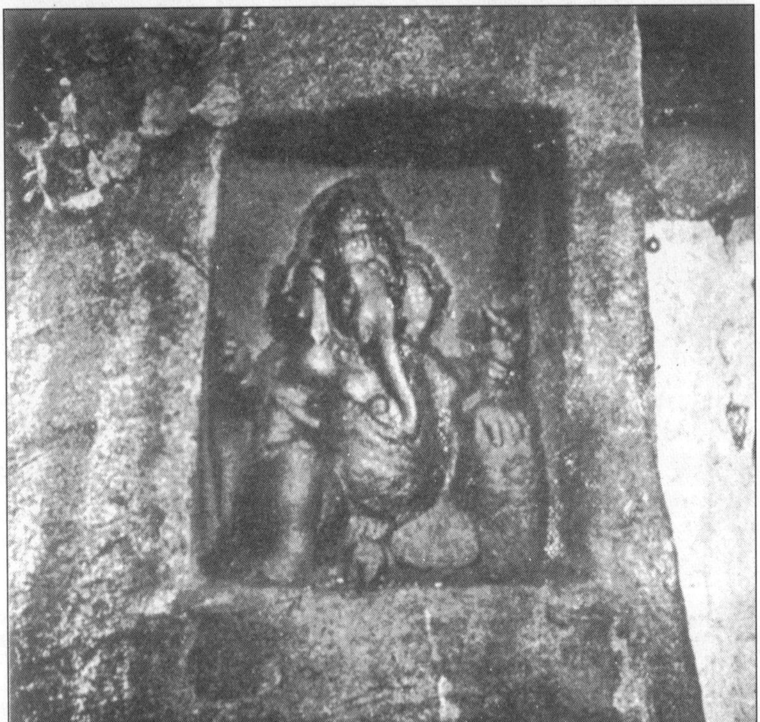

Pulliar at Vallam (7th century).

PLATE XXIX

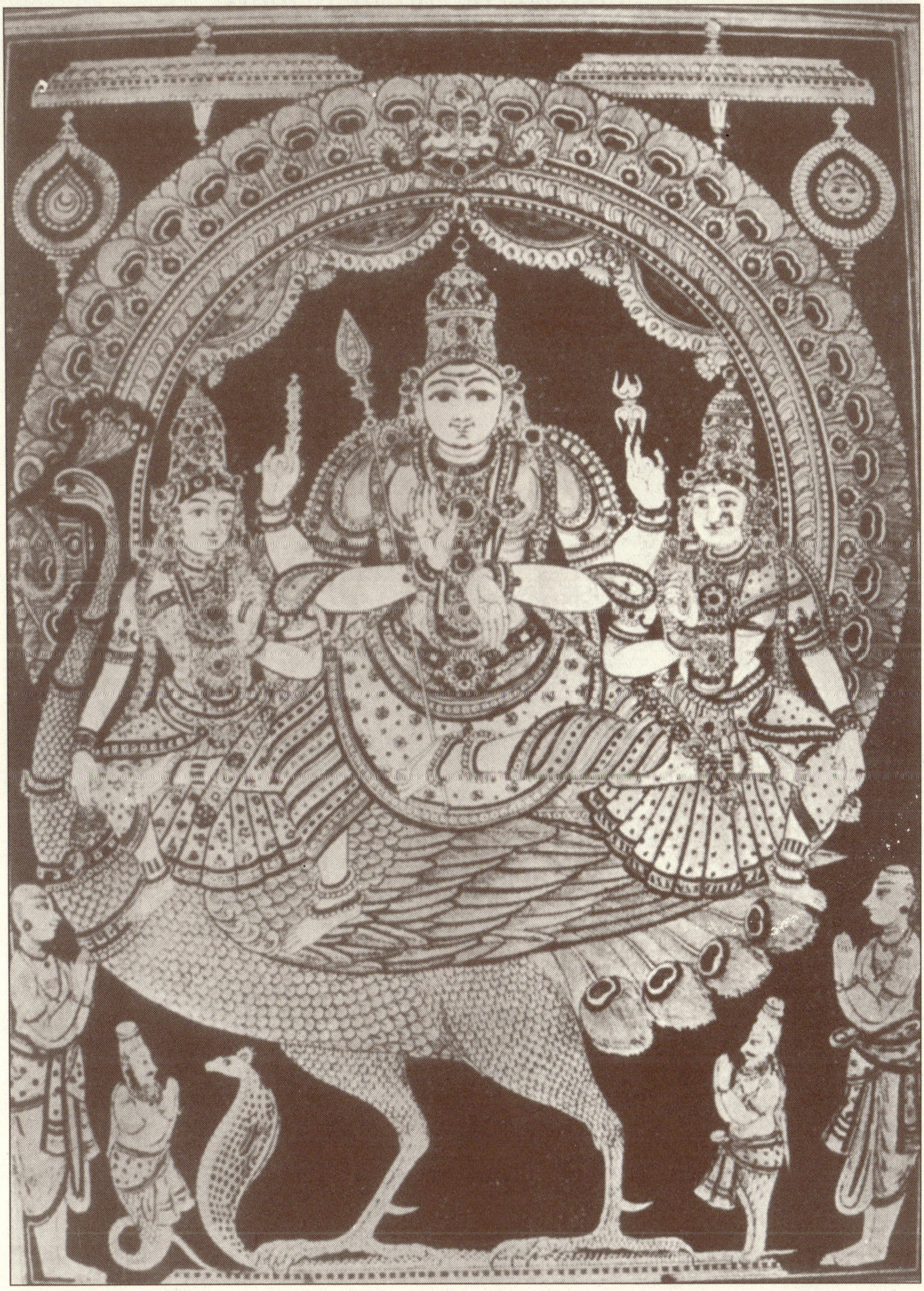

Subrahmaniar on the peacock. Modern image.

PLATE XXX

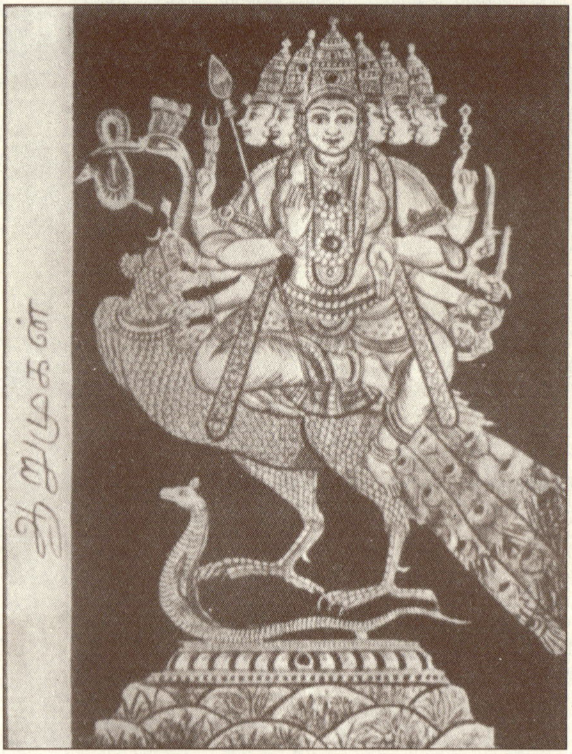

Arumugam (Subrahmaniar). Modern image.

PLATE XXXI

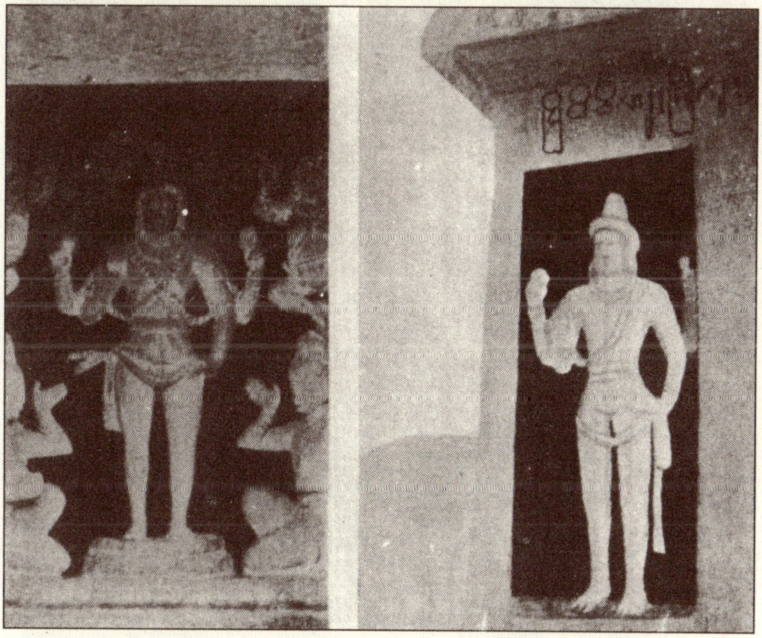

Subrahmaniar at Mavalipuram (7th century).
On the right in the Dharmaraja-ratha ; on the left in the Trimurti cave.

PLATE XXXII

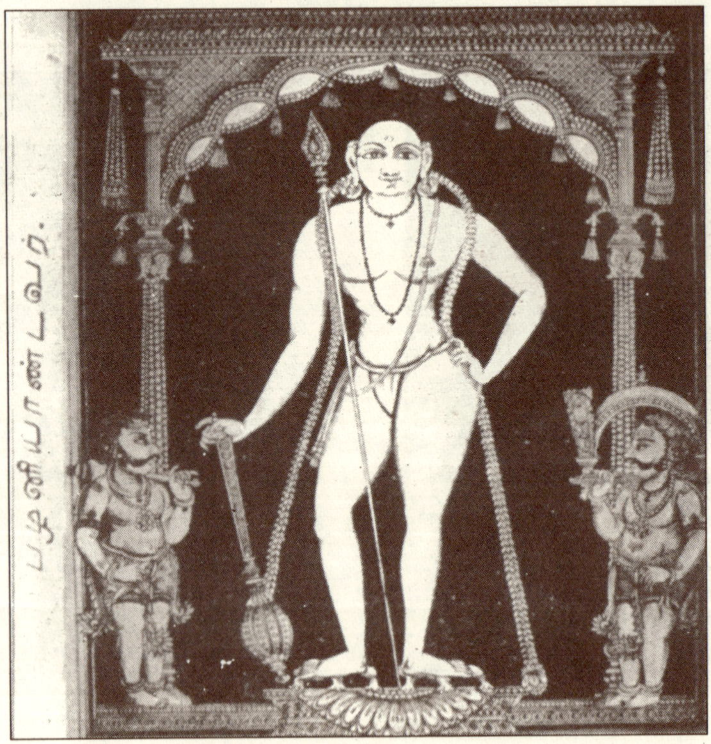

Palani-Andavar. Modern image.

PLATE XXXIII

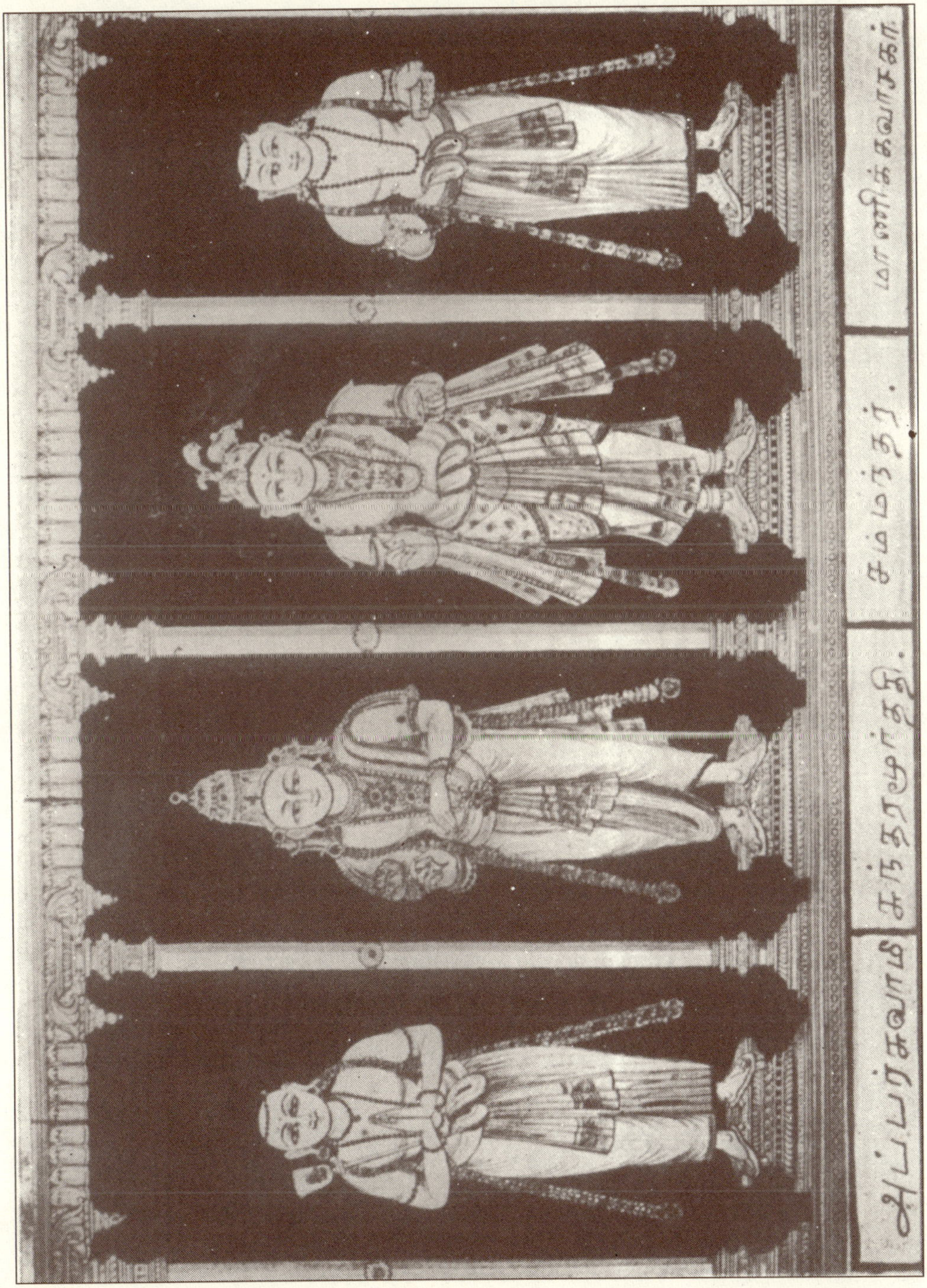

The great Sivaite Saints : Appar, Sundara Sambandar, Manikkavachakar, Modren image.

PLATE XXXIV

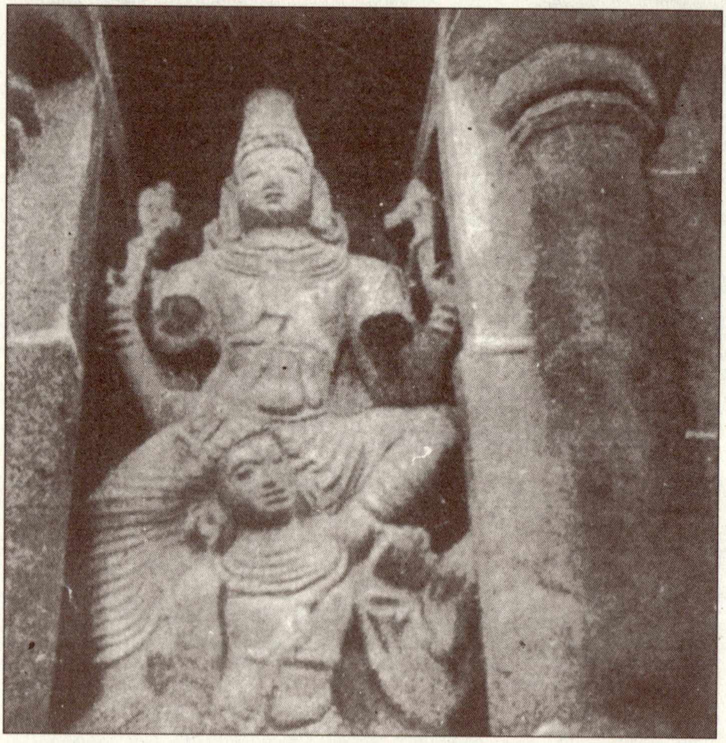

Vishnu (Varadaraja) at Chidambaram (13th century).
(Note the form of the disk.)

PLATE XXXV

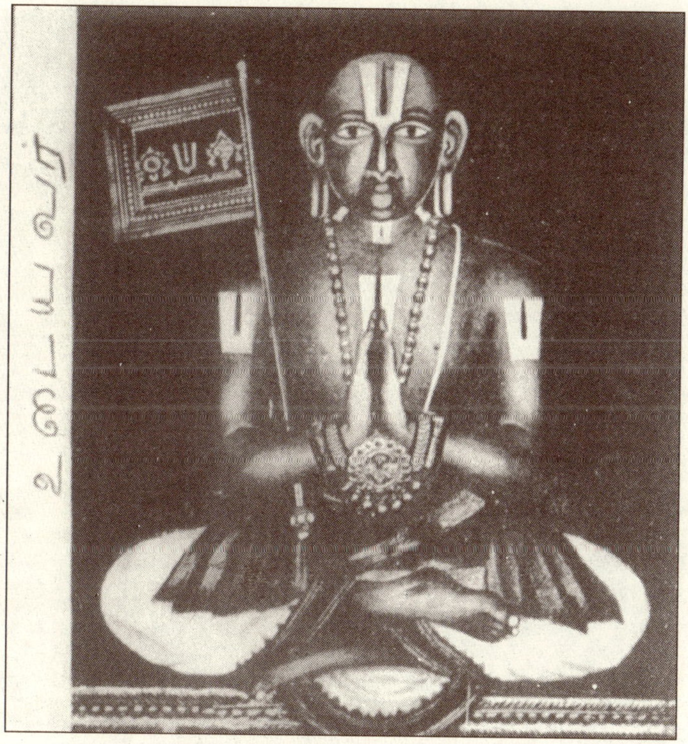

Odeyavar. Modren image.

PLATE XXXVI

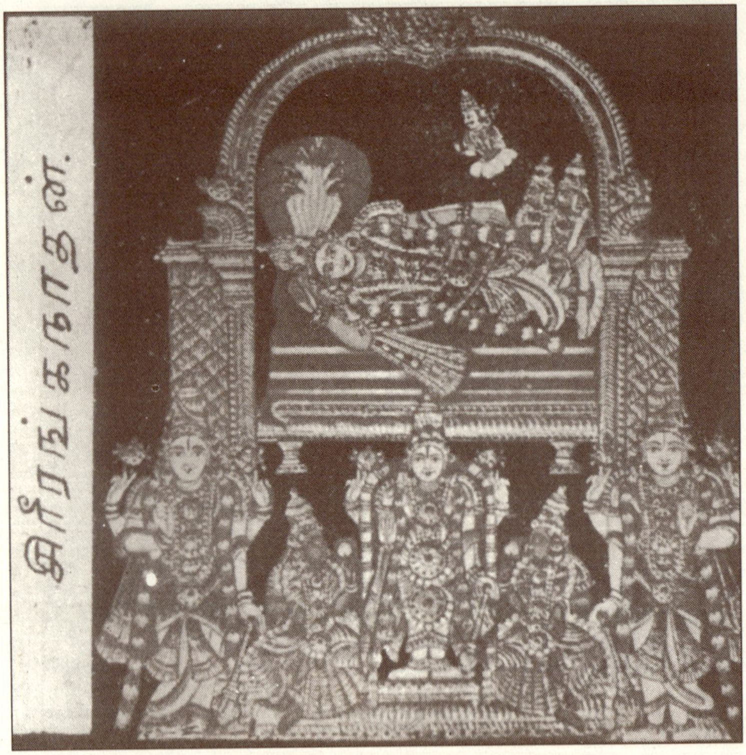

Sri-Ranganatha, Modren image.

PLATE XXXVII

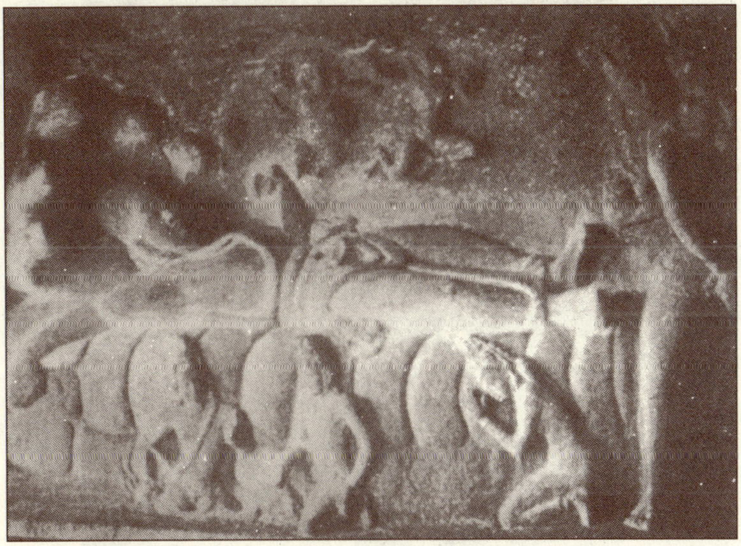

Ranganātha at Mavalipuram (7th century).

PLATE XXXVIII

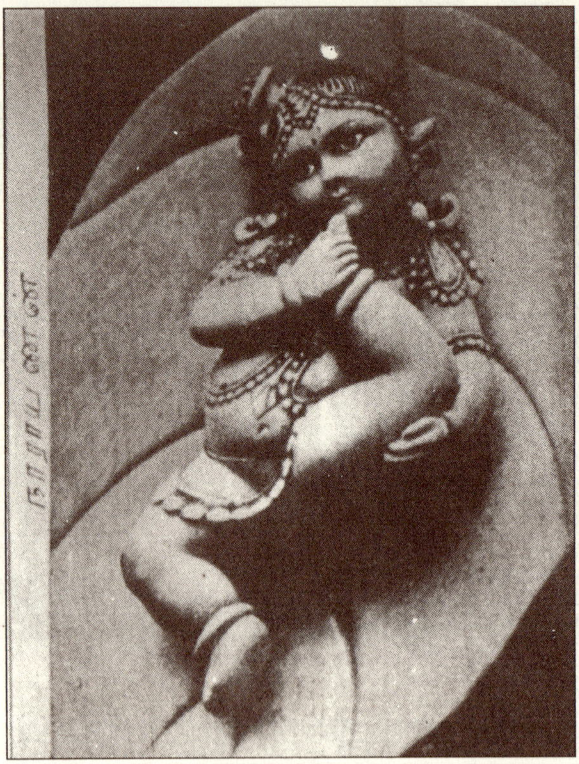

Narayana. Modern image.

PLATE XXXIX

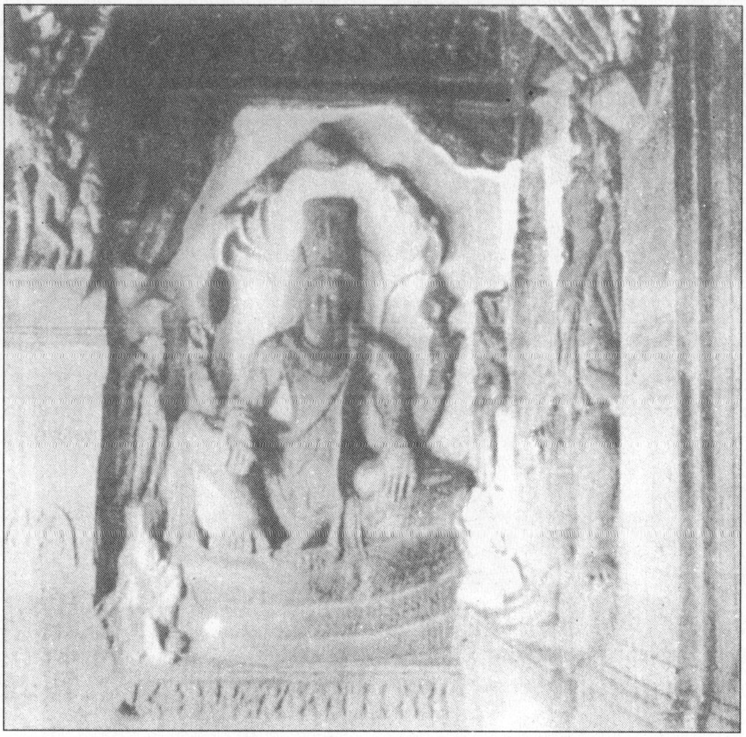

Vishnu seated on the serpent in cave No.3 at Badami (6th century).

PLATE XL

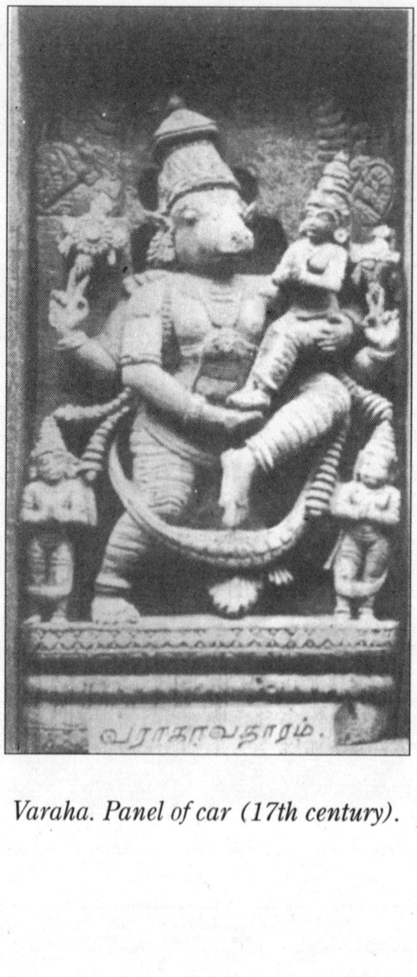

Varaha. Panel of car (17th century).

PLATE XLI

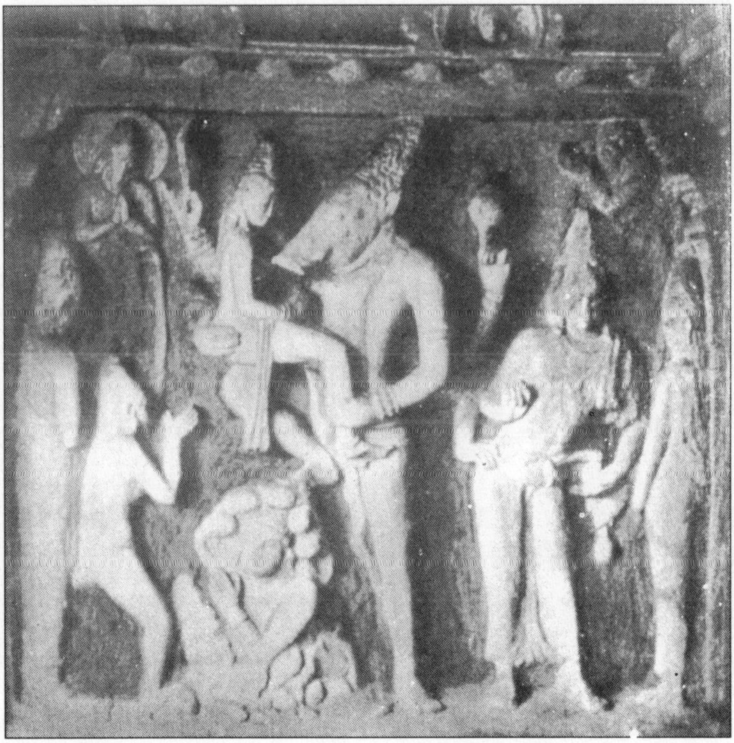

Varaha at Mavalipuram (7th century).

PLATE XLII

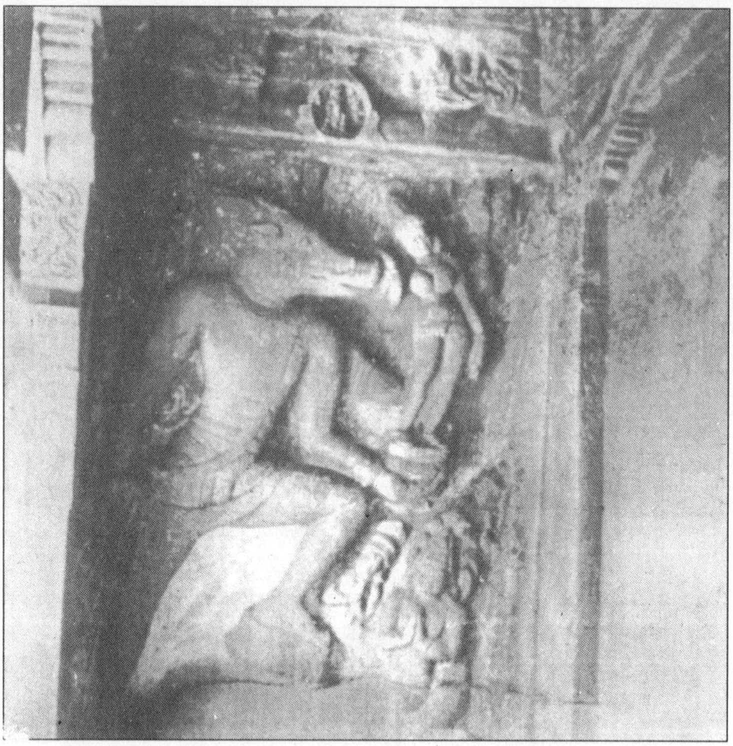

Varaha. Cave No.2 at Badami (6th century).

PLATE XLIII

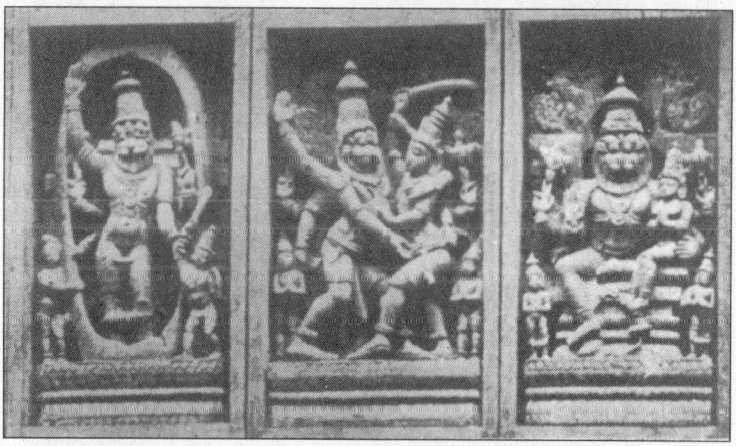

1. 2. 3.

Story of Narasimha : 1. Narasimha coming out of the pillar.
2. Fight of Narasimha and Hiranya. 3. Worship of Narasimha.

PLATE XLIV

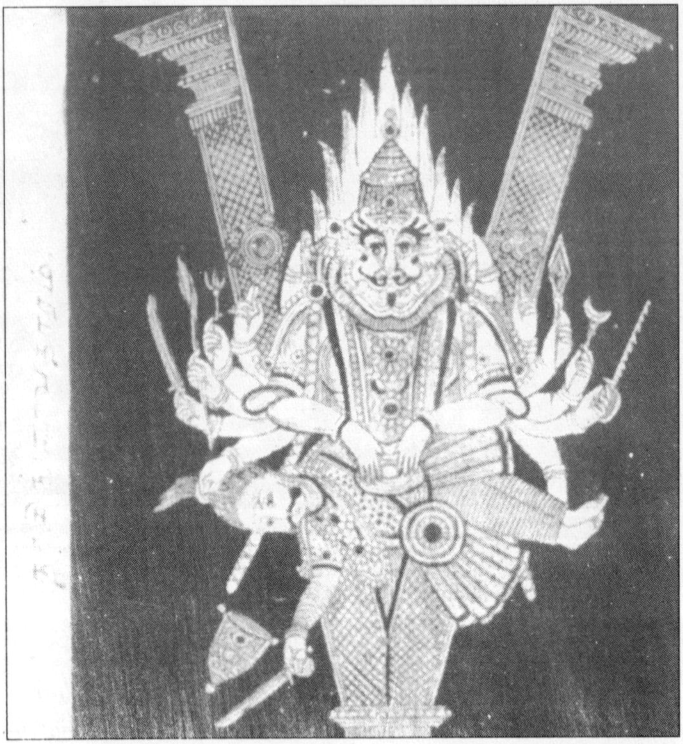

Narasimha tearing out the entrails of Hiranya. (Modern art.)

PLATE XLV

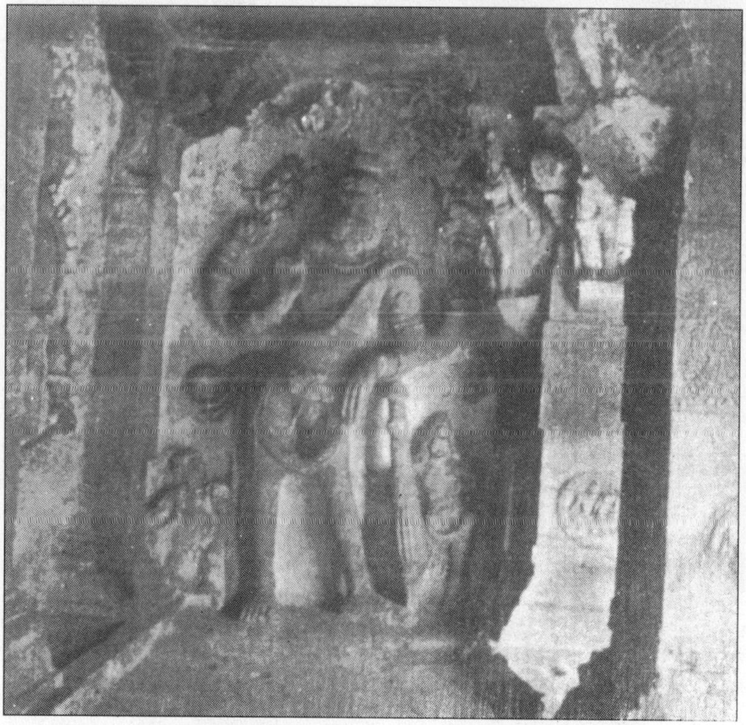

Narasimha at Badami, Cave No.3 (6th century).

PLATE XLVI

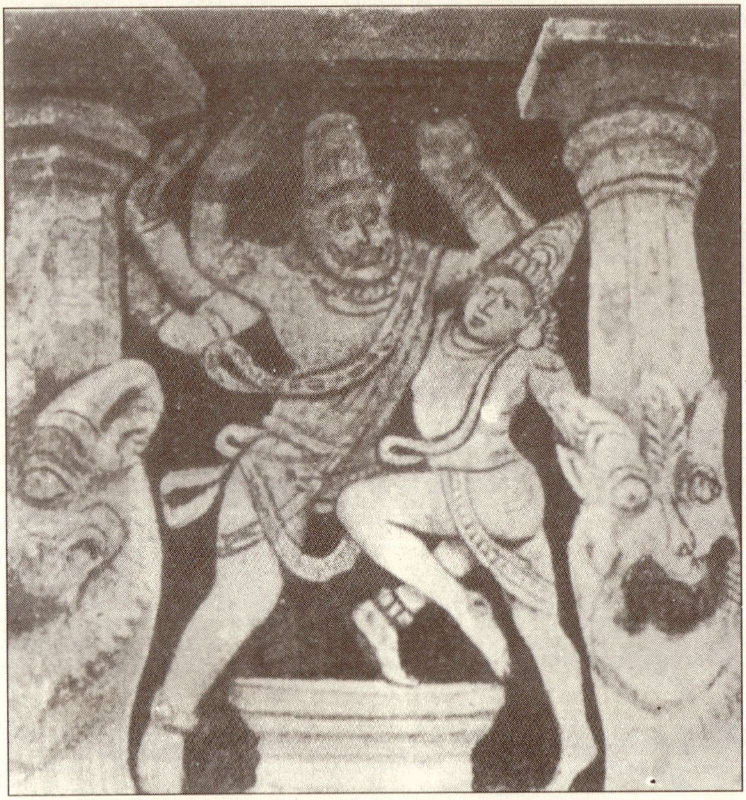

Fight between Narasimha and Hiranya
(Kailasanatha temple at Kanchipuram, 8th century.)

PLATE XLVII

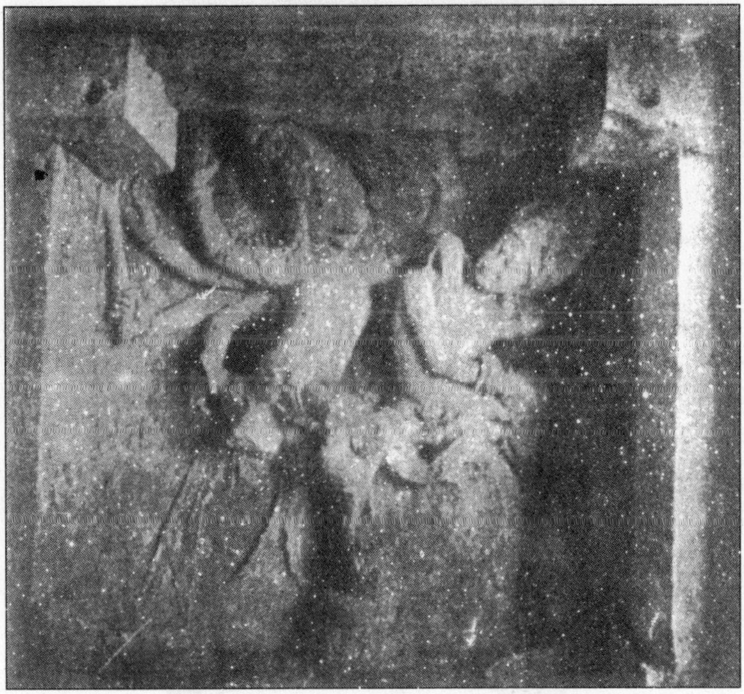

Fight between Narasimha and Hiranya.
(Ellora, Cave of the Avatars, 6th century.)

PLATE XLVIII

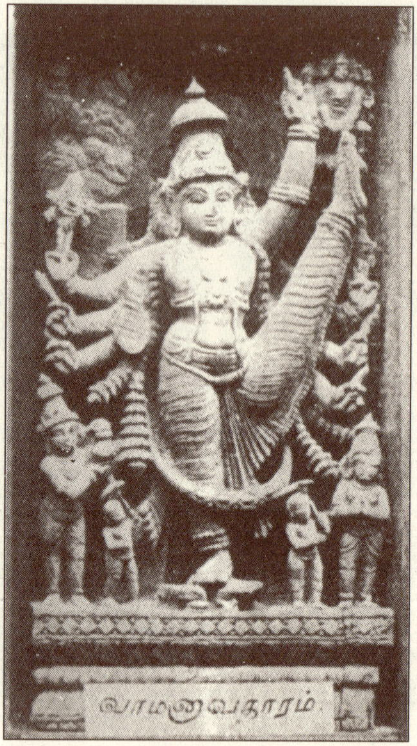

Vamana-avataram. (Panel of car, 17th century.)

PLATE XLIX

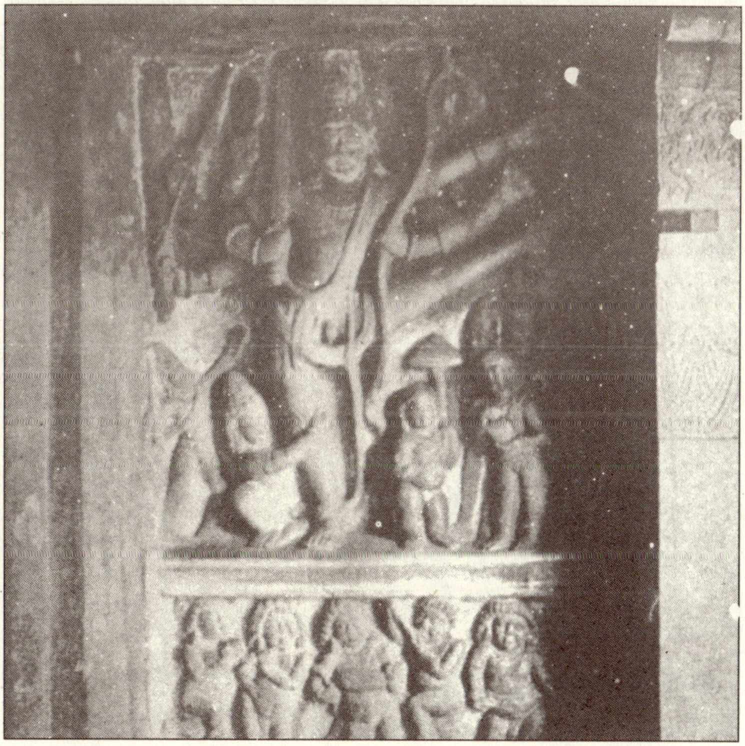

Vamana-Trivikrama at Badami, Cave No.2 (6th century).

PLATE L

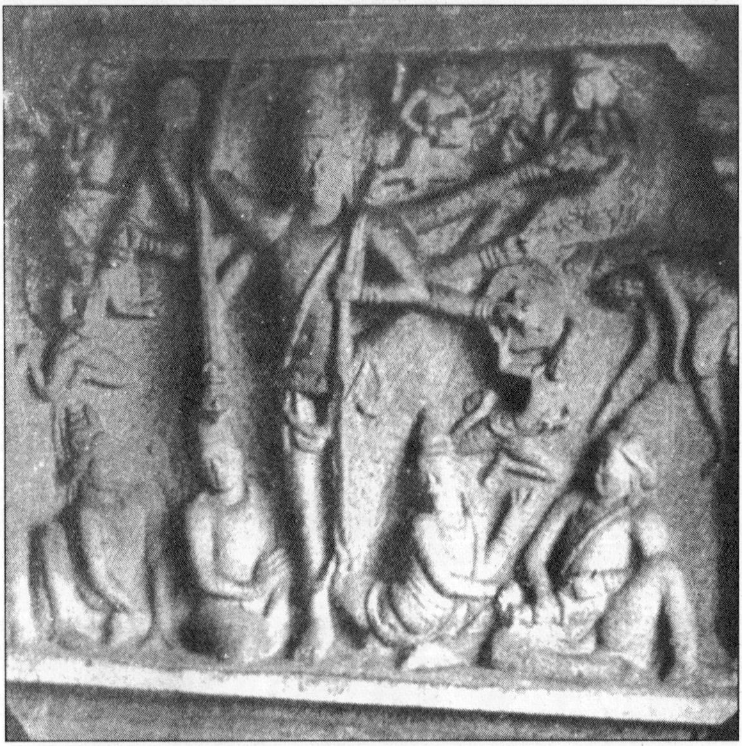

Vamana-Trivikrama at Mavalipuram (7th century).

PLATE LI

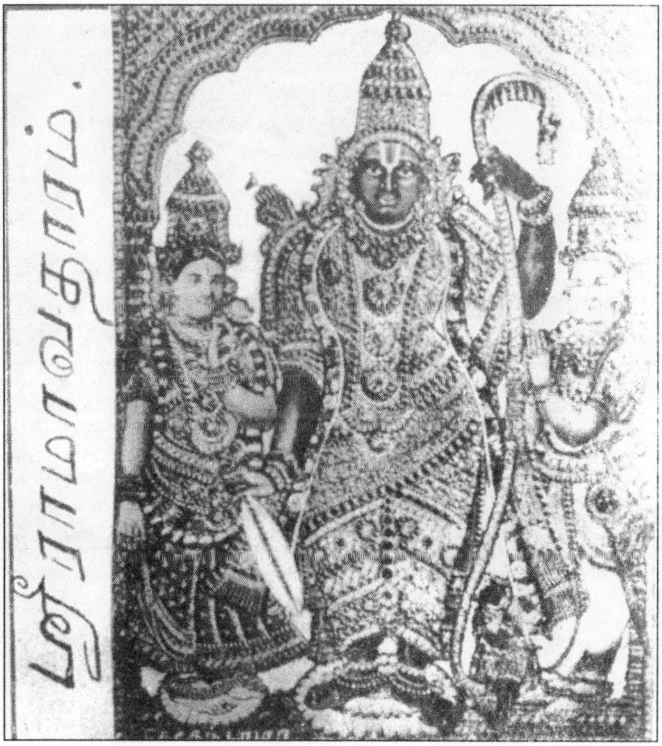

Sri-Rama-avataram : Rama, Sita, Lakshmana and Hanuman.

PLATE LII

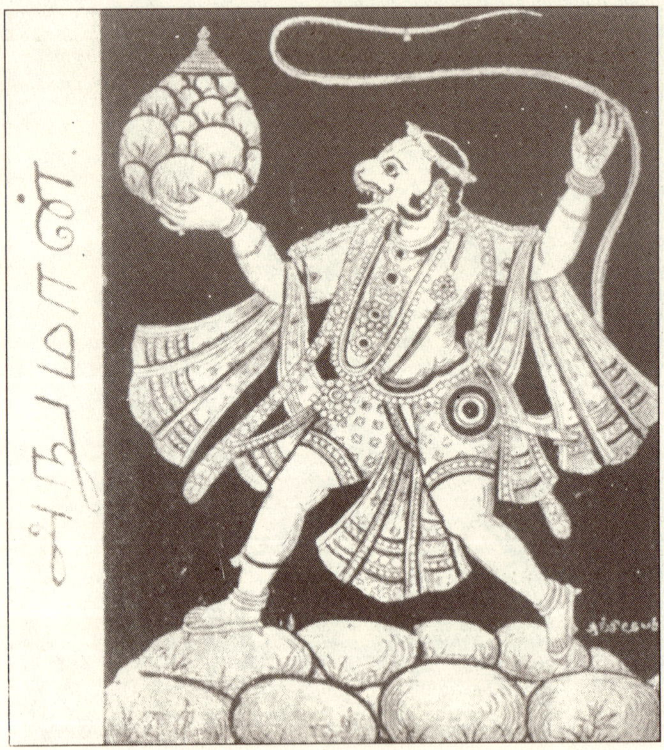

Hanuman. Modren image.

PLATE LIII

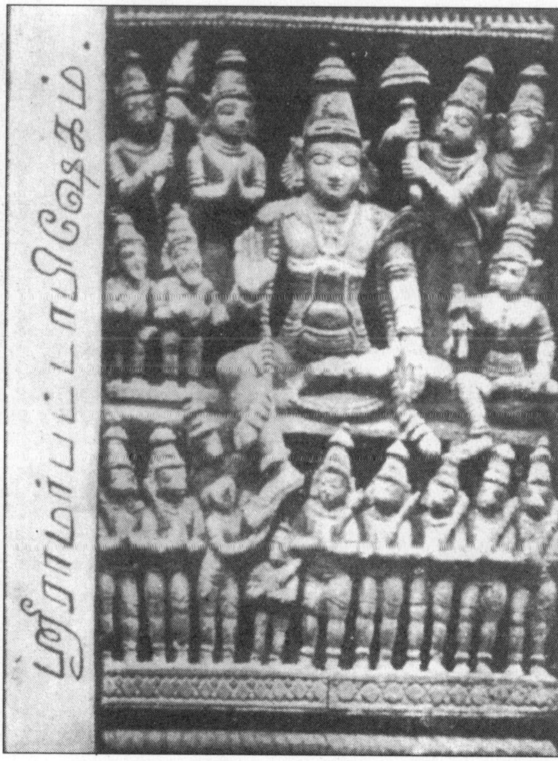

Sri-Rama-pattabhishekan (Consecration of Rama).

PLATE LIV

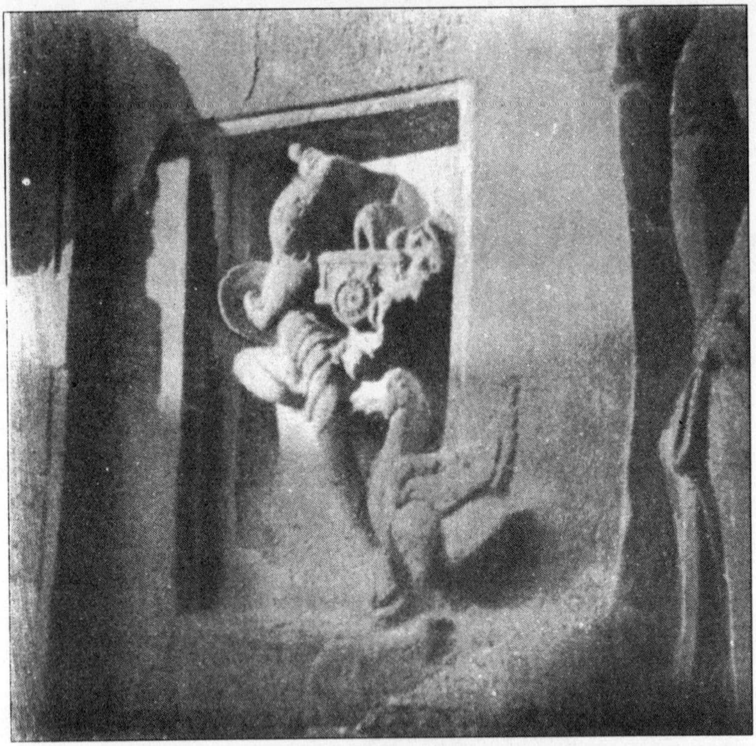

Abduction of Sita. (Kailasa of Ellora, 8th century.)

PLATE LV

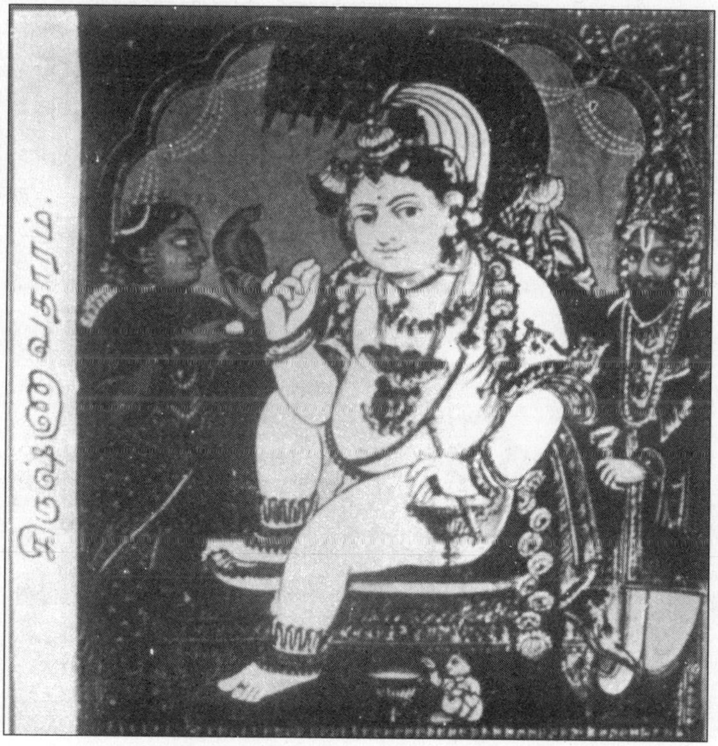

Krishna-avataram. Modern image.

PLATE LVI

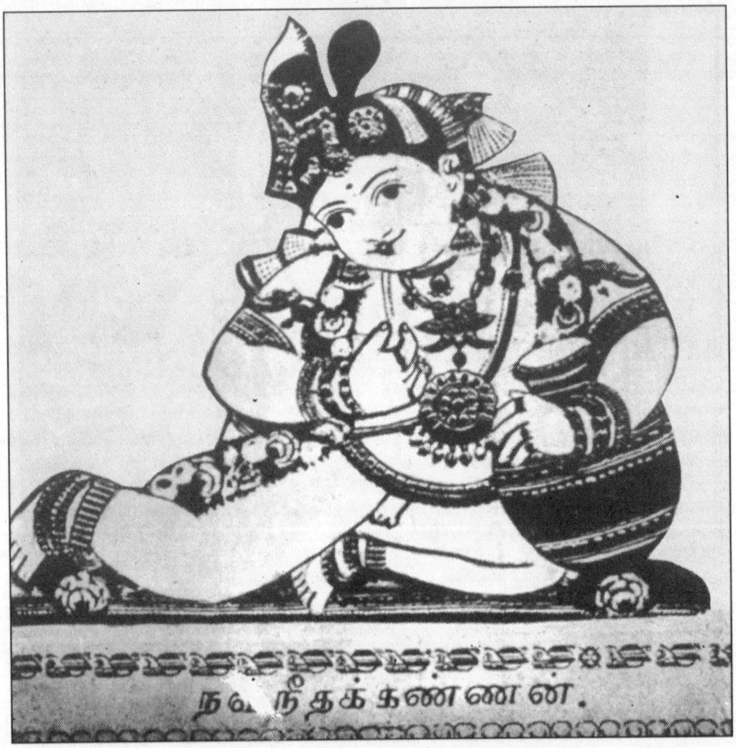

Navanida-kannan (Krishna stealing the butter). Modern image.

PLATE LVII

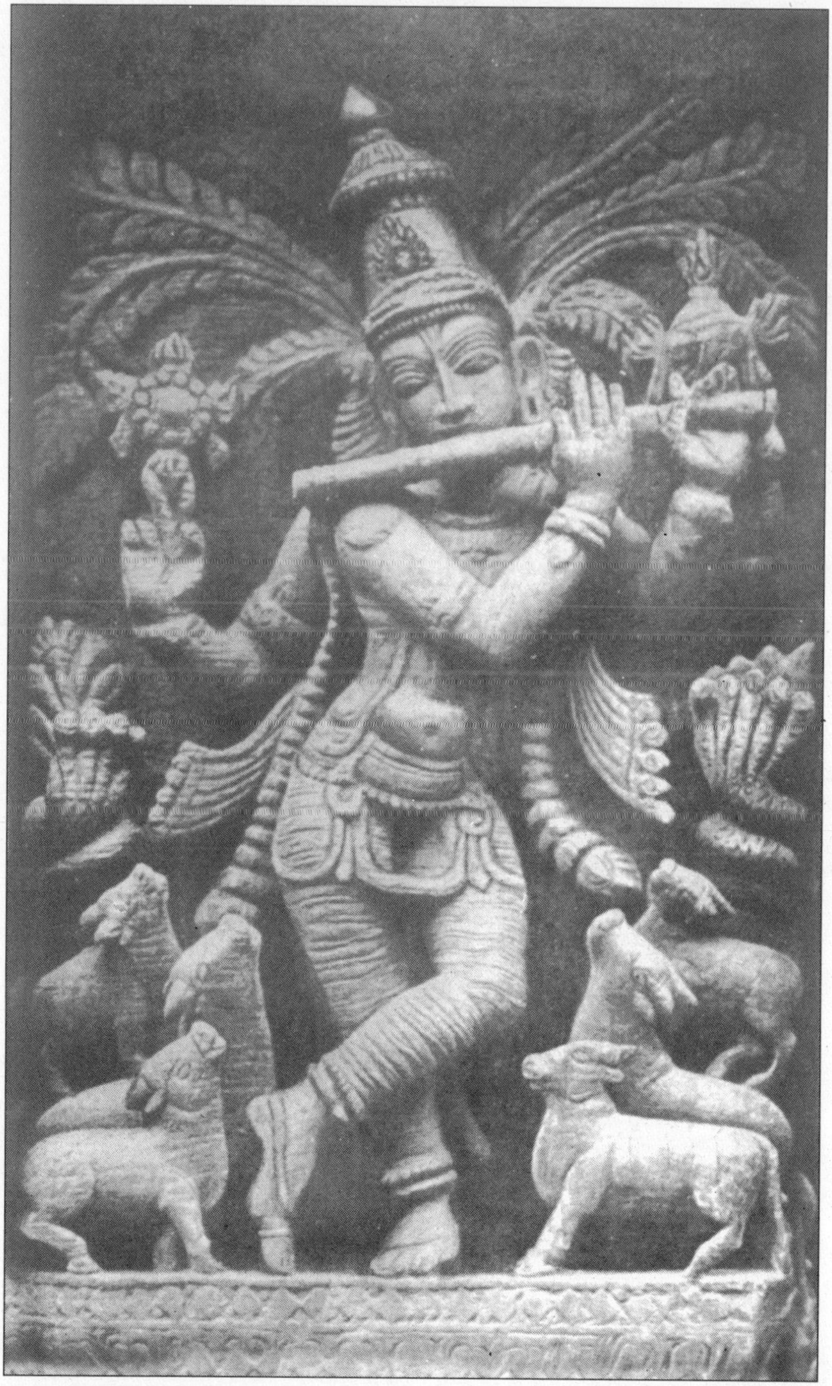

Venu-gopala (Krishna playing the flute). Panel of car (17th century).

PLATE LVIII

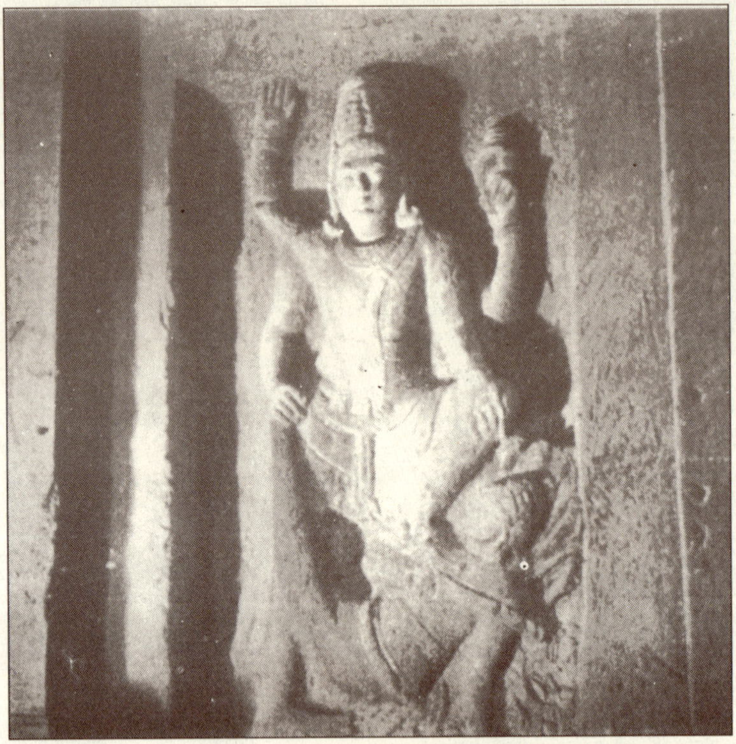

Krishna crushing Kaliya the serpent,
(Kailasa of Ellora, 8th century.)

PLATE LIX

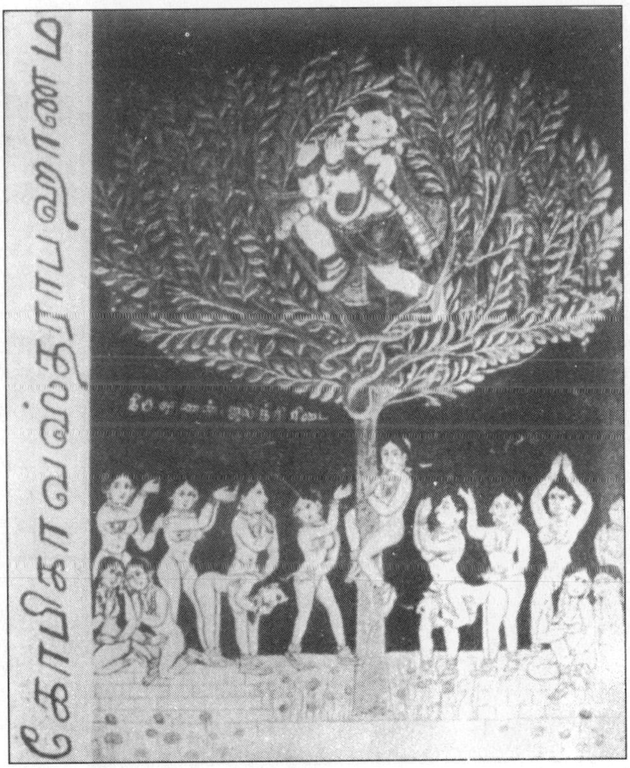

Gopika-vastrapaharana (Stealing of the milkmaids clothes).
(Modren art.)

PLATE LX

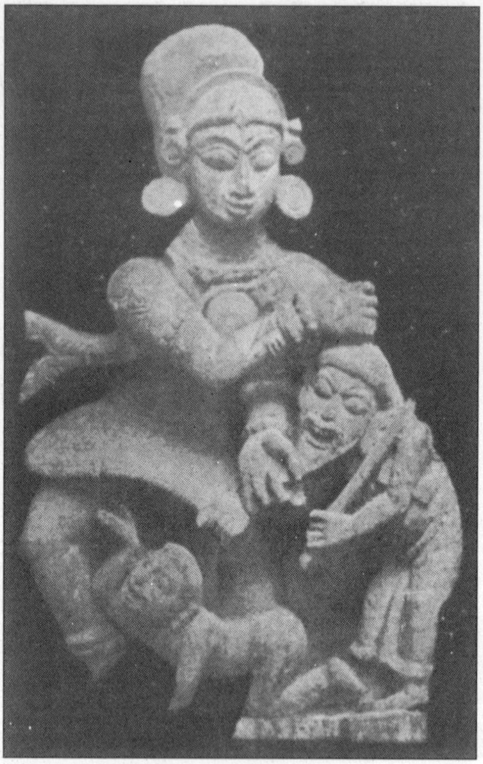

Mohini

PLATE LXI

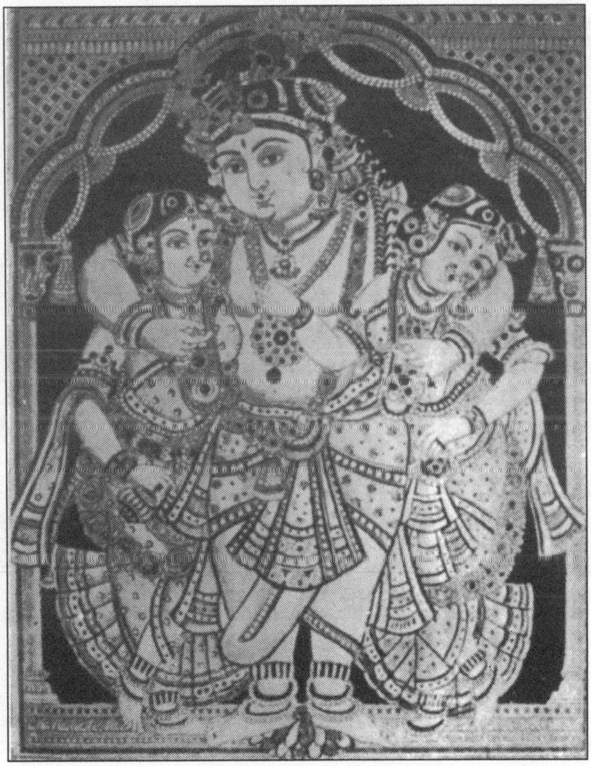

Krishna between Radha and Rukmini. (Modern art.)

PLATE LXII

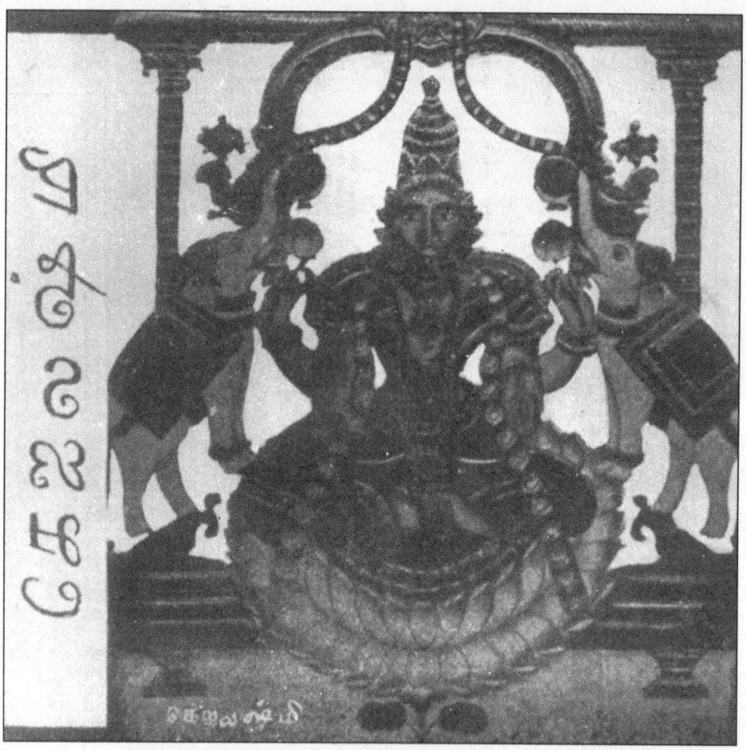

Gaja-Lakshmi. Modren image.

PLATE LXIII

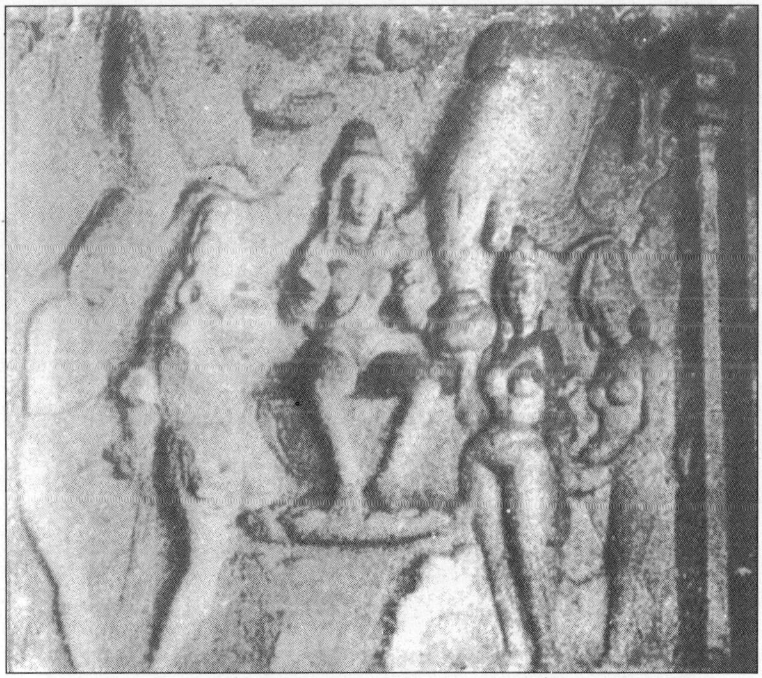

Gaja-Lakshmi at Mavalipuram (7th century).

PLATE LXIV

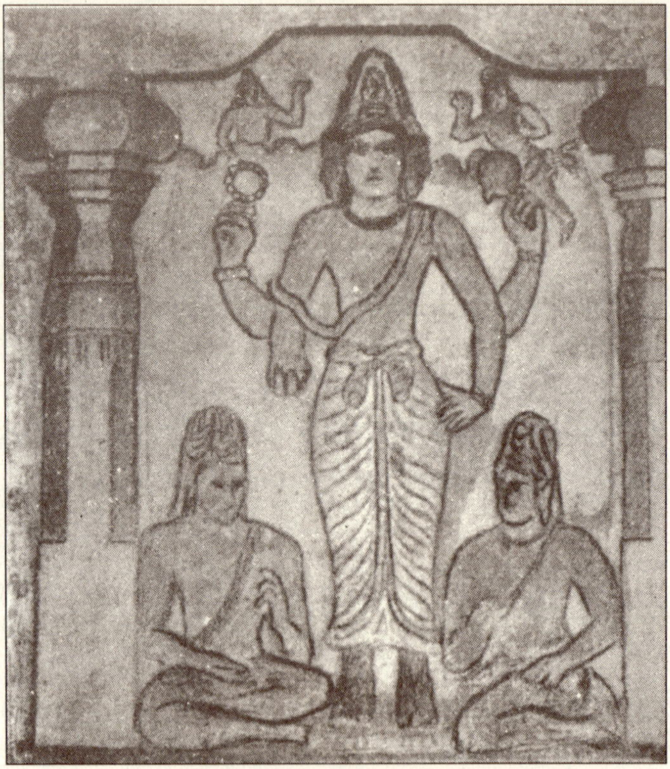

Brahma in a cave at Trichinopoly (7th century).

PLATE LXV

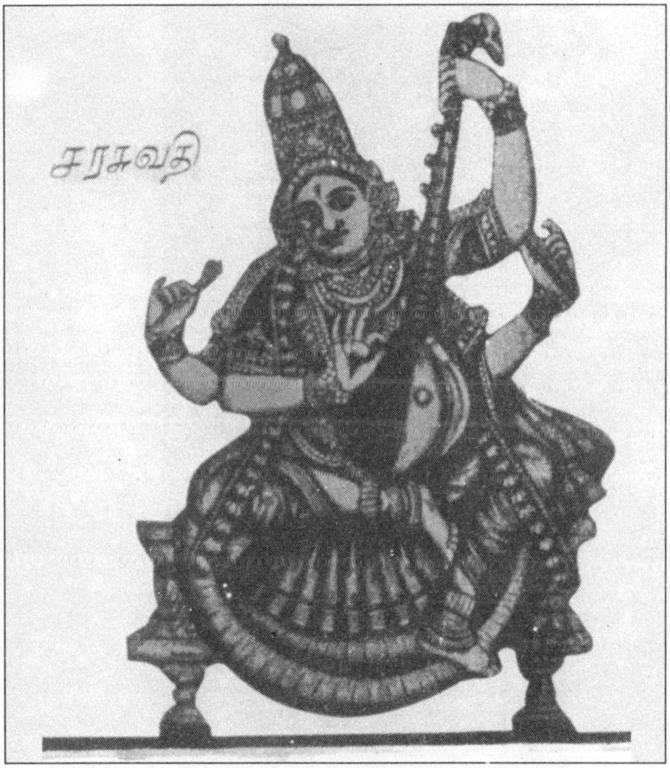

Sarasvati. Modern image.

PLATE LXVI

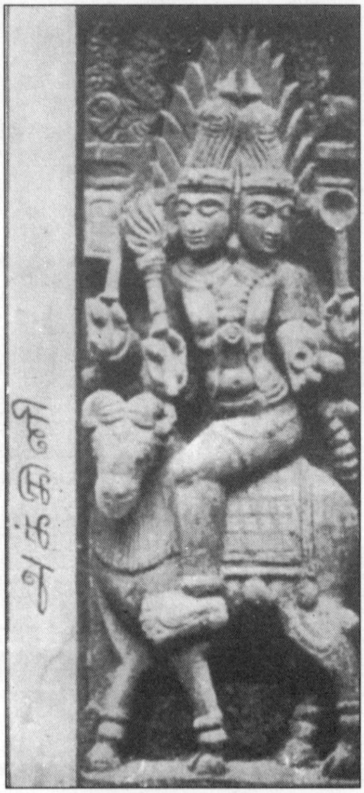

Agni. Panel of car.

PLATE LXVII

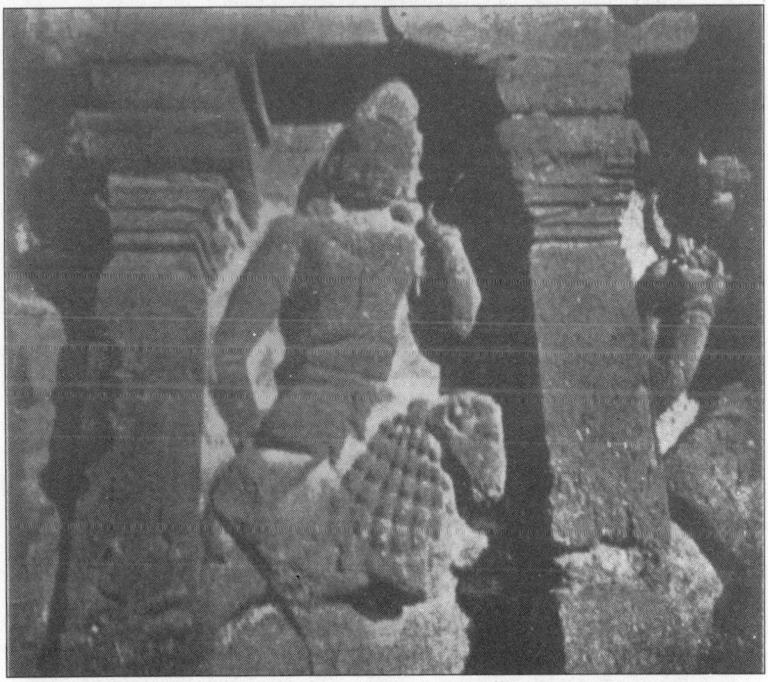

Agni at Ellora, Kailasa (8th century).

PLATE LXVIII

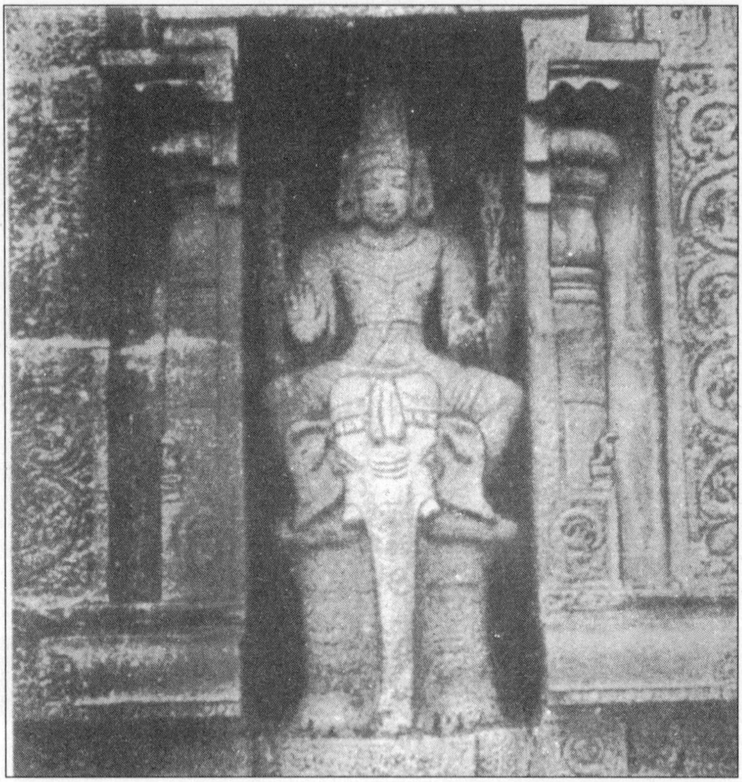

Indra at Chidambaram (13th century).

PLATE LXIX

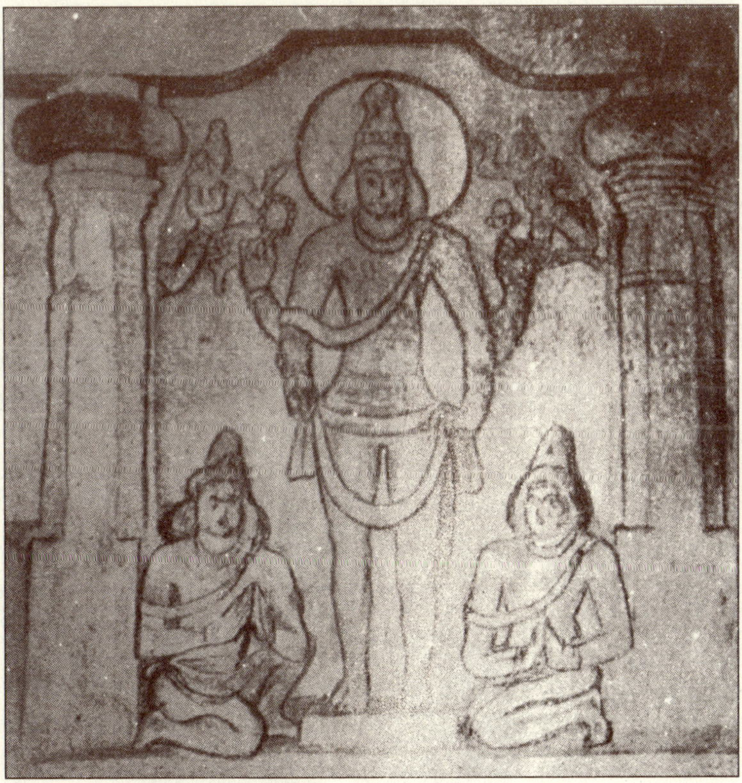

Surya at Trichinopoly (7th century).

PLATE LXX

7th century.

Pallava period

Cave at Trichinopoly.

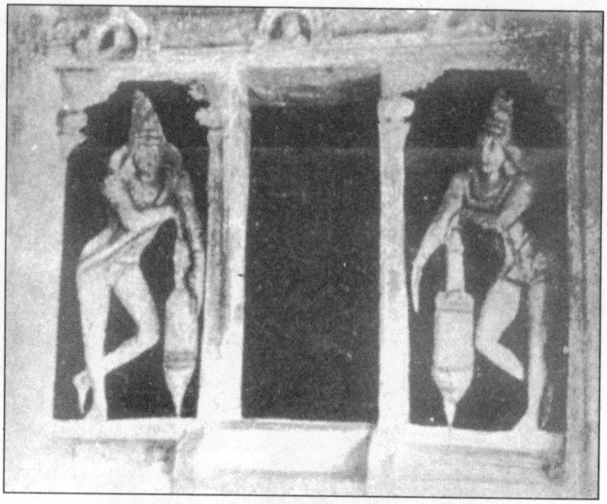

13th century.

Chola period.

Vimana at Tanjore.

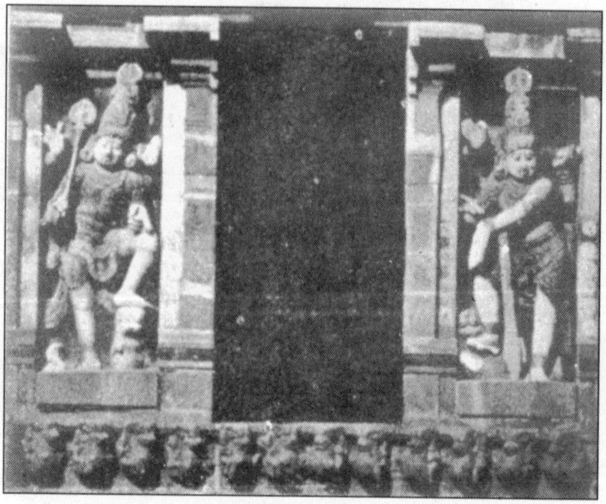

Dvarapalakas.

PLATE LXXI

17th century.

Madura period

Panel of car.

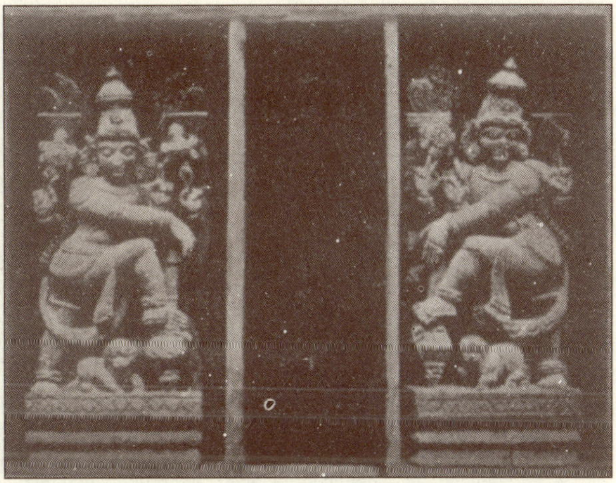

Dvarapalakas.

PLATE LXXII

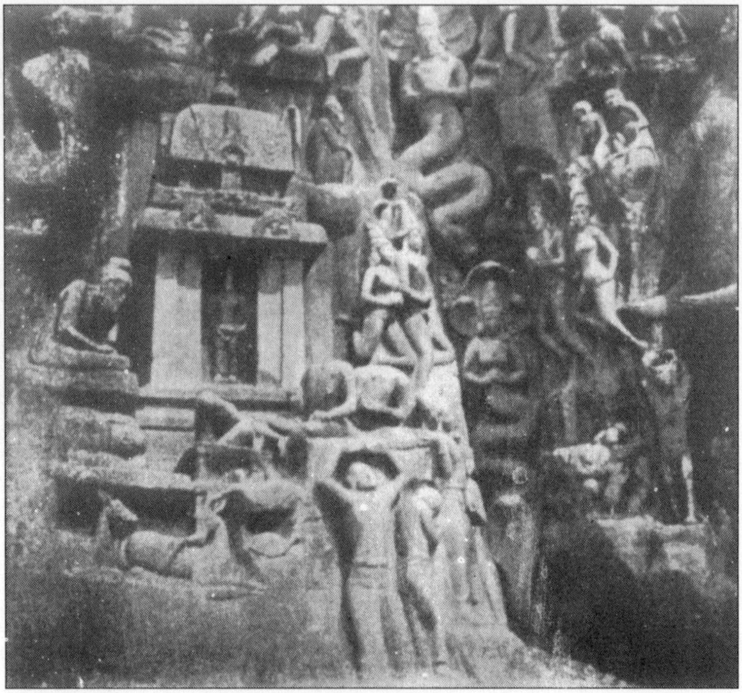

Nagas. Low-relief: Penance of Arjuna, at Mavalipuram.

PLATE LXXIII

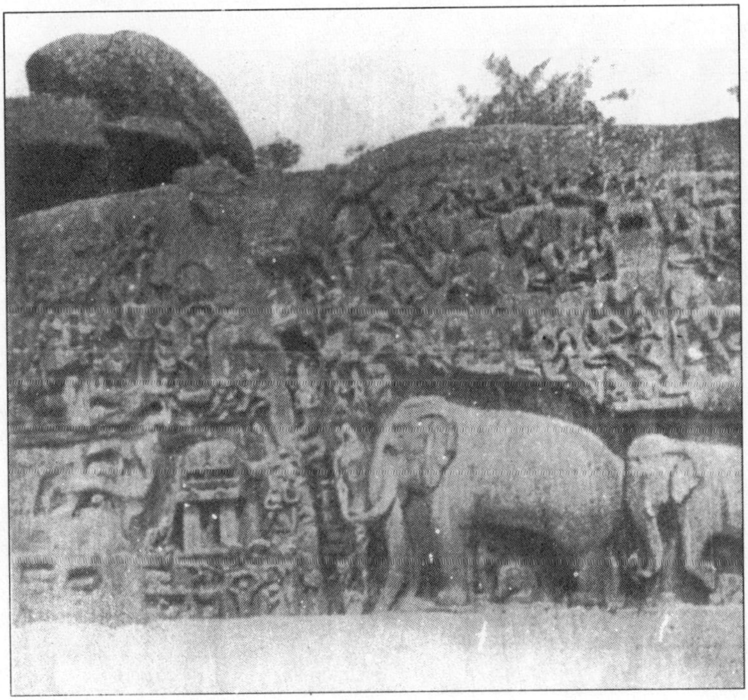

Penance of Arjuna, at Mavalipuram (8th century).

ICONOGRAPHY OF SOUTHERN INDIA

PLATE LXXIV

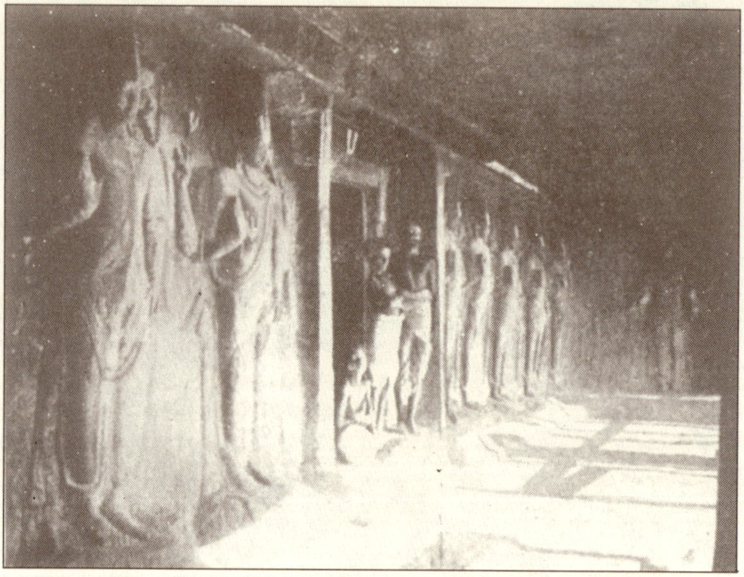

Interior of the cave of Narthamalai (7th century)

PLATE LXXV

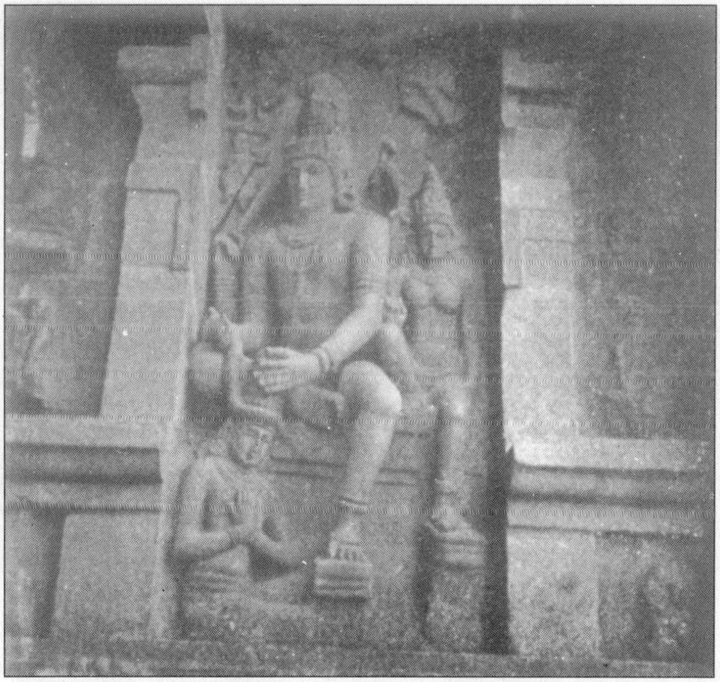

Siva crowning the king Rajendra Choladeva I.
(Gangaikondapuram temple, 11th century.)

PLATE LXXVI

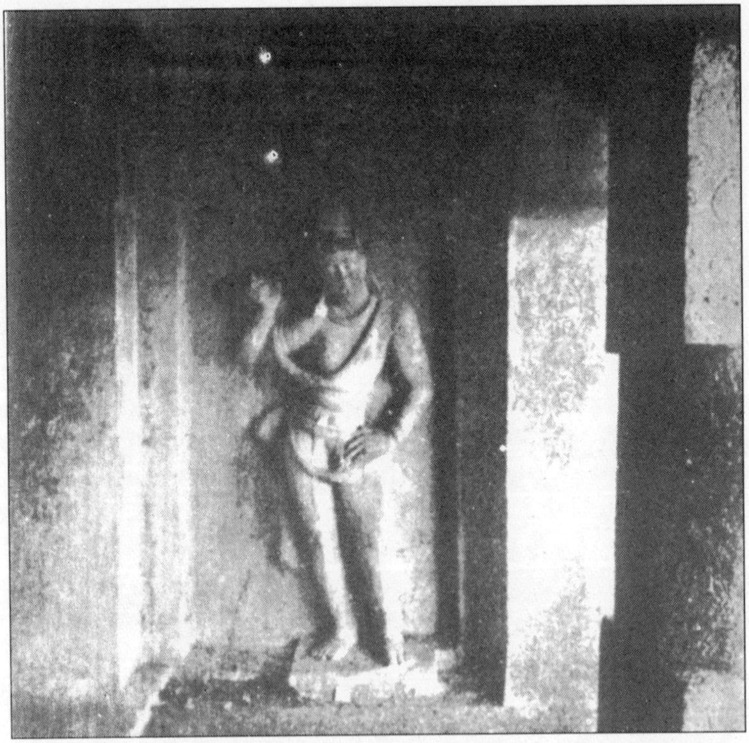

Tirukkalukkundram cave. Prince or Dvarapalaka (7th century).

PLATE LXXVII

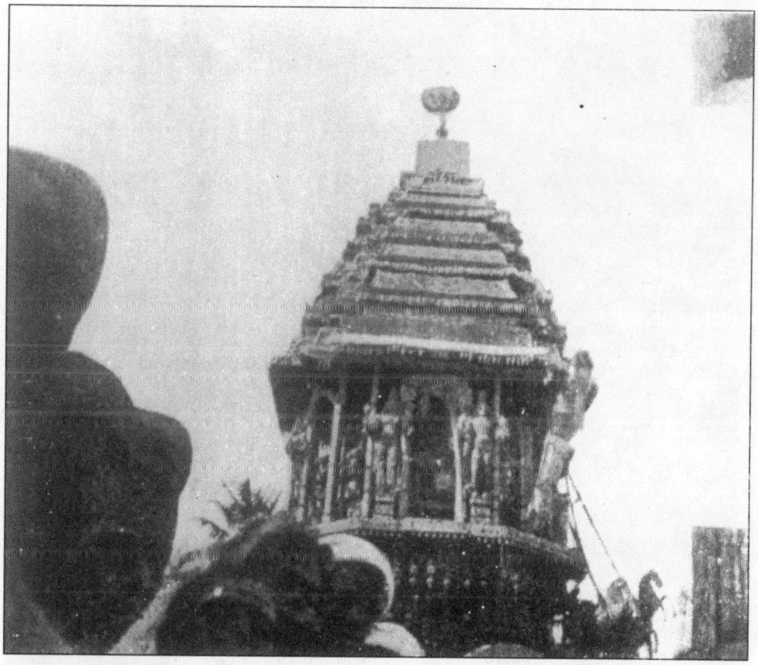

Car at Conjeevaram.

PLATE LXXVIII

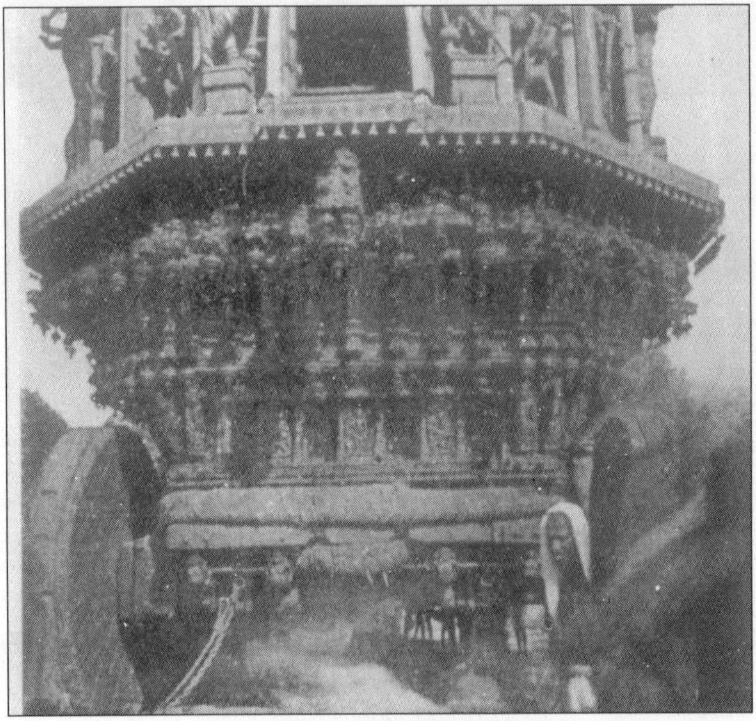

Base of the car at Conjeevaram.